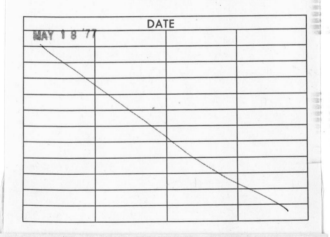

The Arno Press Cinema Program

A COMPARATIVE STUDY OF
SELECTED AMERICAN FILM CRITICS
1958-1974

Joseph Dalton Blades, Jr.

ARNO PRESS

A New York Times Company

New York • 1976

This volume was selected for the
Dissertations on Film Series
of the ARNO PRESS CINEMA PROGRAM
by Garth S. Jowett, Carleton University

Editorial Supervision: Sheila Mehlman

First publication in book form, Arno Press, 1976

THE ARNO PRESS CINEMA PROGRAM
For complete listing of cinema titles see last pages

Manufactured in the United States of America

———··◦◦··———

Library of Congress Cataloging in Publication Data

Blades, Joseph Dalton.
   A comparative study of selected American film critics,
1958-1974.

   (Dissertations on film series)
   Originally presented as the author's thesis, Bowling
Green State University, 1974.
   1. Moving-picutre criticism--United States.
I. Title. II. Series.
PN1995.B497 1976   791.43   75-21429
ISBN 0-405-07532-4

A COMPARATIVE STUDY OF SELECTED

AMERICAN FILM CRITICS, 1958-1974

Joseph Dalton Blades, Jr.

A Dissertation

Submitted to the Graduate School of Bowling Green
State University in partial fulfillment of
the requirements for the degree of

DOCTOR OF PHILOSOPHY

August 1974

FOR MY PARENTS AND MARY-FRANCES, WITH LOVE

ACKNOWLEDGMENTS

There are many people to thank. I am especially indebted to
Dr. Roger D. Gross--teacher, doctoral advisor, scholar, and friend--the
man most closely associated with the evolution of this study. Without
his support, this moment would never have been attained; indeed, the
first day's research would never have begun.

I extend deepest appreciation to Drs. Charles R. Boughton,
Robert K. Clark, Allen S. White, and Ralph H. Wolfe, whose assistance
with and interest in my studies have buoyed me for the last three years.

And for their suggestions, their insights, and their unending
encouragement, for the very shaping of many ideas expressed herein, special,
loving thanks are due Joe Butler, Dr. Lois A. Cheney, Michele Gallery,
Gary Robertson, and Jeanie Robertson.

Finally, and most importantly, a special note of gratitude to my
parents, Dalton and Edna Blades. Their wisdom, faith, and confidence
have long been sources of inspiration.

TABLE OF CONTENTS

I. INTRODUCTION

Arthur Knight has called them "the liveliest art." Pauline Kael "lost it" while watching them. Renata Adler spent "a year in the dark" analyzing them. To Stanley Kauffmann they are "figures of light." What "they" are is the movies.

And in 1973 approximately 250 new ones were released in this country. In an industry that is supposedly on the wane, that is a lot of movies. And for critics, a lot to write about.

François Truffaut, the French filmmaker who began as a critic, recently said:

> It is more difficult to be a [motion picture] critic today because films are so much more varied. Today critics must be specialists. They have to deal with political films, experimental films, entertainment films. This is a problem which must be resolved. I do not mean to be pretentious, but when I was a critic, I was better than all but nine or ten per cent of the people who made the film. Now, of every ten films I see, I don't understand five. Today, I could not be a critic.[1]

In Truffaut's stead, however, many intelligent and sensitive writers do want to be and are film critics. Individually and collectively, and particularly since the late Fifties and early Sixties, movie critics have gained stature. It is apparent that there are more people, writers and readers alike, seriously interested in film as an art form than ever before. For proof, one has only to check the cinema section of any reasonably well-

---

[1] Bob Talbert, "People," Detroit Free Press, November 25, 1973, p. 19-A.

stocked bookstore. More than ever, film reviews have become a part of
our general reading matter. Periodicals now featuring regular movie
departments include everything from America to Zoo World.

As Judith Crist has observed, we belong to a passive era when criticism is needed.[2] She notes quite correctly that printed criticism is on
the rise, so much so that the public at large looks upon the critic as
superstar. That phrase, "the critic as superstar," is not mine or Judith
Crist's. Newsweek gets the credit.[3]

The point is well-taken. Film critics are known nowadays. Whether
or not they are respected is another issue entirely. The role of the critic
is more important than in the past, especially with our current inundation
of entertainment in all the media. Pauline Kael has said that "in the arts,
the critic is the only independent source of information. The rest is
advertising."[4] If you glance at the Sunday New York Times, you'll probably
agree.

In 1972, Frank Beaver published a study of why film was slow in
achieving artistic respectability and why, in consequence, the medium
warranted little "higher" criticism. Beaver asserted that most early
movie reviewers "paid more attention to recapping plots than to the film
methods which produced a unique form of expression. . . ."[5] Critics rarely

---

[2]Robert Downing, "'Defy Herd,' Judith Crist Says," The Denver Post,
July 29, 1971, p. 31.

[3]Arthur Cooper, "Critic as Superstar," Newsweek, December 24, 1973,
p. 96.

[4]Ibid., p. 96.

[5]Frank E. Beaver, "Early Film Criticism: Some Prevailing Attitudes
and Problems," The Central States Speech Journal, Summer, 1972, p. 130.

treated films as if they were worthy of serious examination. They printed reviews that "reflected public taste rather than their own knowledge and sensibilities."[6] As a result, film criticism "remained, at best, a reportorial service for newspaper readers and movie-goers."[7]

Indeed, serious motion picture criticism is a relatively recent phenomenon. Its development began in the Forties with James Agee, whose film columns W. H. Auden revered because they transcended their "ostensible--to me, rather unimportant--subject."[8]

Movie critics before Agee rarely transcended anything. Most of his predecessors in the movie criticism field composed their columns with the dispassion of surgeons. Their dispassion was sometimes subordinated to outright indifference. One prime example, Mordaunt Hall, of The New York Times, had so many shortcomings one barely knows where to begin discussing him. His critiques were compendiums of erroneous plot summaries (and ninety per cent of each review was plot synopsis), weak-wittedness, and amateurish stabs at describing acting performances and filming technique, in painfully stilted composition (not altogether dictated by the Times' conservative

---

[6]Beaver, "Early Film Criticism," p. 130.

[7]Ibid., p. 130.

[8]"Letters to the Editors," The Nation, November 18, 1944, p. 628.

editorial policy).[9] Hall, in his dotage, was succeeded by Andre Sennwald,
then Frank S. Nugent, then the legendary Bosley Crowther--none of them,
except for the urbane Nugent, substantial improvements upon the original.

Agee was decidedly a standard bearer for serious criticism, if only
because his prose revealed intelligence and sensitivity at work. He
brought fresh insight and unprecedented dedication to the art of film
criticism. Luckily, that insight, that dedication, and the profession
itself have endured and expanded with Agee's successors, six of whom are
the subjects of the present study. The six writers comprise part of a
second generation of serious, competent film critics. Like Agee, they
are both literate and qualified to understand the medium.

In this age of "critic as superstar," motion picture critics appear
to be getting more than their share of the limelight. If they are not
trading quips with Dick Cavett, they're being profiled in _Playboy_. Or
joining the campus lecture circuit. Or hosting film weekends at Tarrytown.
Still, for purposes of this study, it is not their peripheral activities
that make these writers important. It's what they write.

----

[9]The gaffes committed by Mordaunt Hall abound in _The New York Times
Film Reviews_ collection, but a few excerpts will suffice. Describing _The
Last Flight_, Hall proclaimed, "There is one scene that is exceptionally
well done. It is where . . ." In _Death Takes a Holiday_, Fredric March's
performance is "pleasing, but his enunciation lacks the shading one would
like to hear." Clearly, the critic, in trying to evaluate the actor's
vocal technique, is just out of his territory. One wishes one had a penny
for every time Hall lauded an actor for his "capital work," as he did,
among others, Elliott Nugent in _The Last Flight_, Margaret Dumont in _Animal
Crackers_, and ZaSu Pitts in _Monte Carlo_; or another penny for each time he
called a sound film "an audible pictorial" (_River's End_, _Animal Crackers_,
and so on). For further illustrations of Hall's blunders and his barbaric
writing style, see _The New York Times Film Reviews_. Arno Press: New
York, 1970.

Their words are often continuing diaries, frequently "guides to what is going on," sometimes vigilant in drawing attention to what would otherwise be neglected, and, in the best instances, informed and thoroughgoing analyses designed to clarify difficult films.

Thus the importance of the six critics chosen for the study. They are men and women who, in their way, are keeping a record of our civilization. It is surprising that their work has been so little documented in a scholarly fashion before now.

This project is designed to fill that gap. It examines the aesthetic principles, critical methods, and style of six currently practicing American film critics. The work is a descriptive examination of those critics, chosen because they are among the most widely read and most influential practitioners of their profession. All have national, perhaps international, reputations. In alphabetical order they are Vincent Canby, Judith Crist, Pauline Kael, Stanley Kauffmann, Andrew Sarris, and John Simon. These six writers represent a variety of approaches, and there are a variety of reasons for choosing them and not other critics.

Vincent Canby was selected because he is the voice of the Times--the New York Times. As the top film spokesman for the newspaper of record, Canby most decidedly has high impact.

Judith Crist was chosen because of her influence on the masses. As a former critic for NBC's Today, and as critic for TV Guide and New York, she is highly visible.

Pauline Kael (The New Yorker) was selected because she commands authority in the right quarters. Unlike Judith Crist, "the people's

critic," Pauline Kael is the "critic's critic."[10] The chapter devoted
to her demonstrates why.

Stanley Kauffmann was selected because he is the country's leading
"highbrow" critic. That means he treats films not as isolated entertain-
ments but in connection with other art forms and life experiences: he
views films as important statements about our political, cultural, and
moral values. Now, at The New Republic, he has a small but select
readership.

Andrew Sarris, of The Village Voice, was chosen for several reasons.
First, he is the leading advocate in this country of the controversial
auteur theory: the film director as author. Secondly, like Pauline Kael,
he is popular with young movie buffs who account for the largest attendance
at today's films. Finally, he has done more extensive writing of film
history than any other leading American movie critic. His collection, The
American Cinema, is the most encyclopedic single volume of film history
and criticism yet published.

John Simon was selected on a number of counts, but basically for his
hard-nosed criticism (some would call it hard-headed) and for his insistence
that critics themselves should be artists. Simon is regarded by both the
general public and his fellows as "the critic you love to hate."[11] Probably
the most acerbic critic, easily the most erudite, and definitely the hardest

---

[10]Harvey Aronson, "Movies and Their Critics--Whoops, We Mean
Reviewers," Cosmopolitan, August 1971, p. 136.

[11]Arthur Cooper, "Critic as Superstar," p. 97.

to please, Simon has been dubbed "Malice in Wonderland."[12] He presently
writes for Esquire, which gives him a reasonably broad forum.

This paper identifies each writer's principles and techniques, then
compares them with the work of the other five. The study is divided into
a chapter-by-chapter look at each critic. Within those chapters is an
analysis of the individual's style, his special areas of concern, his
degree of technicality with regard to the elements of film, and generally
his manner of enlightening and stimulating the reader.

I have posed these questions to each critic: What seem to be the
critic's major concerns in film criticism? What does the writer regularly
emphasize in his critiques--acting, directing, cinematography, music and
sound, story and dialogue, social significance? Is the critic concerned
with the content of the movie or its look or both? Does there seem to
be an actor, a director, a writer, or a genre which the critic unfailingly
praises or damns? Is the critic frank in terms of his assumptions and
prejudices? Is there an identifiable writing style? What is the tone? Has
the critic ever issued a statement of his aesthetic demands? If so, do
his critiques tend to adhere to those demands? What can be determined about
the critic's implicit aesthetic standards? How does the individual apparently
or implicitly view himself--as historian, as dispenser of an individual
opinion, as shaper of public opinion? What objectives does he espouse as
a writer about film? For what kind of reader is the critic writing? Ultimately:
what qualities mark the individuality of this writer, and what can be said
about his influence and importance?

---

[12]Harvey Aronson, "Movies and Their Critics," p. 136.

A concluding chapter summarizes those findings. In that concluding section, I relate the critics by charting what they do and do not have in common.

A bibliography, listing all the materials used in the study, is appended.

II. JOHN SIMON

John Simon is probably the most controversial critic writing in
America today. His bold assertions, his calculated use of unfamiliar
words, his esoteric allusions, and his uncompromising aesthetic principles
have assured him a secure spot in the mainstream of mid-twentieth century
thought. In the realm of drama and film criticism, wherein writing tends,
lamentably, toward a remarkable sameness, John Simon remains unique.

In his scholarship, he bows to no man. As a self-exalted arbiter of
taste, he offers no apology. In his misanthropic view of both theatregoers
and his colleagues, many of whom he damns as "reviewers" or "journalists,"
he pulls no punches. As for his opinions, they are his own alone, and they
are more often outrageous than not. To say there is nothing moderate about
the man is unqualified understatement.

John Ivan Simon was born in Subotica, Yugoslavia on May 12, 1925.
After two years' service in the United States Air Force, Simon was educated
at Harvard (A.B., 1946; A.M., 1948; Ph.D., 1959), where, from 1950 to 1953,
he was a teaching fellow in English and humanities. After that three-year
period at Harvard, during which he completed the course work toward his
doctorate, Simon became an instructor in humanities and comparative literature
at, successively, the University of Washington; Massachusetts Institute of
Technology; and, as "assistant professor of literature," Bard College,
Annandale-on-Hudson, New York, his last permanent educational affiliation
to date.

In 1959, upon his exit from the groves of academe, Simon became an associate editor for the Mid-Century Book Society, where he did his critical teething before embarking on a career in journalism the following year. To his professional credit, he has been drama critic for many distinguished journals: Hudson Review, beginning in 1960; Commonweal, for a brief period in 1967; and New York, where he currently contributes a weekly column and where he has assumed staff position as "contributing editor." From 1963 to 1973, his film criticism appeared regularly in The New Leader. In late 1973 he left The New Leader to assume the movie critic's chair at Esquire. His first byline for Esquire appeared in the October issue.

Simon's books include Acid Test, a collection of theatre reviews, focusing on Broadway of the early Sixties, but with additional commentary on books, the fine arts, film, and poetry; Private Screenings, a volume of his movie critiques from 1963 to 1966; and Movies Into Film, another collection which advances his perspective of the film world to 1970. Ingmar Bergman Directs, Simon's examination of the Swedish filmmaker, came out in 1972. In addition, Simon has co-edited (with Richard Schickel, the erstwhile Life critic now with Time) an anthology of film reviews called Film '67-'68. The critic has recently edited an omnibus of short stories with the overall title Fourteen for Now.[1]

In the Sixties and early Seventies, while gaining a reputation as "a language-oriented critic in a world where the verbal arts are attenuating,"[2]

[1]Barbara Harte and Carolyn Riley, editors, Contemporary Authors, Volumes 21-22. Gale Research Company (The Book Tower): Detroit, Michigan, 1969, pp. 487-488.

[2]Arthur Cooper, "Critic As Superstar," Newsweek, December 24, 1973, p. 97.

Simon became a celebrity to thousands of people who never saw a copy of
The New Leader or New York. His promotion to the ranks of "celebrity"
has all been due to late-night television. As a guest on TV programs
like The Dick Cavett Show, Simon has had an impact.

His video personality may or may not be a reflection of the actual
man, but as a talk-show participant, he seems very much the individual
who might have written Acid Test, Private Screenings, and Movies Into
Film. Dick Cavett's interviews have revealed the critic's sharply defined
tastes, his disdain for audiences and other critics, his dapper dress
(thoroughly befitting a Harvard alum), and his rough-as-a-cob nastiness
externalized in language as refined and articulate off the cuff as it is
in print. Cavett buffs relish the night Simon described the Erich Segal
Love Story (novella and film) in something less than beatific terms to its
creator's face and the time he dubbed Peter Bogdanovich's The Last Picture
Show "dime fiction," then explained its presence on his ten-worst list for
1971.[3]

John Simon stands alone, and he is not widely loved. He has drawn
blood in far too many quarters for that. In an August 1972 Cosmopolitan
article, Harvey Aronson talked to a dozen major American film critics.
"Most critics interviewed for [the] piece smiled when Simon's name came
up."[4] Yet few would comment.

---

[3]Harvey Aronson, "Movies and Their Critics--Whoops, We Mean
Reviewers," Cosmopolitan, August 1972, p. 136.

[4]Ibid., p. 137.

Why this universally peculiar reaction to John Simon? No doubt it was in large measure because the writers Aronson interviewed had, at some time in their careers, felt the wrath of Simon. His condemnation of certain of the leading lights of criticism has sometimes been merciless. Upon more than one occasion, Simon has vented his fury upon Pauline Kael, movie critic for The New Yorker.

Simon's disdain for Ms. Kael stems from their philosophical differences. He sees film as an art form; she sees film as a mode of entertainment which, in instances, reaches the level of art. One of Simon's primary tenets is that criticism should upgrade the medium under discussion, whether film, theatre, sculpture, or dance. In his eyes, Kael's writing does not do this.

Ms. Kael can consider herself in distinguished company. Among other critics Simon holds in distaste are Andrew Sarris (the Village Voice critic and film historian extraordinaire whose bitchy debates with Simon in their respective columns provided spicy copy on entertainment pages for weeks); Clive Barnes, the Times stage and dance critic (he and Simon have engaged in lengthy verbal fisticuffs, in the pages of their publications, if not in public as well); Vincent Canby (first-string film critic for The Times); Judith Crist (who writes film reviews for New York, the weekly journal for which Simon writes about theatre); and Susan Sontag. To Andrew Sarris, Simon is a "professional feuder. . . . He's what everyone thinks a critic is in his worst moment."[5]

Judith Crist has been the butt of numerous Simon jokes, at least one of which was needlessly ambiguous, if not totally pointless; but since it

---

[5]Arthur Cooper, "Critic As Superstar, p. 97.

is emblematic of the chicanery Simon resorts to, it bears repeating.

Concluding his review of The Sterile Cuckoo, Simon took a double swipe

at its star, Liza Minnelli, and Ms. Crist. (It seems indicative of the

critic's methods that when he seeks to smear one of his colleagues, he

does so in the final paragraph of his essay in the form of a swift and

really hurtful zinger, after which he abruptly departs the scene).

> And Liza Minnelli? . . . Despite some talent,
> she cannot fake charm or acceptable looks. For a
> fugitive moment, we can fool ourselves into believing
> that she is a jolie laide, but forthwith she reverts
> to her usual mixture of Judith Crist and the Emperor
> Tiberius.[6]

Like most of Simon's put-downs, this one comes from nowhere. Nothing

else in the review explains or justifies the parting blow. A June 1970

critique of The Beatles' Let It Be film amounts to a follow-up slam.

> One is aware, especially now that their break-up
> has been announced, that the Beatles have progressed
> from the beatific stage to canonization, and that their
> fingernail parings have become priceless. Let It Be is
> a collection of audiovisual nail parings, but not with-
> out a certain morbidly sociological interest.
>
> For this purpose, it is appropriate to consult the
> film reviewer who has attained the highest degree of
> that kind of interest, Judith Crist. "It is a delight,"
> she writes of this movie, "not only for its music but
> for its close-up. . . . of the four young men who have
> affected the lifestyle of one generation and--look around
> you and then back to photos of the fifties--at very least
> the appearance of several generations."
>
> I myself could not find a single outstanding song
> in the film, but that is not the point. The question
> is whether changing the "lifestyle" of one generation
> and the appearances of however many Mrs. Crist thinks
> have zoomed by since the fifties (including perhaps
> those old-timers who haplessly sport the hippie look)
> makes someone a delight to look at. (The Beatles, by
> the way, have not changed the appearance of Mrs. Crist,

[6]John Simon, Movies Into Film, Dial Press, New York, 1971, p. 121.

as you can verify by checking a two-page advertisement
in the women's magazines that features eight pictures
of the lady; the ad is for Pristeen, a product describing itself as a Feminine Hygiene Deodorant Spray).[7]

Back in 1963, before two-page Pristeen spreads were ever dreamed of,

Simon leapt on Ms. Crist and others for their oh-so-quotable rhapsodizing:

Once in a while a movie comes along that makes
poets of our reviewers, and their ball points in a
fine frenzy rolling sprout pure rhymes like "brawling,
sprawling" (Judith Crist), slant rhymes like "rowdy,
bawdy" (Jesse Zunser), and even rhyming pairs like
"roisterous, boisterous . . . uproarious and glorious"
(Justin Gilbert). Obviously a film that elicits such
lyric ejaculations from the reviewers cannot be all
good.[8]

The picture in question was Tom Jones. Whether or not one agrees with

Simon's dismissal of the film, it is certain that the other critics' reviews,

rhymes and all, helped turn it into a box-office bonanza. When the various

award-givers assembled at the end of 1963, Tom Jones was twice blessed.

More prizes were bestowed upon that film than any other film of its year.

Simon has repeatedly recognized the power of the critical press--for

both good and evil. Tom Jones, he believes, was helped immeasurably by

its favorable notices. To contrast the Tom Jones success, Simon cites

numerous examples of films of "artistic value" (Billy Wilder's Ace in the

Hole/The Big Carnival and Stanley Kubrick's Paths of Glory are two) which

died at the box-office due to double ignorance--of critics and audiences.[9]

In certain respects the latter group is as blamable as the former.

---

[7]John Simon, Movies Into Film, pp. 127-128.

[8]John Simon, Private Screenings, Macmillan, New York, 1967, p. 104.

[9]John Simon, Private Screenings, p. 140.

Simon passionately endorsed The Children of Paradise (in its first
uncut New York showing in 1964, and a financial failure), only to end his
piece by reviling the moviegoer:

> [The Children of Paradise] drew no crowds and was
> soon gone.
>
> That is what worries me. Perhaps it is not the
> fault of the movies. Perhaps it is the fault of the
> moviegoers. Or nongoers. Consider some of the best
> films of recent times: Ermanno Olmi's artistically
> daring and humanly simple A Sound of Trumpets and
> The Fiancés, Malle's The Fire Within, Polanski's
> Knife in the Water, and, most recently, Vittorio
> de Seta's heartbreakingly persuasive Bandits of
> Orgosolo--how many of them were still there after
> one, two, or at best three weeks? Only Polanski's
> film had something of a run, but did it get a
> fraction of the acclaim given to that perfect piece
> of pseudoartistic mediocrity Tom Jones? This is,
> for once, not even the fault of the critics, who
> tended to do justice to those films. . . . This,
> then, ladies and gentlemen, is, I fear, your fault
> alone.[10]

Admittedly viper-tongued, Simon is not without his humorous side.
He can even stand back occasionally and view audience "delinquency" and
critical incompetence with a smile. Discussing (in negative terms) Jacques
Demy's Umbrellas of Cherbourg ("a ludicrous movie musical"), the writer
analyzes his amazement over the picture's rampant critical and commercial
acceptance:

> The only reason I have gone into The Umbrellas of
> Cherbourg at such length is that it won, among its half
> dozen important prizes, the International Catholic Cinema
> Award, which I can understand--it is, after all, a songful
> sermon on the Pauline text about the preferableness of
> marrying, however lovelessly, to burning, however pas-
> sionately--and the Louis Delluc Award of the French
> critics, which I cannot understand, except as the complete
> collapse of French film criticism. We are told that in

---

[10]John Simon, Private Screenings, p. 139.

> Paris the opening-night audience wept and the critics
> were ecstatic. It would have made a little more sense
> the other way round.[11]

Although Simon very wisely notes that the movie reviewers can't

always be used as scapegoats, he very nearly contradicts himself with

the frequency and excessiveness of his anti-critics arguments. In one

article, published in 1964, he even finds excuses for the negligent movie-

goer--at the expense of the ever-sinning newspaper and magazine critic.[12]

He asks "What could be some realistic reasons for such large-scale audience

delinquency?" then he replies:

> First-run movie theatres have become too expensive.
> There are too many so-called art houses and they have to
> offer something, consequently, much trashy pseudoart is
> shown; this makes many people lose faith in all films
> and resist even the good ones. There is the assumption
> that it can all soon be seen, cheaper and nearer, as a
> rerun--or even on television--and unawareness that a
> poor first run may effectively prevent there ever being
> any second runs. There is the worsening of taste, pos-
> sibly caused by TV fare; and the rise of an appalling
> cinematic pop art that subverts the younger and more
> enthusiastic movie audiences. There seems to be greater
> confusion in the minds of the reviewers, who find it
> progressively harder, in an era of proliferating pseudo-
> avant-gardes, to distinguish the fine from the fashionable,
> the far-out from the out-of-the-question.[13]

To Simon, the critics--or rather "reviewers" (or "journalists" as

he denigrates them)--are more trouble than they are worth. His dis-

satisfaction extends even to the formerly exalted towers of The Times.

The theory about the life-and-death jurisdiction of The Times in regard

to live theatre in Manhattan is a matter of legend. The same goes for

movies, Simon says. To a reprint of his review of Ermanno Olmi's One

---

[11]John Simon, Private Screenings, pp. 158-159.

[12]Ibid., p. 140.

[13]Ibid., pp. 140-141.

Fine Day at the Seventh New York Film Festival, the writer adds this
retrospective footnote:

> This remarkable film has still not been released.
> The reason? A remarkably wrongheaded and illiterate
> negative review from Vincent Canby in the New York
> Times, enough to frighten Janus Films, which owns
> the rights.[14]

If John Simon considers himself so far superior to the great unwashed
film journalists-reviewers, how is it that he differs from them? The
most significant distinction between him and, say, Judith Crist or Andrew
Sarris or Pauline Kael lies in his demands of movies, stringent ones by
anybody's standards. In attempting to examine Simon as critic, let us
turn first to the most cogent statement of his criteria--his essay "A Critical
Credo."[15] This credo is a schema of the "problems, requirements, and
functions of film criticism and critics. . . ."[16] It provides a clarifi-
cation of Simon's belief that:

> a film critic, or any other kind of critic, must be
> an artist, a teacher, and a philosopher, and that the
> ideal critique is itself a work of art as well as an
> explication of and meditation on the work of art it
> examines.[17]

On this issue of critical responsibility, he echoes the philosophy
of Friedrich Schlegel. Both men make powerful demands of the critic:
they testify to the necessity of the critic to create art, to be just
as artistic as the art work he is criticizing. Simon's colleagues have

---

[14]John Simon, Movies Into Film, p. 395.

[15]"A Critical Credo" was originally a lecture delivered to the Summer
Institute of the National Film Board of Canada.

[16]John Simon, Movies Into Film, p. 1.

[17]Ibid., p. 1.

never expressed themselves quite so passionately about their own writing--at least not in print. We may never know if Judith Crist, from the vantage point of her New York desk, thinks she is creating works of art or not.

Simon's credo begins, "The most important thing to remember about film criticism is that it is not fundamentally different from any other kind of criticism."[18] In one fell swoop, then, he justifies film as art and dignifies his own position as a professional observer of that art. True criticism, he continues, is:

> a kind of poetry, a poetry of hate for what is ugly or false, and of love for what is beautiful and true. I realize that it has become unfashionable in life--let alone in criticism--to use terms like "ugly" and "beautiful," but I accept the charge of being unfashionable with satisfaction and even, I confess, with pride.[19]

Herein he justifies not only his position as critic but his vehement stance of righter or wrongs. He can be as vindictive to a film he hates as to a critic he considers unworthy. Less kind voices would even call Simon a hatchet man. But at least this segment of the manifesto answers those who have considered Simon far too demanding in his tastes and far too vitriolic in his chastisement of works which do not meet his standard of excellence. In the writer's words,

> Different evils need different modes of attack: from Swiftian saeva indignatio to subtle puncturing, from "more in sorrow than in anger" to reductio ad absurdum, one chooses whichever method is most suitable; or, if one is less versatile, whichever method one is best suited to. The critic's words are his tools, or weapons, and he would be foolish and incompetent if he did not use them to the utmost of his, and their, ability.[20]

---

[18]John Simon, Private Screenings, p. 7.

[19]Ibid., pp. 7-8.

[20]Ibid., p. 9.

The sentiment is characteristically well expressed and includes another characteristic dig at his fellow critics (". . . or if one is less versatile, whichever method one is best suited to . . ."). He goes on to differentiate inadequate and indifferent criticism from the superior brand, concluding that the best critics are artists, thinkers, and, above all, teachers.

> . . . what constitutes good criticism? Perhaps it is easiest to begin by defining the commonest kind of bad criticism, which is not criticism at all but reviewing. Reviewing is something that newspaper editors have invented; it stems from the notion that the critic is someone who must see with the eyes of the Average Man or Typical Reader (whoever that is) and predict for his fellows what their reaction will be. To this end, the newspapers carefully screen their reviewers to be representative common men, say, former obituary writers or mail-room clerks, anything but trained specialists. To accept such a reviewer as critic and guide is like expecting school children to teach one another, or patients in a hospital ward to undertake one another's cure. A critic excites the public's curiosity, wonder, suspicion, rage, and enthusiasm; a reviewer elicits mostly one of two reactions: "Good! That's another one I don't have to see!" or "Great! I like it already." Both reactions stifle thought instead of encouraging the audience and, with luck, even the artist to grow.[21]

Simon's definitions are much like those Walter Kerr uses to separate the critic from the reviewer: "Reviewing is . . . a consumer report for the uninitiated; criticism is a conversation with one's equals."[22]

Now we arrive at the crux of John Simon's aesthetic argument, the point at which he diverges from most if not all practitioners of criticism in the 1960's and 1970's. Simon's insistence that man be a thinker carries

---

[21]John Simon, Private Screenings, p. 10.

[22]Andrew Sarris, The American Cinema, E. P. Dutton, New York, 1968, p. 34.

him into the realm of morality. He quotes Oscar Wilde: ". . . the

highest Criticism . . . is the record of one's own soul."

> In other words, the critic must have a world
> view, which, however one may wish to disguise it,
> is a moral position. Nothing is more suspect in
> criticism nowadays than a moral position, and yet
> there can be no criticism without one. The moment
> something appears to us better or worse than some-
> thing else, we are being moralists--for aesthetics
> is the morality of art, just as morality is the
> aesthetics of living.[23]

Therefore, criticism should never be based, as Simon indicates it

commonly is, simply on how well the work in question fulfills its own

aims,

> for by that standard, if it sets out to be only junk,
> junk will have to be found excellent. Essential too
> is an awareness of reconciled opposites: of the joy
> inherent in tragedy and of the pathos no true comedy
> can be without. . . . The fundamental problem, I
> suppose, is that film is being taken, ultimately, as
> an "entertainment" as opposed to a work of art, as if
> art and entertainment were mutually exclusive or, at
> least, separate entities, as form and content or meaning
> and style were once thought to be. While no one today
> would dare to think of form and content as separate or,
> except for purposes of classroom demonstration, separable,
> it still seems the most natural thing to erect a fence
> between the few films that "have something to say" and
> the many that are "merely amusements," and, apparently,
> come up with roughly equal endorsements for films in
> both groups, albeit by a double standard involving
> different scales.[24]

Simon takes up this double standard issue later. In his introductory

essay for Movies Into Film, the critic tries to strengthen his defense.

---

[23]John Simon, Private Screenings, p. 12.

[24]Ibid., pp. 12-14.

He equates movies with entertainment and film with art. The critic, even as the lowly common man,

> can enjoy both Bach and the Beatles, both Kafka and comic strips, both looking at a great dancer perform a perfect arabesque and watching a champion tennis player return an impossible smash. But it is wrong to call the tennis player an artist, wrong to prefer Superman to Joseph K., wrong to equate a popular song with a concerto. Not morally wrong (though, in some cases, that too), but esthetically wrong.[25]

One would be hard-pressed to find a single living, actively engaged critic who would agree with Simon. His detractors would say he is on shaky ground when he complains that what a tennis player does is not art--and on shakier ground yet when he cautions his readers it is wrong for anybody to call it art.

In his rigidity he is in direct disagreement with many of his rival critics, the most formidable of whom is Pauline Kael. Ms. Kael is partially a sociology writer: her New Yorker essays frequently chart audience response. (She sees movies more often than not when they start their commercial engagements. "They have special screenings for the press," she admits, "but they are usually in the morning or afternoon, and I consider it immoral to go to the movies in the daytime.")[26] One of her abiding interests is how spectator response compares with her own.

To be sure, Simon would never align himself with the mass audience, as Kael is wont to do. It would call for too devastating a relaxation of his standards. Recall his horror of having to call junk excellent.[27] When it comes to the bending of Simon's dogma, he is decidedly unbendable.

---

[25] John Simon, Movies Into Film, p. 3.

[26] Douglas N. Mount, "Authors and Editors: Pauline Kael," Publishers' Weekly, May 24, 1971, p. 32.

[27] John Simon, Private Screenings, pp. 12-14.

Stringent as he is, John Simon does not hate all his colleagues.
In fact, he speaks quite affectionately about one group of writers, those
"who have written extensively on other arts besides film . . . [those who]
resist movements, schools, fads. . . ."[28] The individuals who merit his
greatest respect

> write with posterity rather than the mere moment in
> mind, and they are at least as concerned with meanings
> and implications as with the feel of a film. The main
> representatives of this persuasion--Sarris calls them
> "bookish film critics," others call them, contemptuously
> or not, "highbrow"--are Dwight Macdonald, Stanley Kauff-
> mann, Vernon Young, Charles T. Samuels, . . . Wilfrid
> Sheed . . . and myself (if I may be excused the lack of
> false and, very possibly, genuine modesty). I would
> call this group film critics. . . .[29]

On a lower level, but not the lowest, in Simon's eyes are the "movie
critics." In this category fall people who

> do not, as a rule, write on the other arts; they are
> not primarily concerned with film as art--or, if so,
> have a rather demonic or idiosyncratic conception of
> art; they tend to be buffs emeriti (or emeritae), and
> are much more interested in the politics, the social
> (or simply, gregarious) aspects of cinema; they are
> primarily involved with the feel of the film, the
> immediate impact it produces, its relation to the
> temper of the times. They are not, however, to be
> confused with mere reviewers; for their dedication,
> zeal (sometimes fanaticism), and film scholarship
> far exceeds that of the reviewers or journalists
> (of whom Judith Crist can be considered a supreme
> example). In this group I would number Pauline Kael
> and Andrew Sarris, Manny Farber and, with minor
> differences, Penelope Gilliatt, and also, with
> important but not all-important differences,
> Parker Tyler and Susan Sontag.[30]

[28]John Simon, Movies Into Film, p. 5.

[29]Ibid., p. 5.

[30]Ibid., pp. 5-6.

John Simon is well-read, and his erudition extends considerably
beyond his familiarity with the twelve critics listed above. Simon's
academic background in humanities and comparative literature serves
him well. Scarcely a paragraph goes by without reference to a literary
or philosophical (and even occasionally a musical) work. All this cross-
field referencing is allied to Simon's conviction, first promulgated by
Charles Thomas Samuels, that one should not trust a film critic "who writes
only about film."[31] As time-consuming as his writing duties are, Simon
is in frequent attendance at operas, ballets, concerts, and art shows. A
self-proclaimed "pentathlon man," he reviews fiction, poetry, and art in
addition to plays and movies. Whatever the medium, he looks dourly on
journalists who are "in the business of dispensing charity or doing Salvation
Army work in the guise of criticism."[32]

> There is very possibly nothing wrong with a music
> critic who writes only about music, or an architecture
> critic who writes only about architecture. But film is
> both a much newer art than any of the others, and one
> which, as a true Gesamtkunstwerk, subsumes all the others.
> . . . The newness means that there is an insufficient body
> of film criticism, scholarship, and theory available to
> the aspiring critic, and that he had therefore best draw
> in part on the esthetics and methodology of the other
> arts and their criticism--all the more so since every one
> of those arts has to some degree been utilized by the
> cinema. Again, because film is still relatively unex-
> plored and undervalued critically, it has the same fas-
> cination for critics that a barely discovered resort has
> for tourists: it becomes a fad and invites fanatical
> partisanship. So out of both ignorance and overenthusiasm
> it is horribly easy for the film critic to be or become
> one-sided, overzealous, derailed to the point of not making,
> or ceasing to make, sense on his own subject. To prevent
> this from happening, the film critic must be something else
> as well. His experience in other arts and critical dis-

---

[31] John Simon, Movies Into Film, p. 23.

[32] Arthur Cooper, "Critic As Superstar," p. 97.

ciplines will give him that lever and fulcrum with
which Archimedes offered to lift the earth. Certainly
film criticism could do with some heightening.

On the other hand, I hope that I am not guilty of
the charge Andrew Sarris leveled at "too many bookish
film critics," who, he claims, "have perverted the notion
of ecumenical erudition by snobbishly subordinating film
to every other art." I consider film inferior to no art,
but neither do I make the dangerous assumption widely held
by illiterate film critics (or whatever the opposite of
"bookish" ones may be) that film is superior to all other
arts. A critic may be a lover; he must not become an idolater.[33]

And therein lies the justification for all that much-maligned Simon erudition.

Even the most ardent Simon defender (if any such creature exists), would

perhaps agree, however, that the critic's intellectualism, although genuine,

is sometimes misapplied. In those instances, his remarks seem pompous and

out-of-place and his references, intended to elevate and educate the reader,

become tedious, perhaps completely alienating. While describing Fellini's

direction of 8½, Simon attained undreamed-of heights of esoterica:

In Fellini's hands, this approach is rather like
the attempt of a typical Italian composer to forsake
bel canto for the symphonic; 8½ reminds me of those
dreary orchestral works of a Respighi, a Casella, or
a Malipiero.[34]

In a recent theatre review, on a single magazine page Simon quoted from

Diderot's Paradoxe sur le comédien (1773), from Henry Mackenzie's The Man of

Feeling (1771), from Ibsen translator Christian Morgenstern, and, at length,

from Peter Brook's The Empty Space--in addition to mentioning the music of

Liszt, Scriabin, Bartók, Mahler, Elvis Presley, and The Rolling Stones. Space

also permitted a defamatory remark about Lee Strasberg and the Method.[35]

---

[33]John Simon, Movies Into Film, pp. 23-24.

[34]John Simon, Private Screenings, p. 89.

[35]John Simon, "In Praise of Professionalism," New York, September 21,
1972, p. 68.

All this cross-referencing of the arts is viewed with chagrin by at least one of Simon's detractors, Peter Bogdanovich, who challenges Simon's assertion that film criticism is not fundamentally different from other kinds. In his last days as a book and movie critic (before he became known for the direction of Targets, The Last Picture Show, What's Up, Doc?, Paper Moon, et al.), Bogdanovich wrote this criticism of Private Screenings:

> [The author] knows no more about film than the average (even above average) PhD. in Comparative Literature, and his writing isn't good enough to compensate for his ignorance. . . . Unable to discuss a film on its own terms, he usually seeks refuge in a fancy comparative literature phrase. So D. W. Griffith is compared to Achilles Tatius, Richard Lester to John Bunyan, Truffaut's The Soft Skin to Pound's Cantos. . . . Reviewing [Truffaut's Fahrenheit 451] Simon spends most of his space on books vs. movie stuff, then admires an "impressive device"--"closing in with tiny jump cuts," he inaccurately describes it--not knowing it was first used in Hitchcock's The Birds. . . . Film is not literature, comparative or otherwise, and it deserves to be criticized with as much specialized attention and knowledge as any other art. . . . A critic who just hears the words or sees only the most obvious of cinematic "devices" is about as much help as a "legless man teaching running."[36]

Although Bogdanovich does not build a strong enough case for his dismissal of Simon's methods--can literary references in film criticism be all that damnable?--his 1967 attack is so vituperative we can perhaps understand why, in 1971, Simon went completely against the critical majority to pan Mr. Bogdanovich's The Last Picture Show.

J. A. Avant agrees with Bogdanovich's assessment. In a critique of Movies Into Film, Avant verbalized some of the same complaints:

> Simon's reviews are mostly synopses plus superficial value judgments, into which he throws more erudite literary allusions than you can count. Unpleasantly, Simon comes across as male chauvinistic

---

[36]Peter Bogdanovich, Book World, November 5, 1967, p. 6.

and unconsciously right-wing and very uptight, and
the loftiness of his intellectual aspirations often
prevents him from judging a movie . . . on its own
terms.[37]

Here again, we see Simon in diametrical opposition to many of his

contemporaries, many of whom would say "Let's judge a film's worth on the

basis of what it sets out to do." Simon's junk analogy becomes _apropos_

again, short-circuiting any kind of debate.

J. A. Avant may be right: Simon does seem to be a male chauvinist.

Nearly every column testifies to his penchant for being incredibly unchival-

rous to the opposite sex. His sometimes shocking nastiness emerges with

more potency than even the venomous Rex Reed, who at least is customarily

gentle with actresses _d'un certain âge_. Not so Simon. One gets the

feeling that the older the star, the more merciless Simon becomes. Ava

Gardner, Melina Mercouri, Kim Stanley, and Elizabeth Taylor, are among the

not-so-select group of once-luminous stars libeled by Simon.

Ava Gardner, in _Seven Days in May_, the critic writes, "has a problem.

Granted that she is meant to enact a woman left too long on the bough, the

fine line between overripeness and marcescence proves too fine for her."[38]

Melina Mercouri has also fallen victim:

. . . her blackly mascaraed eye sockets gape like twin
craters, unfortunately extinct. Her standard expression
is a bemused, constipated smile which is supposed to
convey everything from mysterious female canniness to
irrepressible hormones, but manages to suggest only
someone trying to look knowing while being talked to
in a language he doesn't know a word of. And speaking
of language, what Miss Mercouri does to English shouldn't
happen to pig-Latin.[39]

---

[37] J. A. Avant, _Library Journal_, January 15, 1971, p. 96.

[38] John Simon, _Private Screenings_, p. 129.

[39] _Ibid._, p. 151.

As for Kim Stanley:

> From auspicious beginnings, Miss Stanley has come
> to the point where her voice is a coyly adenoidal,
> pause-infested quaver, her gestures a ballet of tics,
> and her body a flaccid zeppelin quite unbecoming of
> a profession in which aesthetic standards matter.[40]

Predictably, the unkindest cuts of all are reserved for Liz Taylor. Why,

in this case, should John Simon be different than the movie critics-

reviewers-journalists he so volubly deplores? Worthy of note is the

inevitable literary allusion.

> The once pretty face has become coarse, though
> from a distance it can still look good--but only if
> it avoids any attempt at expression as, to be sure, it
> not infrequently does. Only the bosom keeps implacably
> marching on--or down, as the case may be--but I do not
> feel qualified to be the Xenophon of this reverse ana-
> basis.[41]

And elsewhere, in a review of The Comedians:

> Elizabeth Taylor plays a German woman with what,
> when she remembers it, is a bastard French accent.
> Perhaps she thought of herself as hailing from Alsace-
> Lorraine, and indeed she is portly enough for her head[42]
> to come from one province and her rump from the other.

With comments such as these, Simon descends to the low rungs of

crowd-pleasing journalese, a tendency he would no doubt find unforgivable

were it to emerge in Judith Crist (who it turns out is not entirely without

blame when it comes to cattiness about Mrs. Burton's figure) or Rex Reed

or, to arrive at the bottom rung, Rona Barrett. It is these rather under-

handed tactics which caused Andrew Sinclair to label portions of Private

Screenings as "explosions of squibs and graffiti."[43] Sinclair, who generally

---

[40]John Simon, Private Screenings, p. 129.

[41]John Simon, Movies Into Film, p. 29.

[42]Ibid., p. 308.

[43]Andrew Sinclair, New York Times Book Review, Jan. 14, 1968, p. 12.

liked the book, reprimanded the author for his cruelty. It's something

expected of, to borrow Simon's term, the "journalists." In Simon, it

demonstrates an ingraciousness one might think unbecoming of a Harvard

man. Moreover, it detracts from his self-proud stature as a serious/

highbrow/bookish critic.

With reason, Simon doesn't have many supporters in the critical con-

fraternity. Harold Clurman, the eminent director who is also a drama

critic for The Nation, has censured Simon for utilizing "five columns to

say an actress has big breasts, which he doesn't like. I'd kick him out.

Who the hell cares that he doesn't like big breasts?"[44]

Andrew Sarris looks with equal chagrin on Simon's evident enjoyment

of the pan and the personal slam:

> I think we're all bloody surgeons, we're all
> chopping people up and hacking limbs away like in
> M*A*S*H, the blood squirting all over all the time.
> It's a filthy job. I think we shouldn't enjoy that
> part too much. I think John is like one of those
> surgeons who really hack away and love doing it.
> I mean, when he cuts a limb off, he doesn't do it
> regretfully, or professionally, even, but he does
> it with zest and zeal. I think that's what's bad.
> You should only put somebody down with good reason;
> you shouldn't just do it.[45]

If film studio publicists are to be believed, Simon doesn't always

restrict his hacking to his columns. His everybody-else-be-damned

behavior is carried on even when he is watching movies. Describing

reviewers' screening room attitudes, one publicist has said: "Most critics

are comparatively quiet, but there are exceptions. . . . Like Simon. He

---

[44]Arthur Cooper, "Critic As Superstar," p. 96.

[45]Harvey Aronson, "Movies and Their Critics," p. 137.

can be unbelievable: he talks to himself during screenings; sometimes he's abusive."[46]

Has Simon, then, no points for commendation, no special qualifications, no professional application of his exalted academic standards? To the biased eye, the answer might be no. Many filmmakers, critics, and readers of film criticism, however, fail to look beyond Simon's harsh words. Beneath the acidity is a critical mind working overtime to perfect a craft. Due to his education in other art disciplines, Simon is prepared to analyze most elements of the film art. As John Coleman has emphasized, Simon is "quick to note when someone off-screen, photographer, set designer, script-writer deserves the credit."[47] His comments go beyond the obvious and the superficial, as these excerpts (typical rather than exceptional) demonstrate.

Simon on Nino Rota's contributions to Fellini's I Vitelloni:

> One of the most brilliant features of the film is the musical score by the true maestro, Nino Rota. It consists of only two themes. The first is a soaring, romantic melody that can be made to express nostalgia, love, and the pathos of existence. The other is a march-like, merry tune, carefree and irresponsible; slowed down, with emphasis on the cellos and basses . . . it becomes lugubrious; with eerie figurations in the woodwinds . . . it turns sinister. The quicksilver switches in the music ably support the changing moods of the story.[48]

On Henri Decaé's photography for Sundays and Cybèle, directed by Serge Bourguignon:

> Bourguignon deserves further credit for getting incomparable photographic effects from Henri Decaé, who has worked admirably for directors as different as Truffaut, Claude Chabrol, and René Clément, but who here achieves masterpieces. We are transported

---

[46] Harvey Aronson, "Movies and Their Critics," p. 163.

[47] John Coleman, Book World, April 11, 1971, p. 8.

[48] John Simon, Private Screenings, p. 34.

now into the world of Corot, now into that of Monet
or Seurat; desolate nocturnal city-scapes, enchanted
woods of Ville d'Avray, a solitary gull skimming the
waters of a pond while the small girl's voice pours
out its great yearning, a romantic horseman taking
almost forever to vanish down the corridors of
trees, a miniscule pavilion emerging in the land-
scape so very far away that it hardly has the right
to be there. . . .[49]

On the composer in the same film:

From Maurice Jarre, Bourguignon has elicited a
model musical score, infinitely various (Albioni,
Händel, Charpentier, Tibetan gongs, and Jarre's own
edgy modernism) yet spare and unassuming.[50]

In praise of the screenplay for David Lean's superproduction Lawrence of

Arabia:

. . . unlike other such films, it does not have an
impossible scenario with either typical Hollywood
or typical Christopher Fry dialogue. It is neither
holier nor sillier than thou, does not have Kirk
Douglas making noble speeches from a cross, and
"The Christ," in Lew Wallace's phrase does not
appear in it either in effigy or in person. When
God is mentioned in Robert Bolt's sinewy and
thoughtful dialogue, he is mentioned to good purpose.[51]

On the excellence of the editing in Paul Newman's Rachel, Rachel, a

film of which Simon was not fond: "Newman turned over an enormous mess

of footage to the editor, Dede Allen, and it was that lady, repeating her

wonder-working for Bonnie and Clyde, who turned Rachel, Rachel into the

adequate thing it is."[52]

---

[49]John Simon, Private Screenings, p. 34.

[50]Ibid., p. 50.

[51]Ibid., pp. 52-53.

[52]John Simon, Movies Into Film, p. 318.

His seeking out of deserving contributors to a production is not, perhaps, noteworthy in itself. Other critics do it too. In Simon, though, this practice recurs with almost predictable regularity. Sometimes his plaudits are as impassioned as his put-downs.

Simon can even be kind when he harbors reservations about a film or play, as he did when Dennis Turner's Charlie Was Here and Now He's Gone opened at the Eastside Playhouse in 1971. About that work Mr. Simon said:

> The playwright manages a racy and plausible dialogue, aptly encompassing horror and humor, toughness and tenderness. One of his neat devices is the poetic use of obscenity, which the characters heighten into incantation, litany, emotional purgation. Equally inventive is the game Charlie and Carla play: pretending to be dead or dying so as to force the partner into showing affection, for only when so fooled can these brutalized people break out into loving gestures . . . Carla's monologue to a tied and gagged kidnap victim is true bravura writing. Rosalind Cash's performance, splendid all along, here reaches sublimity, and she is impressively flanked by Joe Morton and Robert Guillaume.[53]

Even though Simon wasn't wholly pleased with the production, he was engaged by the obvious talent at hand. Therefore, he muted his reservations, as well as his characteristic noxious retort.

After critics and audiences in general, two of Simon's primary targets are film buffs and New Wave (nouvelle vague) movies. Both subjects are constant sources of irritation to him. Simon claims that the buff, addicted to movies as a "turn-on" or escape, is one of the major problems in the world of film. He describes the buff as

> someone who lives in and through the movies, who knows all their obscurest data (the obscurer, the better), and who follows his devouring of movies with much pseudo-learned post-prandial chatter, but with virtually no critical standards.[54]

---

[53] John Simon, "Strindberg on the Mat," New York, June 21, 1971, p. 60.

[54] John Simon, Movies Into Film, p. 4.

That is the buff's dilemma in a nutshell. As far as Simon is concerned, all the film addict's movie education is brought to nought by his utter indiscrimination. He further sees buffs as a

> curious coalition of disaffected intellectual drifters, neurotic young women, homosexuals in search of "camp," young people too lazy to read or go to art galleries and concerts, gadgeteers to whom a 16-mm. camera presented itself as a passport to Parnassus--an intellectual demimonde that recognized film as potentially the most energetic art form of our time, but that by its cynicism, pathology, immaturity, or lack of cultivation was hardly in the position to recognize real art when confronted with it. Youth who had never sat down with their Shakespeare--and certainly could not distinguish between a painting and a bit of dribble--mingled with fingernail-biting wives escaping from home-life by sitting through the same double feature twice.[55]

Elsewhere he writes:

> Significantly, popular parlance recognizes the existence of movie buffs and, perhaps, opera buffs, but not theatre buffs, museum buffs, concert buffs. For the movies are the cheapest and most accessible playground for the acquisition of meaningless expertise, and the fellow who can rattle off the filmography of a George Cukor or Douglas Sirk is no better than the guy who memorizes baseball batting averages, but usually much more pretentious.[56]

Pretentiousness is one of Simon's pet peeves. Next to the "meaningless expertise" acquired by the movie buffs, he finds pretentiousness more abundant in the films of the New Wave than anywhere else. This movement of the late Fifties and early Sixties out of France was in revolt against the slick, commercial studio product. The revolt took the form of conspicuous technique (or avoidance of conventional technique): intentional jump-cutting, elimination of montage, elimination of special effects (e.g., dissolves,

---

[55]John Simon, Private Screenings, p. 154.

[56]John Simon, Movies Into Film, p. 4.

fades), and the use of the hand-held camera. Simon harbors a further

dislike for any critic who supports the New Wave, or supported, actually,

since nouvelle vague techniques have been absorbed into even the most

conventional movies. Susan Sontag was one of the New Wave advocates; she

has particular admiration for one of the Wave's chief exponents, Jean-Luc

Godard. (Godard's devices have their roots in Brecht. Among the elements

of a Godard film are the use of signs, posters, and inscriptions to make

points, the division of a work into episodes, references to literary works,

references to contemporary issues, actors stepping out of character to

address the audience (camera) directly--all of which Simon finds pretentious,

repetitious, and vastly uncinematic. One might have predicted the critic

would delight in the literariness and theatricality of it all).

Simon labeled Godard's **Vivre Sa Vie** "trashy" and "pretentious" in

distinct contrast to Ms. Sontag's evaluation of the film as "one of the

most extraordinary, beautiful, and original works of art. . . ."[57] Simon

recalled the lady essayist's enthusiasm for Godard in a later acerbic indict-

ment: in a 1965 pan of Godard's Contempt, the critic concludes, "Until we

get an article from Miss Sontag proclaiming Contempt a near-masterpiece,

we shall have to consider it trash."[58]

Perhaps the most remarkable quality of John Simon's writing, however,

is not the content, individual as his opinions may be, but the form. No

matter what Simon thinks about the inseparability of form and content, it

is not only academicians who divide the two for purposes of analysis. (Res-

---

[57] John Simon, Private Screenings, p. 153.

[58] Ibid., p. 167.

ponsible actors and directors do it as well). Unlike some of his colleagues in criticism, Simon is a distinctive stylist. His prose is instantly identifiable. His critical essays, when they stick to the issues and omit side-discussions of actresses' breast size, are triumphs of scholarly elucidation.

Joined with other elements of his style that have already been noted is his ability to carry a metaphor amazingly far. In his review of a recent Broadway comedy he stated:

> The basic conceit in How the Other Half Loves, an otherwise ordinary farce, is to make the same set serve as the house of two quite different couples. Distantly related by ties of business, acquaintance-ship and adultery, they inhabit the same stage space alternately or even simultaneously, but the Fosters do not see the Phillipses and the Phillipses do not see the Fosters--that is, when they are not visiting each other. There is also a third couple, the pathetic Detweilers, used and abused by both the others. These wretches are even seen at dinner parties at both the Fosters and the Phillipses on consecutive evenings, but seated at the same dinner table that stands for two different places on two different nights. This clearly makes the British author, Alan Ayckbourn, the conqueror of space/time, the Einstein of farce. If marital capers pay off handsomely at the box office, how much more Emolument is there in marital capers squared, for which his formula is $E=mc^2$.[59]

The unsuccessful revival in 1971 of Arthur Miller's adaptation of An Enemy of the People gave Simon another chance for metaphor-stretching:

> There is a famous line in Pope's "Eloisa to Abe-lard": "The world forgetting, by the world forgot"; omit the first "l" and it applies . . . to . . . Arthur Miller, whose 1950 adaptation of Ibsen's An Enemy of the People is being given at Lincoln Center. It is odious to present a modern master as rewritten by a contemporary second-rater, especially when the adapter's

---

[59] John Simon, "Unstrung Quartet," New York, April 12, 1971, p. 58.

greatest weakness is his language and when his version
reduces an aristocratic play that exalts the visionary
individual over the purblind majority to a mere justification of Miller and his fellow-leftists during the
McCarthy persecutions.[60]

As noted, Simon has a fondness for florid rhetoric. Witness how

esoteric he becomes when he himself is complaining of esoterica: speaking

of the decline in quality of the New Wave films, Simon states,

> The New Wave is succumbing to a kind of Byzantinism
> that is no longer making it new, only esoteric, in-group-
> oriented and self-indulgent. Perhaps this is the ineluc-
> table trajectory of innovation, but if so, the New Wave
> is traversing it with alarming speed.[61]

In a comparable flight of fancy, he describes the dialogue in The

Umbrellas of Cherbourg as "of a banality unsurpassed by the pure dross

distilled in the alembics of Hollywood."[62]

The Simon style has its pitfalls. Sometimes it traps the writer into

verbal self-consciousness ("The time is the last gasp of the Duce's era,

with the Germans being booted out of the boot of Italy, and tempers,

spirits, and discipline cracking amid the bootlessness of it all.")[63] or,

to expand the previous example (from Luciano Salce's The Fascist/Il federale),

overly-cute puns; in commenting on The Virgin and the Gypsy, the film of

D. H. Lawrence's novella, Simon contrasts the performances of co-stars

Mark Burns and Franco Nero:

> . . . Mark Burns capably conveys a solidity that stops
> short of stolidity, a calmness not without heat below.

---

[60]John Simon, "Abelard's Loss--and Ibsen's Too," New York, March 29,
1971, p. 57.

[61]John Simon, Private Screenings, p. 149.

[62]Ibid., p. 158.

> The great lacuna of the film . . . is Franco Nero's
> Gypsy. Nero may be the reason for spelling the word with
> a "y"--so gypped do we feel by his nonperformance. Unlike
> the Major [Mark Burns], this Gypsy suggests nothing with
> his empty blue-eyed stare; yet desire, the Gypsy's absurd
> but absolutely natural craving for Yvette, and the salutary
> response it kindles, are the subject of the story. In the
> film, the Major's repressed stirrings toward Yvette register
> more strongly than the Gypsy's undivided desire. Nero
> fiddles while Mark burns.[64]

When they aren't so protracted, Simon's witticisms work. In March

of 1970, the critic wrote that "Fellini Satyricon is barely satiric and

a huge con."[65] Its brevity sustains the joke.

Proud of his command of the English language, Simon's pen can be

poisonous to those who breach accepted linguistic etiquette. When Elia

Kazan's America America premièred, Simon, who didn't like the work, took

its creator to task for his uncommaed title: "Kazan would always rather

say a thing doubly than singly, but, to find time for so much duplication,

he must breathlessly hurtle over the decencies of punctuation."[66] At the

conclusion of his The Greatest Story Ever Told pan, Simon poked fun at an

earlier critique of the same film written by Bosley Crowther: "Crowther

assures us that [director George] Stevens' 'reverence should captivate the

piously devout.' But what does it do for those whose religiosity, or

English, is not redundant?"[67]

---

[64] John Simon, Movies Into Film, p. 64.

[65] Ibid., p. 211.

[66] John Simon, Private Screenings, p. 120.

[67] Ibid., p. 175.

Simon's precision in language is rarely matched by his fellows in criticism, so he takes it upon himself to reprimand writers for their less than crystalline prose. Andrew Sarris, John Thomas, and Richard Roud are three of the many critics who have received public grammar lessons from John Simon.

Sarris once wrote:

> Tragedy and comedy float in such free orbits in Godard's sensibility that we often seem to be stuck in a steady stew of tromedy. Catherine's put-down of Robert [in Masculine-Feminine] is perhaps the most excruciatingly moving scene of a male Waterloo on the field of femaleness in all the history of dramatic and cinematic art. . . .68

which drew this response from Simon:

> Consider, first, the distressing diction. Why do we need the barbarism "tromedy," when we have the perfectly good word "tragicomedy?" What is a "steady stew?" Sarris is obviously trying to improve on "steady stream," which, at least, makes sense, whereas "steady stew" is either nonsense or rank pleonasm. As for "a male Waterloo on the field of femaleness," it is a superb specimen of catachresis. If we now proceed to the meaning of all this, it would appear that because Godard recklessly mingles the brutal and the facetious, which Sarris chooses to dignify with the terms "tragedy" and "comedy," he is to be credited with the invention of a new genre, "tromedy." And it further appears that a seemingly improvised scene in which a dull girl tells an oafish young man in clumsy and trivial words that she won't go out with him is not only one of the summits of cinematic art, but also one of the triumphs of world drama. This would be merely comic if it were not for the fact that such movies, and such movie criticism, are taken seriously by large numbers of viewers and readers, which makes it all rather tromic.69

68John Simon, Private Screenings, p. 318.

69Ibid., pp. 318-319.

Simon is still out to destroy Godard and the New Wave when he assails
a pro-Godard article by John Thomas. In Film Society Review (October 1966),
Thomas had written about Godard's The Married Woman:

> With Godard's film . . . we are challenged to split
> our attention; at the same time really see, really hear,
> what's happening on the screen. Not only does Godard
> brilliantly evoke the modern world with its constant
> and conflicting sensory impressions, but he challenges
> us with the context of the film to wake up and overcome
> it.[70]

Thomas' comments brought forth this response, quite rightly, from John Simon:

> It is not clear from that final "it" whether what
> we are supposed to overcome is the modern world or the
> context of Godard's film. The antecedent, I suppose, is
> "conflicting impressions," which would require a plural
> pronoun, but the decencies of rational discourse are not
> for the Godardians.[71]

A monograph on Godard, written by Richard Roud, film critic of

The Guardian, is deemed

> so frilly, pretentious, ill-written, and foolish that
> I can see no reason for taking up any more of our time
> with it. At best, one can laugh at it as at a C-grade
> Hollywood horror movie laying claims to metaphysical
> significance; if you light upon it at a bookstore, open
> it at random and get a few chuckles. And an idea of
> what, nowadays, passes for film criticism.[72]

Simon's own sentences never fail to parse; and, as one who upholds
the highest literary standards of Western civilization, he is always
prepared to jump on any writer who resorts to bad English. In his review
of Norman Mailer's pictorial biography of Marilyn Monroe, Simon drew
attention to Mailer's deficient grammar.

---

[70] John Simon, Private Screenings, p. 319.

[71] Ibid., p. 319.

[72] John Simon, Movies Into Film, p. 410.

Vulgar errors abound. Most typical is the mixed
metaphor, as when Marilyn is "a sweet peach bursting
before one's eyes" while looking "like she'd stepped
fully clothed out of a chocolate box for Valentine's
Day"--a chocolate-covered peach, presumably, to whom,
in the next sentence, "sex was, yes, ice cream."
Such an indigestible diet of metaphors leads inevitably
to the scrambling of digestive and other organs; so
Darryl Zanuck, a hundred pages later, finds Marilyn's
surpassing his low estimate of her "ulcerous to the
eye of his stomach," and Marilyn's vacuous countenance
becomes "in part the face DiMaggio has been leaving
in her womb." I haven't the space here for examples
of mere errors of grammar and syntax, misuse of words,
illiterate inversions, and the like; at least let me
instance the carelessness that exudes from repetitions
like "receive a good reception" and "Dougherty's
version is by way of Guiles: 'Are you happy?' he
decides to ask by way of a greeting."

The tastelessness is less in the prurience than
in the ineptitude. We read, for example, that "a male
photographer wants to photograph his woman nude, ideally
her vagina, open and nude"--as if a vagina were not ipso
facto open and nude. We read that "more than one Hollywood star would yet brag of early morning blow jobs fresh
as milk while having his studio lunch in the commissary"--
where it is rather hard to determine what is blown and
what is eaten, and just where "breakfast" stops and lunch
begins. Again: "Darryl Zanuck liked to put his own meat
into a star's meat, so that the product was truly stamped
Twentieth Century-Fox. In his eyes [Marilyn] had to be
Schenck's meat and Hyde's potatoes. No glory to his own
sausage." We begin to wonder what oral-infantile fixation
obliges Mailer to keep mixing up sex and eating, the erotic
and the esculent?[73]

Something of a literary showman, Simon's own oeuvre, as we have seen,

contains smatterings of Latin and dollops of French and German. An

exacting grammarian in his own language, he is adept at other tongues as

well. Within his command are French, German, Spanish, Hungarian, and

perhaps others--all of which are put to good use when the critic attends

special art house showings of films in their original language. (Simon

---

[73]John Simon, "On Screen: Mailer's Mystic Marriage," The New Leader,
September 17, 1973, pp. 22-23.

is an ardent spokesman for the subtitle and against dubbing). Thus he
is able to comment on the execrable dialogue in a 1963 Hungarian film--
"dialogue (I happen to know Hungarian) almost as bad as the subtitles--thus
'Edited' in the credits emerged as 'Compilated!'"[74]

"No doubt about it," Simon affirms, "the worst subtitles are still
preferable to dubbing," then he appends, "but must we really have the
worst subtitles?"[75] In an effort to elevate the medium, Simon is stringently
critical of the treatment of foreign films in this country. Indeed, he
frequently laments the fact we do have the worst subtitles. In Love at
Twenty, the narrator

> observes at one point, "Ils se parlaient stéréophonie,"
> which, of course, means, "They talked about stereo."
> But to the subtitle writer it is, "They talked stereo-
> phonically," which if it had any meaning, might imply
> that they blared at each other from every nook and
> cranny. Not only is this inaccurate but, worse, it
> suggests a pretentiousness of diction wholly alien to
> the gifted Francois Truffaut.[76]

Simon has caught mistranslations in other films as well. In Henri-
Georges Clouzot's The Truth,

> the accused Brigitte Bardot is told by the judge that
> already as a little girl she stole her sister's doll.
> The word used for "steal"--a deliberately somewhat
> grandiloquent one to poke fun at bureaucracy--was
> dérober, and, sure enough, in the fractured French
> subtitle this came cut as "already as a little girl
> you would take the clothes off your sister's dolls,"
> implying that, instead of being merely selfish and
> childishly amoral, the unhappy girl was a lesbian
> fetishist and incestuous voyeur.[77]

---

[74]John Simon, Private Screenings, pp. 97-98.

[75]Ibid., p. 62.

[76]Ibid., p. 63.

[77]Ibid., p. 63.

Such mistranslations make important changes in the story line and/or character developments. It is to Simon's credit that he is campaigning for improvement in this area. When it comes to stamping out barbarisms in the subtitling trade, he is virtually a lone crusader. If any other critics are concerned with the subtitle problem (and Stanley Kauffmann, for one, is), they have yet to voice their distress with the volume and the regularity of John Simon. His drive for improved translating is indicative of his solidly professional interests. When he concerns himself with worthwhile matters such as these, one can almost forgive Simon his rude, ungentlemanly tongue, that is to say his repeated references to Elizabeth Taylor's expanding frame.

Perhaps there is something to be said for Simon's modus operandi; perhaps his scathing indictments of ills in the movie industry will fall on sympathetic and, hopefully, influential ears. Until Simon begins to see some kind of advance, it is likely the venom will continue to flow from his pen.

That venom is apparent in equal proportions in his stage criticism. Yet Simon defends his inflexibility; his severity does not, he says, make him a hater of theatre. In a rather frank admission, he once wrote in his New York theatre column,

> In an average week, I get about two or three fan
> letters to some nine or ten pieces of hate mail. I
> enjoy both equally, though, naturally, I am more grate-
> ful for the former. . . . Most interesting is the demand
> that because the ["hate"] letter-writers (often backed
> up by friends) disagree with me--or because I don't
> seem to like any play and, therefore, theatre much--I
> be summarily sacked.

Now there are three points explicit or implicit
in this that bear examination. First, the notion that
a critic who likes few of the plays or productions he
sees must ipso facto dislike theater. This is bad logic
and worse mathematics.[78]

Simon's stringent criteria are defensible, he says, because, unlike

many of his contemporaries, he sees himself as speaking to the ages. He

continues:

Literary and dramatic values are always formulated
by the supreme court of time, also known as posterity.
If works and writers are considered worthy, it is because
they have survived the test of time. Now glance at the
number of new plays that open in a given season; then
look up in the authority of your choice (lexicographic,
scholarly or critical) the number of surviving plays from
any season ten or more years ago. Finally, decide
whether the number conforms more to the seasonal number
of raves dished out by me or by--you supply the name.

That, of course, leads to the second question: are
my few laudatory notices given to the right plays? If
"right" means from the point of view of time, we--or,
more likely, our successors and descendants--will have
to wait and see. . . .

Who is the complainer? He or she may be a literate,
theater-loving outsider; or, more often, a vociferously
self-satisfied pretender, whose lack of culture and dis-
crimination is reflected in his or her inability to cope
with the English of mere letter-writing, never mind the
vastly more complex and subtle language of art. Let us
take him to be an average concerned citizen who likes
theatergoing, reads the reviews in The Times, and perhaps
even an occasional theatrical book. He knows something.
But what of the critic who, from infancy, has loved theater,
been involved with it in one way or another, seen it and
read about it much more than the most dedicated dilettante,
traveled all over in search of it, and cultivated a
number of arts related to it (extending from opera and
ballet to music and painting)? Indeed, a critic who can
endure what is hurled at him almost daily under the abused
rubric of theater, must be either a strong-stomached and
weak-minded ostrich who can placidly swallow anything, or
someone who, despite his passionate jeremiads, continues
to believe and love the theater, and exults in its rare
but genuine glories. . . .

---

[78]John Simon, "Who Pens the Poison?," New York, August 21, 1972, p. 39.

I wonder: do these superiorly enlightened con-
sumers write similarly insolent letters to engineers,
physicists, biochemists, twelve-tone composers, struc-
tural anthropologists, to name but a few? Of course not,
because they realize that they know little or nothing
about engineering, dodecaphony or enzymes. And yet (to
take engineering) have they not crossed innumerable
bridges? Well, is theater less of an art and skill--less
of a discipline with its rules, devices, structures,
esthetics, problems, imponderables--than bridge-building?
. . .

. . . the expert can detect both hidden failures and
virtues--along, of course, with obvious ones, if any.
His expertise--in perception, comparative assessment,
and expression, if he is a drama critic--is not available to the common man, or even to the frequent theater-
goer. This fact has to be accepted in the case of the
qualified drama critic just as in that of any other
expert. Not slavishly accepted, to be sure; certainly
not to the extent of abrogating cultivation of one's
private thought and taste. But it has to be reckoned
with at least to this degree: "Damn it, there is a good
chance that, in the long run, he may be right.'" Then,
if one still wants to write a dissenting letter, based
on cogently developed arguments or facts that the critic
overlooked, very good. But the mere loudness of one's
opinions, even backed up by a large number of similar
loud-minds, is meaningless.

What is essentially quaint, lastly, is the assumption
of these gab-gifted amateurs that, because of their
presumed numerousness or actual vociferousness, the
dissenting critic should be fired. If criticism were
merely a business (as, alas, it is for some), the customer might be "always right." But serious criticism
is an art, a mode of perception and expression, an
ability to evaluate based on multiplicity of experience
and--less definably--taste. And here mass opinion has,
historically, more often proved wrong than right. The
critic, like any other artist, would be suspect if he
did not--by not being only of his time--antagonize the
multitude.[79]

Once again, Simon emphasizes that criticism is an art. His fierce

pride in being an artist is obvious. He positively revels in being a

serious critic with perception, taste, and the ability to evaluate and

---

[79]John Simon, "Who Pens the Poison," p. 39.

clearly express his evaluations. In the past, it has been the
expression of those evaluations which has clearly divided John Simon
from "the average concerned citizen" and the critical majority. If
Simon is indeed America's least influential critic, as he is generally
conceded to be,[80] then it is surely because his standards make him the
most demanding one.

---

[80] Harvey Aronson, "Movies and Their Critics," p. 135.

III. PAULINE KAEL

Pauline Kael and film criticism go hand in hand. One without the
other seems hard to imagine. Ms. Kael has called movies "the most total
and encompassing art form we have." She has written of the critic,

> He is a good critic if he helps people understand
> more about the work than they could see for themselves;
> he is a great critic, if by his understanding and feeling
> for the work, by his passion, he can excite people so
> that they want to experience more of the art that is
> there, waiting to be seized.[1]

As reporter Harvey Aronson has noted, Pauline's passion for movies is
obvious: she wants the public to see and enjoy films.

Richard Schickel, the motion picture critic for Life magazine at the
time of its demise, has observed that Pauline Kael never engages in small
talk or general conversation. "She only talks about movies. She only
seems to think deeply about movies. She's a bit of a monomaniac. I don't
say that really criticizing her; that's just the way she is."[2]

Pauline Kael began writing about films in her native San Francisco.
The movie habit struck her, as it did so many others, during her school
days. Kael was a student at the University of California at Berkeley from
1936 to 1940, but she left without taking a degree. After leaving school,
she made contributions to what are traditionally termed "the little magazines" and she operated a twin-art theatre in San Francisco. To exploit

---

[1]Harvey Aronson, "Movies and Their Critics--Whoops, We Mean Reviewers,"
Cosmopolitan, August 1972, p. 137.

[2]Ibid., p. 137.

her writing skills, Kael prepared incisive program notes for the patrons
of her movie house. (Later, these same notes were used by film societies
throughout the country). In her spare time, she participated in radio
broadcasts about film over the Pacifica network in Berkeley. All these
matters occupied her from 1953 into the early Sixties.

By 1964, Ms. Kael was well-established in the Bay Area as a walking
encyclopedia of film history and as a perceptive and fastidious critic.
(In 1964, she was granted a Guggenheim Fellowship for further study in film).
As far as the majority of the United States was concerned, however, Pauline
was an unknown--and not a well-paid unknown.

When interviewed at the 1965 New York Film Festival, Kael admitted,

> It's nearly impossible for a serious film critic
> to make a living wage in the U.S. . . . In ten years
> I made under $2,000 from film criticism. . . . It's
> always been for fun and love, never for profit.[3]

During low salary periods, she worked as a cook, a seamstress, a copywriter,
and a ghostwriter.[4] Among the limited-circulation journals which printed
her essays were Partisan Review, Sight and Sound, Massachusetts Review,
Kultur, Art Film Publications, Second Coming, Film Culture, Moviegoer, and
the Berkeley-based Film Quarterly. She also rose to the ranks of Atlantic
Monthly with a piece entitled "Are Movies Going to Pieces?" For the most
part, though, Pauline was strictly underground.

I Lost It At the Movies changed all that. I Lost It At the Movies
assembled in one volume Kael's pre-1965 radio commentaries, published reviews,
and essays. For a hardcover book of film criticism, it sold relatively well,

---

[3] Ruth Ross, "Perils of Pauline," Newsweek, May 30, 1966, p. 80.

[4] Harvey Aronson, "Movies and Their Critics," p. 137.

and even better (150,000 copies in 1966 alone) when Bantam issued the paperback edition.[5] Before long, most regular moviegoers were well acquainted with the name of Pauline Kael. Fame and notoriety were just around the corner.

In 1965, the year of I Lost It At the Movies, Kael moved East to become the resident film critic for McCall's. This assignment turned out to be one of short tenure. In May of 1966, Kael was relieved of her McCall's duties--ostensibly because, in the editor's words, "her reviews became more and more uniformly unfavorable--not only to all films, but questioning the motives of the people who made the films."[6] Moreover, her comments "became less and less appropriate for a mass-audience magazine. . . . [Hiring] her was . . . a noble experiment. The experiment did not work out."[7] A more realistic reason for her dismissal is that she lambasted a lot of Hollywood epics which (a) were expensive to produce; (b) were expensive to promote; and (c) were adored by the public at large, including subscribers to McCall's. Understandably, The Sound of Music, with its family appeal, its slick production values, and its lies about the hard facts of life, headed Kael's list of films to deplore. Her written attack on that film (she called it "The Sound of Money") caused considerable commotion at McCall's headquarters.

Shortly after her departure therefrom, several developments on the brighter side took place. First, Kael was hired as "occasional critic"

---

[5]Ruth Ross, "Perils of Pauline," p. 80.

[6]Ibid., p. 82.

[7]Ibid., p. 82.

for The New Republic. Her "Movies" column ran sporadically from November
1966 to August 1967. Then in 1968 her second collection of film criticism
went into print. An Italian movie poster inspired the title--Kiss Kiss
Bang Bang. Those four words, Kael stated at the time,

> are perhaps the briefest statement imaginable of the
> basic appeal of movies. This appeal is what attracts
> us, and ultimately what makes us despair when we begin
> to understand how seldom movies are more than this.[8]

Kiss Kiss Bang Bang collects the critic's writings from 1965 to 1967,
with an additional 153 pages devoted to "Notes on 280 Movies (From Adam's Rib
to Zazie)." The latter section is a compilation of many of the program
notes written in Kael's California days. Of course, the reviews for McCall's
are also included, along with previously published essays from other mass-
circulation magazines.

In 1967, William Shawn of The New Yorker invited Pauline Kael to become
his fall-through-winter film critic (rotating every six months with Penelope
Gilliatt). Kael gladly accepted the berth, which she maintains to this
day. Going Steady, the third collection of her material, reprints her
"Current Cinema" columns from January 1968 to March 1969. In her foreword
to Going Steady Kael reflects on that often bleak period before she became
a regular contributor to The New Yorker:

> Although I had been writing and broadcasting about
> movies since 1953, I had never had a regular weekly
> column and I had just about given up hope that it was
> really possible to be a movie critic when The New Yorker
> offered me one. . . . This book . . . is, I think, in
> some ways the best writing that I've done because I
> had for the first time in William Shawn an editor who
> loves movies and who never said those obscene words:
> "Our readers won't be interested in all that." He

---

[8]Pauline Kael, Kiss Kiss Bang Bang, Little Brown and Company, Boston,
1968, p. iii.

> gave me the space I needed to develop a sustained
> position from week to week, and, for the first time,
> that total independence from advertisers and from the
> anxieties about reader response that makes criticism
> possible.[9]

Kael's most recent opuses are The Citizen Kane Book and Deeper Into

Movies. The former is a volume divided between the shooting script for

the Orson Welles classic and Kael's accusatory critique of it, "Raising

Kane." Deeper Into Movies places between covers the critic's late 1969-

to-1972 New Yorker writings. In 1974 the collection won a National Book

Award in the arts-and-letters category.

Readers of any of these works--I Lost It At the Movies, Kiss Kiss

Bang Bang, Going Steady, "Raising Kane," Deeper Into Movies--come at once

in touch with the Kael aesthetic. It is an undisguised aesthetic, one

not difficult to fathom. Particularly when one views the attitudes within

an entire collection, certain Kael characteristics become instantly apparent:

the author's disgust at the pretense in art-house movies; her heavy

dependence on autobiography; her taking rival critics to task, a proclivity

which has diminished over the years; her love of kitsch; her distrust of

the auteur school of criticism; and her abiding love for the entertainment

value in movies--continuing in the tradition of James Agee, whose Time

and Nation critiques of the Forties had a liberating effect on the world

of motion picture criticism. Probably the first serious--and intellectual--

movie critic, Agee converted that particular kind of dramatic criticism

into an art. As opposed to his colleagues, he had a peculiar talent for

writing about movies in a non-stuffy, uncondescending way. A trend-setter,

-----

[9]Pauline Kael, Going Steady, Little, Brown, and Company, Boston,
1971, pp. vii-viii.

he was descriptive in terms of what made movies, both Hollywood fluff
and European neo-realism, work or fail. And again, in this respect, Agee
is revisited in the writings of Kael.

Ms. Kael's particular interest and style tend to set her apart from
other current commentators on film. Let us look first at her disdain for
what were hailed in the Fifties and Sixties as "art" films. Most of the
so-called art pictures of that period were foreign, and Kael was quick to
point to their high-flown dialogue, their pretentiousness of approach and
artiness of cinematography, and, in some cases, their virtual vacuousness.
As she asserted in "Are Movies Going to Pieces?,"

> There is more energy, more originality, more
> excitement, more art in American kitsch like Gunga
> Din, Easy Living, the Rogers and Astaire pictures
> like Swingtime and Top Hat, in Strangers on a
> Train, His Girl Friday, The Crimson Pirate, Citizen
> Kane, The Lady Eve, To Have and Have Not, The
> African Queen, Singin' in the Rain, Sweet Smell
> of Success, or more recently, The Hustler, Lolita,
> The Manchurian Candidate, Hud, Charade, than in
> the presumed "High Culture" of Hiroshima, Mon
> Amour, Marienbad, La Notte, The Eclipse, and the
> Torre Nilsson pictures.[10]

A few critics clash with Ms. Kael over such statements. Philosophical
differences often bring Kael and Esquire film critic John Simon into opposing
camps. Simon sees film strictly as an art form; this position presupposes
a rather stringent aesthetic stance. Few films come anywhere near Simon's
standards. On the other hand, Kael sees film (the word "movies" is her

---

[10]Pauline Kael, I Lost It At the Movies, Little, Brown and Company,
Boston, 1965, p. 22.

preference)[11] as a mode of entertainment which sometimes attains the status of art.

To John Simon's way of thinking, Kael's criteria allow too much pseudo-art to slide by undamned. Her unbounded joy at moviegoing, her frequent wallowings in the pleasures of _kitsch_ and "trash," and her "swooning [over a picture] in the pages of _Life_ . . . "[12]--these things rub Simon's puritanism the wrong way. Kael is summarily dismissed by him as a "curious combination of lively shrewdness, sentimental-hysterical self-indulgence, and dependably plebeian tastes. . . . "[13]

As previously noted, Kael speaks quite personally about her sensations in watching film. She is unblushing in her admission that, upon occasion, she sees wealth in "trash." (_The Thomas Crown Affair_, she says in her landmark essay "Trash, Art and the Movies," is "pretty good trash, but we shouldn't convert what we enjoy it for into false terms derived from our study of the other arts. That's being false to what we enjoy.")[14]

Hers is a frank explication of those baser, non-critical moments in all of us--even as the man who derives pleasure from watching stag movies, although he realizes there is not an iota of art in them. The stag films satisfy another longing altogether. Art has nothing to do with it. But

---

[11] Indeed, during her stay at _The New Republic_ as a semi-regular film critic, Kael changed the title of her column from "Film" to "Movies." Stanley Kauffmann, returning to _The New Republic_ after absenting the drama desk at _The Times_, switched the heading back to "Films" when he replaced Kael.

[12] John Simon, _Private Screenings_, Macmillan, New York, 1967, pp. 42, 203.

[13] _Ibid._, p. 311.

[14] Pauline Kael, _Going Steady_, p. 112.

Ms. Kael is saying that there is a vast range of quality even in the stags.
To elucidate her position, we can turn to her review of Sidney J. Furie's
Lady Sings the Blues, the biography of Billie Holiday:

> "Lady Sings the Blues" fails to do justice to the
> musical life of which Billie Holiday was a part, and
> it never shows what made her a star, much less what
> made her an artist. The sad truth is that there is no
> indication that those who made the picture understand
> that jazz is any different from pop corruptions of
> jazz. And yet when the movie was over I wrote "I love
> it" on my pad of paper and closed it and stuffed it back
> in my pocket.[15]

She goes on in that review to say that certain movies have a "chemistry
of pop vulgarization [that] is all-powerful." Lady Sings the Blues has
"what makes movies work for a mass audience: easy pleasure, tawdry electri-
city, personality, great quantities of personality."[16]

While John Simon would balk at the rationale here (steeped as it is
in self-analysis and sociology), other critics and moviegoers find this
frankness, combined with Kael's standards, a more tenable approach to
criticism. Whatever else you say about it, you must admit that Kael's
rationale is never cloaked. You always know what she is thinking and why--
and her prose is straightforward.

Kael's autobiographical interpolations are alternately praised and
condemned, but John Simon's accusation that their use is "irrelevant when
[not] downright embarrassing"[17] seems a strident overstatement. The fol-

---

[15]Pauline Kael, "The Current Cinema: Pop Versus Jazz," The New Yorker,
November 4, 1972, p. 152.

[16]Ibid., p. 152.

[17]John Simon, Book Week, April 4, 1965, p. 4.

lowing excerpt is probably the most blatantly personal passage available
in the Kael oeuvre. Is it indicative of a healthy, sincere approach, a
markedly original springboard to analysis, or is it merely an indulgence?
Each reader must judge for himself.

> When Shoeshine opened in 1947, I went to see it
> alone after one of those terrible lovers' quarrels
> that leave one in a state of incomprehensible despair.
> I came out of the theater, tears streaming, and over-
> heard the petulant voice of a college girl complaining
> to her boyfriend, "Well I don't see what was so special
> about that movie." I walked up the street, crying
> blindly, no longer certain whether my tears were for
> the tragedy on the screen, the hopelessness I felt for
> myself, or the alienation I felt from those who could
> not experience the radiance of Shoeshine. For if
> people cannot feel Shoeshine, what can they feel? My
> identification with those two lost boys had become so
> strong that I did not feel simply a mixture of pity
> and disgust toward this dissatisfied customer but an
> intensified hopelessness about everything. . . . Later
> I learned that the man with whom I had quarreled had
> gone the same night and had also emerged in tears. Yet
> our tears for each other, and for Shoeshine did not
> bring us together. Life, as Shoeshine demonstrates, is
> too complex for facile endings.[18]

With her subjective faculties glaringly apparent, Kael provides open
evaluations based on a combination of her education (both scholastic and
experimental film work), her years of movie-viewing, and her personal
tastes.

Of inestimable value in Going Steady is "Trash, Art and the Movies"
(reprinted from Harper's). This lengthy essay expands the quotation on
page 50 in praise of American film studio product at the expense of "High
Culture" (like Hiroshima, Mon Amour, and Last Year at Marienbad). The

---

[18]Pauline Kael, I Lost It At the Movies, p. 102.

attitude Kael expounds here places her in diametrical opposition to John Simon, Stanley Kauffmann, and all other "purists."

In "Trash, Art and the Movies," the critic articulates her credo. That credo, essentially, is that "art" can rear its head in the most unlikely places--maybe even, John Simon be damned, on a tennis court, maybe at a Beatles concert, maybe within a comic strip. Of course, along the way there is the admonition, "all art is entertainment but not all entertainment is art."[19] And on this side of the coin, Ms. Kael takes into account, as previously stated, that there are certain kinds of "entertainment" we enjoy knowing full well they are devoid of artfulness. <u>Lady Sings the Blues</u> is Kael's special case. That movie, for instance, is artistically flawed, but the critic found a wealth of good things to say about it anyway.

Kael writes,

> Unlike "pure" arts which are often defined in terms of what only they can do, movies are open and unlimited. Probably everything that can be done in movies can be done in some other way, but--and this is what's so miraculous and so expedient about them--they can do almost anything any other art can do (alone or in combination) and they can take on some of the functions of exploration, of journalism, of anthropology, of almost any branch of knowledge as well. We go to the movies for the variety of what they can provide, and for their marvellous ability to give us easily and inexpensively (and usually painlessly) what we can get from other arts also. They are a wonderfully <u>convenient</u> art.[20]

In many instances, "trash" is defensible--although not, as Kael emphasizes, defensible on intellectual grounds. By "trash," the writer

---

[19]Pauline Kael, <u>Going Steady</u>, p. 107.

[20]<u>Ibid</u>., p. 99.

means the out-and-out genre films which attempt neither innovation nor
profundity and certainly don't strike out in any new directions: her
examples of such movies include Wild in the Streets, Planet of the Apes,
The Manchurian Candidate, and The Thomas Crown Affair. Most "trash" is
for pure enjoyment. It is fun for the duration. Some of it is mindless.
But Kael makes a case for the good mindless fun-for-the-duration picture
as opposed to the bad one. Here again she exhibits her individuality--
although, not surprisingly, there are one or two other non-purists with
a reputation for praising pure entertainment products without resorting
to puffery. Maybe Judith Crist and Andrew Sarris fit into that category.

As we have seen, Pauline Kael is, in some respects, an affective critic;
but she never indulges in simply relating how something affected her. Like
all the writers in this study, her professional attitudes and methods
drive her to probe more deeply than that. In a sense, she writes what is
commonly named "criticism of commitment"--that is, evaluating a film
according to the way it affects society. Kael uses this principle at times,
although it is not her chief guideline for criticism.

Kael is also rather special in her recognition that moviegoers

> get little things even in mediocre and terrible movies--
> José Ferrer sipping his booze through a straw in "Enter
> Laughing," Scott Wilson's hard scary all-American-boy-
> you-can't-reach face cutting through the pretensions of
> "In Cold Blood" with all its fancy bleak cinematography.
> We got, and still have embedded in memory, Tony Randall's
> surprising depth of feeling in "The Seven Faces of Dr. Lao,"
> Keenan Wynn and Moyna Macgill in the lunch-counter sequence
> of "The Clock," John W. Bubbles on the dance floor in
> "Cabin in the Sky," the inflection Gene Kelly gave to the
> line, "I'm a rising young man" in "DuBarry Was a Lady,"
> Tony Curtis saying "avidly" in "Sweet Smell of Success."[21]

---

[21]Pauline Kael, Going Steady, p. 102.

Yet no matter what the content of the work or the specialness of an isolated moment, Kael feels that one's pleasure need not have justification. To give pleasure (on the filmmaker's part) and receive it (on the filmgoer's) is justification enough.

Kael also speaks to those people who maintain that trash corrupts.

> Can one demonstrate that trash desensitizes us, that it prevents people from enjoying something better, that it limits our range of aesthetic response? Nobody I know has provided such a demonstration. Do even Disney movies or Doris Day movies do us lasting harm? I've never known a person I thought had been harmed by them, though it does seem to me that they affect the tone of a culture, that perhaps--and I don't mean to be facetious--they may poison us collectively though they don't injure us individually. There are women who want to see a world in which everything is pretty and cheerful and in which romance triumphs ("Barefoot in the Park," "Any Wednesday"); families who want movies to be an innocuous inspiration, a good example for the children ("The Sound of Music," "The Singing Nun"); couples who want the folksy blue humor ("A Guide for the Married Man") that they still go to Broadway shows for. These people are the reason slick, stale, rotting pictures make money; they're the reason so few pictures are any good. And in that way, this terrible conformist culture does affect us all. It certainly cramps and limits opportunities for artists.[22]

Kael then contends it is this slickness, this predictability, in addition to a sameness, which drives people away from movies, accounting for a diminishing attendance over the years since television's dominance. A large part of the older audience, she says, gives up movies plainly because "they've seen it before."[23]

---

[22]Pauline Kael, Going Steady, p. 117.

[23]Ibid., p. 128.

> One's moviegoing tastes and habits change . . .
> and the big change is in our habits. If we make any
> kind of decent, useful life for ourselves we have
> less need to run from it to those diminishing pleasures
> of the movies. When we go to the movies we want some-
> thing good, something sustained, we don't want to settle
> for just a bit of something, because we have other things
> to do. If life at home is more interesting, why go to
> the movies? And the theatres frequented by true movie-
> goers--those perennial displaced persons in each city,
> the loners and the losers--depress us. Listening to
> them--and they are often more audible than the sound
> track--as they cheer the cons and jeer the cops, we may
> still share their disaffection, but it's not enough to
> keep us interested in cops and robbers. A little nose-
> thumbing isn't enough. If we've grown up at the movies
> we know that good work is continuous not with the
> academic, respectable tradition but with the glimpses
> of something good in trash, but we want the subversive
> gesture carried to the domain of discovery. Trash has
> given us an appetite for art.[24]

Ultimately, that is why trash (and near-trash) is most defensible.

When it comes down to it, enough trash makes us long for finer things--art,

if you will. At least that is what Pauline Kael thinks. Newsweek's

Joseph Morgenstern has praised Kael for having

> the wit and maturity to see most movies for what they
> are, "a tawdry corrupt world," but she also has the
> childist delight to see what movies might be. . . .[25]

"Good movies," Kael writes in Going Steady, "make you care, make you believe

in possibilities again."[26]

Another trademark of Kael's--one mentioned but not heretofore discussed,

and yet one that characterizes her above all else--is her continuing exploration

of the sociological implications of the cinema. No other critic quite so

---

[24]Pauline Kael, Going Steady, p. 129.

[25]Joseph Morgenstern, "The Moviegoer," Newsweek, February 23, 1970,
p. 100.

[26]Pauline Kael, Going Steady, p. 88.

untiringly and intelligently probes the audience aspect of movies, that
is, the psychology of watching movies and the sociology of response to
them. One literary critic concludes his _Going Steady_ review by praising
Ms. Kael as "always informative because of her unique grasp of movies
both as business and as social institutions. . . ."[27] One should add
that she also sees the possibilities in cinema for creations of art. Her
critiques are dotted with passages about _why_ we, the audience, go to movies

> (The question most people ask when they consider
> going to a movie is not "How's it made" but "What's it
> about?" and that's a perfectly legitimate question. (The
> next question--sometimes the first--is generally "Who's
> in it?" and that's a good, honest question.)[28]);

what _gratifications_ we derive from specific movies

> (We generally become interested in movies because
> we _enjoy_ them and what we enjoy them for has little to
> do with what we think of as art.);[29]

and _how_ makers of movies trade on that knowledge (recall what good psycholo-
gists the producers of _Lady Sings the Blues_ were). "Let's clear away a
few misconceptions," Kael has pleaded.

> Movies make hash of the schoolmarm's approach of
> how well the artist fulfilled his intentions. Whatever
> the original intention of the writers and director, it
> is usually supplanted, as the production gets under way,
> by the intention to make money--and the industry judges
> the film by how well it fulfills that intention. . . .
>
> The intention to make money is generally all too
> obvious. One of the excruciating comedies of our time
> is attending the new classes in cinema at the high
> school where the students may quite shrewdly and accurately
> interpret the plot developments in a mediocre movie in

---

[27]C. T. Samuels, _The New York Times Book Review_, February 22, 1970, p. 6.

[28]Pauline Kael, _Going Steady_, p. 98.

[29]_Ibid._, p. 102.

terms of manipulation for a desired response while the teacher tries to explain everything in terms of the creative artist working out his theme--as if the conditions under which a movie is made and the market for which it is designed were irrelevant, as if the latest product from Warners or Universal should be analyzed like a lyric poem.[30]

Kael's pragmatic outlook often obliges her to see or re-see films with the public, in contrast to her colleagues who overwhelmingly prefer private screening sessions. In a sense, her semi-sociological methods make her among the most interesting, perhaps _the_ most interesting, of all recent critics.

Kael wrote in 1964,

> I had gone to see a famous French film, Georges Franju's _Eyes Without a Face_, which had arrived in San Francisco in a dubbed version called _The Horror Chamber of Dr. Faustus_ and was playing on a double-horror bill in a huge Market Street theater. It was Saturday night and the theater, which holds 2646, was so crowded I had trouble finding a seat.
>
> [The patrons] were so noisy the dialogue was inaudible; they talked until the screen gave promise of bloody ghastliness. Then the chatter subsided to rise again in noisy approval of the gory scenes. When a girl in the film seemed about to be mutilated, a young man behind me jumped up and down and shouted encouragement. "Somebody's going to _get_ it," he sang out gleefully. The audience, which was, I'd judge, predominantly between fifteen and twenty-five, and at least a third feminine, was as pleased and excited by the most revolting, obsessive images as that older mostly male audience is when the nudes appear in _The Immoral Mr. Teas_ or _Not Tonight, Henry_.[31]

Here, as elsewhere, Kael's special and very valuable contribution to film criticism is her cultural and social commentary, coupled with her insistence that art can be "fun." This fun factor is a notion which

---

[30] Pauline Kael, _Going Steady_, p. 93.

[31] Pauline Kael, _I Lost It At the Movies_, pp. 6-7.

further marks the critic's distinctiveness. Besides, one can't imagine

many other critics going to some of the theatres Ms. Kael does or

reporting on some of the films she does. Not many reviewers would take

upon themselves an excursion to a Market Street dive to see a movie

titled The Horror Chamber of Dr. Faustus.

In a recent publication of audience reactions, Kael explored her

own response to Bernardo Bertolucci's Last Tango in Paris:

> This is a movie people will be arguing about, I
> think, for as long as there are movies. They'll argue
> about how it is intended, as they argue again now about
> "The Dance of Death." It is a movie you can't get out
> of your system, and I think it will make some people
> very angry and disgust others. I don't believe that
> there's anyone whose feelings can be totally resolved
> about the sex scenes and the social attitudes in this
> film. For the very young, it could be as antipathetic
> as "L'Avventura" was at first--more so, because it's
> closer, more realistic, and more emotionally violent.
> It could embarrass them, and even frighten them. For
> adults, it's like seeing pieces of your life, and so,
> of course, you can't resolve your feelings about it--
> our feelings about life are never resolved. Besides,[32]
> the biology that is the basis of the "tango" remains.

Pauline Kael's obvious concern, her passion, for movies is at work here.

One senses her commanding need to communicate through print. Only a

writer deeply in love with the art form he is writing about could express

what Kael does. Like a lover, she waxes ecstatic over success and, when

she witnesses failure, again like a lover, or, perhaps more correctly, like

a loving parent, she chides the wrongdoer. Very few critics can equal Kael's

passionate prose: even though Vincent Canby probably liked Robert Altman's

The Long Goodbye just as much as Kael--it was on his year-end best-list

---

[32]Pauline Kael, "The Current Cinema: Tango," The New Yorker,
October 28, 1972, p. 138.

for 1973 and he wrote the film a laudatory notice--The New Yorker critic
let her readers know in unqualified terms how she felt about the movie.
While Canby hailed The Long Goodbye as "thoroughly entertaining . . . very
funny . . . an original work, complex without being obscure, visually breathtaking without seeming to be inappropriately fancy. . . ."[33] Kael's joy
at the movie was more obvious, her prose more unbridled; within her seven-
page review-essay, she called Altman's work

> a knockout of a movie that has taken eight months to
> arrive in New York because after opening in Los Angeles
> last March and being badly received . . . it folded out
> of town. It's probably the best American movie ever
> made that almost didn't open in New York.[34]

Another controversial film of 1973 found Kael and Canby sharing identical sides of the critical fence. Both reviewers championed the virtues
of Bertolucci's Last Tango in Paris, starring Marlon Brando. Here is what
Kael wrote for The New Yorker:

> Last Tango in Paris was presented for the first
> time on the closing night of the New York Film Festival,
> October 14, 1972; that date should become a landmark in
> movie history comparable to May 29, 1913--the night
> "Le Sacre du Printemps" was first performed--in music
> history. . . . [Tango] must be the most powerfully
> erotic movie ever made, and it may turn out to be the
> most liberating movie ever made. . . . Bertolucci and
> Brando have altered the face of an art form.[35]

--all this in "trying to describe the impact of a film that has made the
strongest impact on [her] in almost twenty years of reviewing."[36] Charac-

[33]Vincent Canby, "For 'The Long Goodbye,' A Warm Hello," The New York
Times, November 18, 1973, p. D-1 and D-6.

[34]Pauline Kael, "The Current Cinema: Movieland--The Bums' Paradise,"
The New Yorker, October 22, 1973, pp. 133 and 139.

[35]Pauline Kael, "The Current Cinema: Tango," The New Yorker, October 28,
1972, p. 130.

[36]Ibid., p. 138.

teristically, Canby showed more reserve, speaking of the film in these terms: "beautiful, courageous, foolish, romantic, and reckless . . . [a] superlative production by Bertolucci [and] an extraordinary performance by Marlon Brando."[37]

The point of these comparisons is that, while Kael and Canby may be equally _devoted_ movie buffs, Kael's passion is more apparent in print. She can convey her unbounded passions far more dramatically than any of her colleagues. That is her hallmark. With a snatch of autobiography here, a salvo there, and a nod to the stature of popular culture along the way, Pauline Kael definitely calls them as she sees them. Indeed, with regard to _Last Tango_, she infuriated more than one critic with her references to how the film personally affected her; the hyperboles she heaped on the director and his star; and the shocking implication that a mere piece of celluloid should be ranked anywhere near the rarefied straits reserved for "Le Sacre du Printemps."

If Kael is to be criticized, as, in fact, she was, for adding fuel to the fire of _Tango_'s promotional campaign (her review became a two-page ad in the Sunday _Times_, then was used in blown-up lobby displays), then she is to be congratulated for her occasional trumpeting of a film that otherwise would have disappeared altogether. This is a practice she has in common with Judith Crist. _McCabe and Mrs. Miller_, an earlier Robert Altman work, is one instance. That film was failing commercially in its initial playdates. Warners, the releasing studio, was about to abandon the movie to saturation

---

[37]Vincent Canby, "Tango--Erotic or Exotic?," _The New York Times_, January 28, 1973, pp. D-1 and D-3.

and neighborhood bookings. Before they could, Kael published her affirmative critique, and the critique helped change the tide somewhat. In going to bat for McCabe and Mrs. Miller, she almost singlehandedly salvaged it--"almost" for two reasons: first, Judith Crist took pains to promote the picture too, and second, the film, while widely released made only a marginal profit at the box-office.[38] Still, Kael--because her commitment to the movie was strong--did her best to save it. That effort, for McCabe and Mrs. Miller, as well as for other pictures, is to her credit.

As recently as October of 1973, Kael requested and got a private showing of the lengthy Jean Eustache epic, The Mother and the Whore, starring Jean-Pierre Léaud. The French Film Office made arrangements for the special screening. Reports contended that Kael's special interest in the film resulted from a "downbeat notice" written by Nora Sayre for The Times.[39] Presumably, Kael knew that the Times' negative review could destroy the film's chances to be picked up for United States distribution. Eustache's work had its theatrical première in Manhattan in February 1974. Kael's review, a generally positive notice, appeared in The New Yorker's March 4 number. So far, however, her affirmation hasn't offset the Times pan.

Kael's subjectivity and her enjoyment of many non-art films have often come under attack. Writing in her own defense, she has asserted

> I'm not sure most movie reviewers consider what they honestly enjoy as being central to criticism. Some at least appear to think that that would be relying too

[38]"Big Rental Films of 1971," Variety, January 5, 1972, p. 9.

[39]"As N. Y. Film Fest Fades," Variety, October 17, 1973, p. 6.

> much on their own tastes, being too personal instead
> of being "objective"--relying on the ready-made terms
> of cultural respectability and on consensus judgment.
> . . .[40]

Pauline Kael's low opinion of her fellow critics reached its peak in

the years before 1970. Since then she has mellowed somewhat. But her

first two books are littered with derogatory remarks directed toward John

Simon, Judith Crist, Arthur Knight, Bosley Crowther, and Dwight Macdonald.

Although her vehemence of tone has softened lately, as recently as 1968 she

was proclaiming,

> Because of the money and advertising pressures
> involved, many reviewers discover a fresh masterpiece
> every week, and there's that cultural snobbery, that
> hunger for respectability that determines the selection
> of the even bigger annual masterpieces. In foreign
> movies what is most often mistaken for "quality" is an
> imitation of earlier movie art or a derivation from
> respectable, approved work in the other arts--like the
> demented, suffering painter-hero of Ingmar Bergman's
> "Hour of the Wolf" smearing his lipstick in a facsimile
> of expressionist anguish. Kicked in the ribs, the press
> says "art" when "ouch" would be more appropriate. When
> a director is said to be an artist (generally on the
> basis of earlier work which the press failed to recognize)
> and especially when he picks artistic subjects, like the
> pain of creation, there is a tendency to acclaim his new
> bad work. This way the press, in trying to make up for
> its past mistakes, manages to be wrong all the time.[41]

More than once Kael has cast aspersions on her colleagues' integrity.

Reviewing the spy film Our Man Flint, she addended

> If your local critics or TV reporters are kind
> to this film, you might bear in mind that 78 of them
> were invited on a publicity junket to Jamaica, as part
> of the film's budget.[42]

---

[40]Pauline Kael, Going Steady, pp. 108-109.

[41]Ibid., p. 108.

[42]Ruth Ross, "Perils of Pauline," p. 82.

Such are the tactics of Ms. Kael. It's all a part of the style that
her readers have come to know, love, and expect.

The candor of her prose, in addition to her devotion to the medium
and her interest in pop culture, have made Kael a controversial figure.
In her years of writing--from Film Quarterly to McCall's, from The New
Republic to The New Yorker--she has established quite a following. Even
though Kael is an opponent of all cinema cults, she has acquired something
of one all her own. Her fans number into the thousands--and a devoted tribe
they are. In 1969, at the San Francisco Film Festival, an American filmmaker had commenced a diatribe against Kael when someone in the audience
sprang up and shouted: "I think Pauline Kael's work will outlive your own."[43]

Kael's devotees are attracted to her zeal, her iconoclasm, and her
independent nature. But movie buffs and readers of movie criticism in
general support Kael for yet another reason: the tone of her writing--that
is, the attitudes she has toward her work and her readers. Filmmaker and
teacher Lee Bobker has asserted that in reading Kael, one "feels involved
in a friendly conversation. . . ."[44]

A cursory examination of Ms. Kael's compiled work reveals that she
makes frequent use of the pronouns "we" and "us" and of "our" to rope the
reader into a kind of shared experience. No doubt her following has risen
partly because her examples of common occurrence are so well chosen. Very
often she relates experiences that are directly linked with readers, particularly if those readers are within the general age bracket of the critic.

---

[43]Joseph Morgenstern, "The Moviegoer," p. 100.

[44]Lee R. Bobker, Elements of Film, Harcourt, Brace and World, New
York, 1969, p. 293.

The following excerpt from her essay "Movies on Television" demonstrates this experiential technique at its best:

> Now these movies [being shown on television] are there for new generations, to whom they cannot possibly have the same impact of meaning, because they are all jumbled together, out of historical sequence. Even what may deserve an honorable position in movie history is somehow dishonored by being so available, so meaninglessly present. Everything is in hopeless disorder, and that is the way the new generations experience our movie past. . . .
>
> There are so many things that we, having lived through them, or passed over them, never want to think about again. But in movies nothing is cleaned away, sorted out, purposefully discarded. . . . Watching old movies is like spending an evening with those people next door. They bore us, and we wouldn't go out of our way to see them; we drop in on them because they're so close. If it took some effort to see old movies, we might try to find out which were the good ones, and if people saw only the good ones maybe they would still respect old movies. As it is, people sit and watch movies that audiences walked out on thirty years ago. Like Lot's wife, we are tempted to take another look, attracted not by evil but by something that seems much more shameful--our own innocence. We don't try to reread the girls' and boys' "series" books of our adolescence--the very look of them is dismaying. The textbooks we studied in grammar school are probably more "dated" than the movies we saw then, but we never look at the old schoolbooks, whereas we keep seeing on TV the movies that represent the same stage in our lives and played much the same part in them--as things we learned from and, in spite of, went beyond. . . .
>
> There are those of us who, when we watch old movies, sit there murmuring the names as the actors appear (Florence Bates, Henry Daniell, Ernest Thesiger, Constance Collier, Edna May Oliver, Douglas Fowley), or we recognize them but can't remember their names, yet know how well we once knew them, experiencing the failure of memory as a loss of our own past until we can supply it (Maude Eburne or Porter Hall)--with great relief. After a few seconds, I can always

> remember them, though I cannot remember the names of
> my childhood companions or of the prizefighter I
> once dated, or even of the boy who took me to the
> senior prom.[45]

Again, Kael gives the reader a dose of autobiography, but this time it is laced with common experience. Kael wins over the reader. Nodding in agreement, he has a tendency to remark, "Yes that's exactly how it is. I've undergone the same sensation."

Widely published as she is, it is not solely through the printed word that Kael is recognized. Like most of her fellow journalists, she is a frequent lecturer at universities and film societies. Then too, due to the continued popularity of late-night TV talk shows, many journalists, reviewers, and critics, formerly faceless, have become known to thousands of Americans. In the late Sixties and early Seventies, by way of her appearance on the Dick Cavett program, Kael joined that throng. Like her colleagues of the critical press--Walter Kerr, Judith Crist, John Simon, Rex Reed--she has attained an identity with televiewers, thus making her, if not a household name, at least a celebrity in the quarters where it most counts: among the young, college-educated media enthusiasts who keep tabs on drama and film criticism.

Pauline Kael is widely proclaimed the most influential film critic now working in the United States, even though The New Yorker has a relatively small circulation compared to The Times, where Vincent Canby is first-string critic, and The News, where Rex Reed currently has a sounding board. Probably the critic best known to the general public is

---

[45]Pauline Kael, Kiss Kiss Bang Bang, pp. 217, 218, 225, 226.

Judith Crist, the scribe for TV Guide and New York who last year completed a ten-year stint as film reviewer for NBC's Today program. But Pauline, in a very real sense, is even more powerful in her influence. That influence derives from the fact that she is the reviewer most read by moviemakers. (A recent survey-interview conducted by Harvey Aronson for Cosmopolitan magazine established this.)[46] Furthermore, Pauline, "the critic's critic," is read by the right kind of people outside the industry. Richard Schickel, of Time magazine, has said of her,

> Pauline has a following among young people who are deeply interested in film. It's important to understand that only a very few movies are of interest to the masses. . . . The New Yorker may be a small magazine by our standards of numbers, or by television's standards. But Pauline is talking quite directly to the very people who still go to movies on a more or less regular basis. So that she has influence out of proportion to her readership numbers.[47]

That phenomenon puts her in an enviable position.

In a Book Week article of a few years ago, Saul Maloff declared that reading Pauline Kael is "better than going to the movies." Assertions of that nature reek of overstatement. Still, when you consider Kael's background, her stature, her longevity, her influence on her readers, the respect of her peers, and her unique aesthetic standard, you imagine there may be a touch of truth in what Maloff says.

Certainly that upraised voice at the San Francisco Film Festival was not out of bounds: Pauline Kael's writing may well outlive the work of many of the filmmakers who revile her.

---

[46] Harvey Aronson, "Movies and Their Critics," pp. 134-163.

[47] Ibid., p. 135.

IV. STANLEY KAUFFMANN

Journalists are repeatedly cautioned about a handful of topics which are potential danger zones in the media. One of the most controversial subjects of all, fully equal to sex and politics, is religion. On that touchy matter, editors normally insist that their reporters and critics maintain a hands-off attitude. If the subject is broached, one must keep an equilibrium in diction, respecting both the devout and the doubtful.

While many critics labor overtime to hide their religious convictions under a cloak of darkness, Stanley Kauffmann boldly asserts his world view. His beliefs are not remarkable, except that he brings them up from time to time in his film writings. Kauffmann's lead-off paragraph for a review of George Stevens' The Greatest Story Ever Told couldn't be plainer:

> Sometimes I am more relieved than at other times that I am not a Christian; these occasions include the experience of most films about Jesus. I am again glad of my graceless state, which freed me from at least one kind of offense, all through the latest, longest, most lavish solecism, The Greatest Story Ever Told. A sociologist might find an interesting correlation between a decline in religious influence and the increase in religious films. Possibly it is no coincidence that recent years, which are festooned with such ethical garlands as Bobby Baker's doings and mass cheating at the Air Force Academy, have seen large audiences flocking to The Ten Commandments, Ben-Hur, King of Kings. One emptiness recognizes another.[1]

---

[1]Stanley Kauffmann, A World on Film, Harper & Row, New York, 1966, p. 28.

The flow of motion pictures with religion-based themes has waned in the years since Kauffmann wrote that denouncement; but the critic has discovered that he doesn't require a Ben-Hur or a King of Kings to proclaim his skepticism. A revival of Jean Renoir's Grand Illusion or the American première of Chloé in the Afternoon by Eric Rohmer is sufficient occasion. Grand Illusion is Renoir's masterpiece about war (specifically World War I) and the decline of both Christianity and aristocracy; in Kauffmann's view, that grave decline can be perceived by even "[t]hose of us who happen to be neither aristocrats nor devout Christians. . . ."[2] As for Chloé in the Afternoon, director Rohmer "tells us, in effect, that God wants us to be happy and unhappy (a thesis I can support after a change of nouns). . . ."[3] Kauffmann, both privately and publicly, has been advocating a change of nouns for a long time. And that is only one philosophical factor which places his film criticism in a category all its own.

A native New Yorker, Stanley Jules Kauffmann was born in Manhattan in 1916. He received his education at New York University (the College of Fine Arts), where he graduated with a baccalaureate degree in 1935. Like most of his colleagues now active in the profession, Kauffmann's interest in critical writing began during his college years. In reminiscing about that era, the critic recalls a landmark date:

> I discovered film criticism some time in 1933.
> Up to then, although I had already been an avid movie-
> goer for some ten years, it had not occurred to me
> that films could be discussed in terms relative to
> those used by good critics of the theater or literature

---

[2] Stanley Kauffmann, A World on Film, p. 4.

[3] Stanley Kauffmann, "On Films," The New Republic, October 14, 1972, p. 22.

> or music. Then one day in my college library I picked
> up a copy of The Nation and read a review by William
> Troy--I can't recall the title of the film--in which
> he compared a sequence of a new film with a similar
> sequence in a previous one to show relations of style.
> I'm not sure that my jaw actually dropped, but that's
> the feeling I remember.[4]

In an introduction to his anthology American Film Criticism, which he

edited with the help of Bruce Henstell, Kauffmann mentions yet another

date important to his career as critic: 1958. "That was the year in which

Agee on Film was published, a year that marks the beginning of change in

general attitudes toward serious film criticism."[5] It was, furthermore,

the year in which Kauffmann began his long association with The New Republic.

From March 3, 1958 to the present, Kauffmann has been the magazine's regular

film critic. In August 1966, he took a year's vacation from writing about

film (he had been awarded a Ford Foundation Traveling Fellowship to study

cinema); but as contributing editor for The New Republic he continued to

provide copy, in the guise of political commentary and book reviews. Pauline

Kael wrote most of the movie columns for the journal in Kauffmann's absence.

Kauffmann originally came to The New Republic after a decade in publishing.

From 1949 to 1952 he was an associate editor of Bantam Books. In 1952,

he became editor-in-chief of Ballantine Books, an association which lasted

through 1959, with the budding critic adopting a consulting editorship for

the last two years. But by 1958, he was firmly rooted on The New Republic

staff. By that time it had been decreed (by editor Gilbert Harrison presumably)

that Kauffmann should be the magazine's one and only film specialist, rather

than one in a rotating pool of writers.

---

[4]Stanley Kauffmann, ed., American Film Criticism (From the Beginnings
to Citizen Kane), Liveright, New York, 1972, p. ix.

[5]Ibid., p. ix.

Since beginning his present career in 1958, the critic has written, in addition, for The Reporter, Saturday Review, Horizon, and Theatre Arts. Widespread fame eluded him, though, until he covered the winter 1966 theatre season for The New York Times. (His stay at The Times was short-lived because, contrary to editorial expectation and policy, his reviews were not, to quote Walter Kerr again, "consumer report[s] for the uninitiated. . . ."[6] Editors of The Times were reputedly discontent with Kauffmann, and he was no fan of that journal's policies and space restrictions; so, by mutual consent, his assignment with the newspaper of record was terminated.)

Unlike the vast majority of practicing journalists, Kauffmann has gained an enviable reputation in non-critical fields. As a novelist, he has had seven works published here and abroad--including The Hidden Hero, The Tightrope, A Change of Climate, Man of the World, and If It Be Love; and he has written a script for children's theatre (Bobino).[7]

Once in a while, Kauffmann reviews a stage production for The New Republic, but his main concentration is film. Judging by the quantity of his writings about movies, one may assume he is more devoted to them than any of the other arts.

Kauffmann's criticism has been collected in two volumes: A World on Film and Figures of Light. The former is the compilation of eight years of film reviewing (early 1958 to late 1965) for The New Republic. In addition to his weekly film commentary, the book preserves pieces from

---

[6]Andrew Sarris, The American Cinema, E. P. Dutton, New York, 1968, p. 34.

[7]The Author's and Writer's Who's Who, Hafner Publishing Company, Darien, Connecticut, 1971, p. 445.

other periodicals, some revealing second-thoughts, and a concluding
essay on "the film generation." Figures of Light, too, is largely a
collection of his "Films" column reprints. Herein, Kauffmann appraises
every important cinematic "figure of light" from Who's Afraid of Virginia
Woolf? (1966) to Catch-22 (1970). A World on Film appeared in 1966.
Figures of Light followed in 1971. As if these volumes were not testament
enough to Kauffmann's prolificacy, in 1972 he edited American Film Criticism,
an omnibus of pre-James Agee criticism subtitled "From the Beginnings to
Citizen Kane." With its careful documentation, American Film Criticism
proves Kauffmann to be what admirers, as well as detractors, have been
calling him for years: a scholar. The critic's broad knowledge of film
history and criticism surfaces in chapter annotations, an extensive index
and bibliography, and his career biographies of many important newspaper
and magazine reviewers of the pre-Citizen Kane age.

Kauffmann's reputation for scholarship is well-founded. It is a
factor not to be ignored in any of his movie criticism--from the earliest
examples (meaning 1958) to the most recent. One of his specialties is
making observations about films based on material from another medium. More
often than not, Kauffmann makes a point of reading the original (if he
hasn't already read it, or seen it, if a stage derivation is the case) prior
to writing his review.

Back in 1958, the film version of Shaw's The Doctor's Dilemma was
released, to extensive critical and public apathy. Kauffmann's analysis
of that film is model Kauffmann. Besides clarifying the essentials of
plot, stars, directing, costuming, and so forth, the analysis demonstrates
how well-read this critic is--in this instance, his familiarity with the

original playscript. Kauffmann describes at the outset some of the

"necessities" for transferring Shaw from footlights to celluloid:

> The producer who attempts to adapt a Shaw play
> for films soon realizes, if he is perceptive, that
> it is impossible; he must allow Shaw to adapt the
> film form to his play. For Shaw is a dramatist in
> the classical tradition: almost everything in his
> plays happens through the words. . . .
>
> It is therefore suicidal, for a Shaw film, to
> start by seeing how many words you can leave out.
> . . . When you make your Shaw film, use the best
> camera crew and cutter you can get, but place your
> chief bet on Shaw.[8]

The reviewer then proceeds to list what is missing in the film script

and the resultant inadequacies:

> Anatole de Grunwald, the producer and adapter,
> has committed the error of errors: he has tried to
> movie-ize the play. He has sliced the script to the
> bone and beyond; and because he has not condensed
> proportionately, he has distorted the story and theme.
> For what he has taken away of Shaw's play, he tries
> to compensate by giving us some shots of Harley Street,
> old motor cars, a quarrel with a butcher, a Hampstead
> pawnshop. It is, mildly speaking, an unfair exchange.
>
> I don't suggest that every word of the play should
> or could have been retained. I'm not shocked by, for
> instance, the moving of the Jennifer-Ridgeon scene
> at the end of Act III from the artist's studio to
> Ridgeon's house. But the general implication of
> this script is that if only poor old Shaw had had
> MGM around when he was writing this play, they could
> have shown him how to save time; and if only he could
> have written directly for films instead of the
> miserably limited theater, he would himself have done
> things like bringing in the recovered Blenkinsop at
> the end and having the dead artist speak on the sound
> track to his wife.
>
> When Shaw was himself on hand during the filming
> of Pygmalion, Major Barbara, and Caesar and Cleopatra,
> he supplied extra material as a kind of lubrication to

---

[8]Stanley Kauffmann, A World on Film, p. 90.

slide the camera from one place to another. De Grunwald
lacked that advantage, and it must be admitted that,
in his inserted scenes, he has at least had the courtesy
to use no dialogue at all or to use lines lifted from
other places in the play. But here again, in my view,
he has erred; instead of trying to write Shaw scenes
without Shaw, he should have plumped heavily for making
the most of the Shaw scenes he had.

Yet even this maimed script could have been much
more effective if it had been directed by someone who
understands the Shaw style. Anthony Asquith, a
competent film hand per se, does not. . . .

What he has done is to hire the best cast he could
find and to say, in effect, "Look, chaps, I'm going to
be terribly busy with camera set-ups. I'll just have
to leave the lines to you." The result is that we see a
number of good actors fending for themselves, with no
sense of overall scene structure and with much left
unrealized in each of their parts. . . . Only Robert
Morley, perfectly cast as B.B. and knowledgeable about
Shaw, gets considerable out of his part. Schutzmacher,
whose flavor contributed so much to the play's world,
has been completely deleted.

The pleasant surprises of the film are Dirk Bogarde as
Cubedat and Leslie Caron as Jennifer (here made Ginevra
and a Breton). [Bogarde] has been cheated of his grand
climactic credo; the film, frightened of large utterance,
simply has him murmur "Michelangelo . . . Rembrandt . . .
Velasquez" and another phrase or two, then he dies. He
is thus also cheated of his wonderful dying line, reported
by Walpole: "He wants to know is the newspaperman here."
. . .

Miss Caron is by no means ideal for Jennifer; she
is more a kitten than a young priestess. But she
persuades us of her utter devotion to her husband
as man and genius, and her playing of the death scene
is irresistible. The script cheats her, too; she is
robbed . . . of the meat of Act V in which the doctor
admits that he allowed her husband to die, she is
touched by his candor and states her faith in her dead
husband and his obedience to him through remarriage.
The script omits Ridgeon's reaction to the news of
her remarriage, the crucial line: "Then I have com-
mited a purely disinterested murder"; and thus we are
nicely protected from Shaw's truth.[9]

---

[9]Stanley Kauffmann, <u>A World on Film</u>, pp. 91-92.

Kauffmann does a similarly thorough job of explaining the differences

between Faulkner's The Sound and the Fury and the Hollywoodized version

thereof. But he postpones discussion of the Faulkner novel to show he is

more than conversant with the oeuvre of Anton Chekhov too. Tongue firmly

in cheek, he uses The Sea Gull as a springboard to describing what can

happen with screen versions of classic works.

> A recurrent debate about criticism of films and
> plays is whether adaptations ought to be considered
> in relation to their originals or as entities in
> themselves. Where the original is a work of little
> importance or reputation, the question can be begged.
> Otherwise, in my view, reference to the original is
> unavoidable. Imagine going to see a film advertised
> as Chekhov's Sea Gull and finding that in it Trigorin
> has been made a Mongol (to suit a Mongolian star),
> that he does not seduce Nina but has taken a Daddy
> Longlegs interest in her which blossoms into cozy
> marriage, and that the character of Konstantine has
> been excised.[10]

Kauffmann continues: "Far-fetched as that sounds, it is a fair analogy

with what has been done in the film of Faulkner's The Sound and the Fury."[11]

Then he reports the exact alterations of plot and character relationship

that screenwriters Irving Ravetch and Harriet Frank, Jr. have made.

> Quentin (Caddy's brother) has been completely
> eliminated, along with about half the novel. Jason
> has been made a Cajun to fit Yul Brynner's accent.
> He is no longer Caddy's brother; he is the son of
> Father Compson's second wife by her previous marriage.
> Thus there is no blood relationship between him and
> the younger Quentin (Caddy's daughter), and the
> antagonism between them can blossom into love and
> probably marriage. This from a novel which Irving
> Howe calls one of the three or four twentieth-century
> works of prose fiction in which the impact of tragedy
> is felt and sustained, a novel which ends with Quentin's

---

[10]Stanley Kauffmann, A World on Film, p. 93.

[11]Ibid., p. 93.

flight with a carnival showman and the certainty that,[12] whatever happens to her, the Compson family is doomed.

The critic goes on to bemoan further omissions and substitutions; he reveals his careful reading and thorough recollection of the novel. Nonetheless, not to slight individual contributors to the film, he leaves ample space to relate who among the cast and behind-the-scenes personnel merits commendation or blame.

This process of meticulously detailed accounts of textual revisions is typical of Stanley Kauffmann's style. He echoes the procedures repeatedly throughout his work, in critiques of films as diverse as Lolita and Catch-22.

In Lolita, the Kubrick adaptation of Nabokov (with a scenario by Nabokov himself), the "prose texture" of the novel is gone and the protagonist's "sexual penchant" has been "normalized" (Lolita is twelve in the novel, fifteen or sixteen in the movie).[13] In Catch-22, Joseph Heller's tone is absent, that "cool extension of the horror and the ridiculousness that are already present in the world: as in Kafka."[14]

Kauffmann characteristically examines these changes at length, with vivid, bountiful examples from each picture. All along the way, he provides striking analogies that are the marks of a highly literate man. (The alternative explanation is that Kauffmann is a pretentious bastard who can't keep his typing finger away from high-flown literary allusions; but this proposition does not seem to be the case: Kauffmann never lords

---

[12] Stanley Kauffmann, A World on Film, p. 93.

[13] Ibid., p. 113.

[14] Stanley Kauffmann, Figures of Light, Harper & Row, New York, 1971, p. 272.

his expertise or erudition over the reader. His literary references never strike one as superfluous, as straining for effect.)

His reference to other works of prose may be extensive, as here--

> Shortly after I saw Ingmar Bergman's Persona for the first time, I discovered the writings of R. D. Laing. Laing is a Scottish psychiatrist, blazingly humane, who is trying to understand (among other things) how madness becomes the sanity of the mad. A passage from his book The Divided Self might serve as epigraph for Persona:

>> The unrealness of perceptions and the falsity and meaninglessness of all activity are the necessary consequences of perception and activity being in the command of a false self--a system partially discovered from the "true" self. . . .[15]

By contrast, the critic's references may be simply en passant (a brief mention, in his Bonnie and Clyde review, of Lionel Trilling, who observed that the traditional literary ballad usually concerns an act of violence).[16] Extended or concise, Kauffmann's choices are always illuminating, never self-conscious. His literary style is as lucid as it is scholarly.

It is worthy of note that, although Kauffmann is widely read, he is not always a "purist" like John Simon and other of the "highbrow" critics.[17] That is, cinema is not always looked upon as a reduction of literature. Upon occasion, Kauffmann has seen film adaptations of literary works which transcend their origins. Whenever this happens, the critic tirelessly charts the

---

[15]Stanley Kauffmann, Figures of Light, pp. 13-14.

[16]Ibid., p. 19.

[17]See the discussion of "highbrow" critics in the John Simon chapter.

improvements, reversing the process utilized in the negative notices for

The Doctor's Dilemma, The Sound and the Fury, Lolita, and Catch-22.

One adaptation that Kauffmann found better than its source was

The Collector, the tale of the introverted butterfly collector who kidnaps

a young woman:

> John Fowles' tour de force novel, The Collector,
> has been turned with considerably more force in the
> film version directed by William Wyler. . . . The film
> version is ideal for Fowles' project, for it is complete
> without the entire second half of the book, which
> reviewed events that had already been seen from one
> viewpoint. . . .
>
> In the novel the young man is impotent; by
> removing that element, the screenplay becomes more,
> not less, truthful--it avoids some facile Freudianism
> and achieves wider humanity.[18]

Likewise, John Braine's Room at the Top

> has been blessed with a film incarnation which is, in
> my view, better than the original. . . .
>
> Neil Patterson's screenplay, praised by Braine,
> has strengthened the story line by rearrangement,
> excision and development and has . . . improved the
> characterization.
>
> [Director Jack Clayton] has made the very tempo
> of the film match the stages of the story. For a
> while the pace is swift, restless, impatient. . . .
> Then as the relationships form and deepen, the
> tempo gradually broadens--the way compulsive
> conversation with a stranger evolves into easy,
> relaxed conversation with a friend.[19]

In a moment of candor, Kauffmann once admitted, "I'm not worried about

desecration. Who wants to protect art that can't take care of itself?" He

---

[18]Stanley Kauffmann, A World on Film, pp. 132-133.

[19]Ibid., pp. 177-178.

added, "Remember those silly protests some years ago against the jazzing up of Bach?"[20] Silly protests? By reading some of Kauffmann's criticism, one might have thought he would have been in the forefront of such protest. The present admission is something of a shock coming from the pen of a highbrow. It's a sentiment John Simon isn't prepared to share.

One stylistic habit they do share--and a further sign of Kauffmann's intellectualism--is their constant reference to other art forms. Kauffmann frequently finds scenes or sequences in movies analogous to novels, essays, paintings, musical compositions, and dramatic literature. He moves with apparent ease from an allusion to Flaubert in one review to a quotation from Heraclitus in another.

Kauffmann's evaluation of Alain Resnais' film style in Last Year at Marienbad is a study in erudition. The critic compares the director's work to the graphic arts:

> Resnais has combined the loneliness of the di
> Chirico surrealist vista with the exploded time of
> Picasso's cubism, but with this simple yet important
> difference: he has not distorted any of his elements.[21]

In a similar manner, Kauffmann writes that the lovers in Elvira Madigan (Thommy Berggren and Pia Degermark) have faces "out of Degas. . . ."[22]

The critic's estimation of Orson Welles' The Trial is made clearer when he caps it with this musical analogy:

> [The Trial] lacks integral design and accomplish-
> ment. Kafka's or anyone else's. Welles stands where
> he stood, a spoiled big-baby prodigy who cannot resist

---

[20]Stanley Kauffmann, Figures of Light, p. 174.

[21]Stanley Kauffmann, A World on Film, p. 249.

[22]Stanley Kauffmann, Figures of Light, p. 35.

> showing off and who would be unbearable except that
> his showing off is often so magnificent. . . . [He]
> is not capable of dedicating himself to an author,
> he just wants chances for virtuosity. The effect
> here is like turning Joan Sutherland loose in Wozzeck
> and telling her to improvise.[23]

Elsewhere, Kauffmann calls on Guillaume Apollinaire and André Breton to help explain surrealism in the films of Luis Buñuel. With the particular aid of Breton, Kauffmann traces Buñuel's surrealist vision from its initial stage of incongruous shocks (e.g., slashing an eyeball with a razor in Un Chien Andalou) to its present mature state since The Milky Way in 1970. Of late, the filmmaker's concept is more closely aligned with Breton, who expressed a belief "in the future resolution of the states of dream and reality, in appearance so contradictory, in a sort of absolute reality, or surréalité. . . ."[24] Kauffmann demonstrates, by referring to Breton and Apollonaire (who originated the term surréalisme in 1917), how Buñuel's films now show resolution between the states of dream and reality. The Milky Way, Kauffmann implies, is more coherent because Buñuel "has come back to Surrealism with greater purity. . . ."[25]

Judging by his compiled works, Kauffmann is as comfortable writing about surrealism as he is, say, Thoreau. Indeed, Thoreau's Walden has found its way into one of Kauffmann's movie columns. A few short months before posting his notice on Buñuel's The Milky Way, the critic concluded his Alice's Restaurant critique with this reflection:

---

[23]Stanley Kauffmann, A World on Film, p. 120.

[24]Stanley Kauffmann, Figures of Light, pp. 233-234.

[25]Ibid., p. 234.

> During the best sequence, the last, I thought of
> Walden, the last chapter. Thoreau tells us that he
> left the woods for as good reason as he went there.
> This man who left society because (for one thing) he
> disliked its routines tells us that he had been in the
> woods only a week when he noticed that he had already
> beaten a path, from his door to the pondside. Some
> such idea may have been in [director Arthur] Penn's
> mind in his conclusion. Alice is in the doorway of
> the church, which she is soon to leave to found a commune.
> Loneliness is in the air. As the light changes, the
> camera moves in slow circles without ever leaving her
> face: away from her and back to her in slow circles.[26]

His true catholicity of reading taste is indicated in Kauffmann's

reviews of Godard's Breathless and Resnais' Last Year at Marienbad. The

former, to Kauffmann, recalls Shaw and Camus,[27] while the latter makes him

think of Archibald MacLeish, whose "familiar line tells us that a poem should

not mean but be; a film, Resnais obviously thinks, should not mean but see."[28]

Essayists. Novelists. Dramatists. Composers. Painters. All of them

in their turn are grain for Kauffmann's grist. What is significant here is

not the mere fact that this critic uses enlightened analogies, but that he

does so consistently. For Kauffmann, these referents are common practice.

For most other film critics, they would be out of the ordinary.

A side pleasure of Kauffmann's obvious intelligence and education is

that the man avoids pedantry every step of the way. In a lighter moment,

he has even been known to dash off a witticism or two: ridiculing the

excessive virtue of all the "good people" in Chaplin's The Great Dictator,

Kauffmann relates how "they settle on a storybook farm where they dine on

an outdoor table under a grape arbor in a picture so itchily pretty that it

---

[26]Stanley Kauffmann, Figures of Light, p. 200.

[27]Stanley Kauffmann, A World on Film, p. 240.

[28]Ibid., p. 249.

would give Currier the Ives."[29] With knowing puns of that brand, Kauffmann
impresses the reader; here is an urbane writer who can sense the down-to-
earth element of fun in moviegoing.

Kauffmann is a hip scholar, yet one never gets the impression of the
great academician slumming. The critic doesn't drift to extremes: he
refuses to use contemporary jargon to placate the masses; and he never talks
down to his audiences. There is no condescension with Kauffmann.

Devotees of Stanley Kauffmann point with pride to the considerable space
he gives in each review to the major elements of cinema: acting, screenwriting, directing, cinematography. His readers are treated to discussions
rife with expertise. For instance, his response to an actor's performance
is rarely stated in general terms. A member of the Washington Square
Players from roughly 1931 to 1941, Kauffmann knows something about acting
and expresses that knowledge lucidly in his reviews. None of Mordaunt
Hall's "He/she was adequate" will do. He lists detailed reasons for pleasure
or displeasure, sometimes citing specific behavioral observations.

Kauffmann is perhaps most eloquent on Marlon Brando, the actor about
whom, to date, he has seemed most enthusiastic. In a 1958 evaluation of
The Young Lions, the critic wrote:

> Brando begins with a good actor's instrument--his
> body. Not a huge man, he is both solid and lithe. We
> are all perhaps too much aware of the effect of his
> chest through a torn undershirt; but more to the point,
> he seems to carry in him a silently humming dynamo of
> energy, bridled and instantly ready. Whenever he moves,
> something seems to impend. There is in acting, indis-
> putably, an element that is often called star quality;
> partly it is this constant hint of possible lightning.

---

[29]Stanley Kauffmann, A World on Film, p. 162.

His face is enormously more expressive than one
expects. It is not the soulful mask of a Barrault or
Fresnay, yet it has more than the forceful masculinity
of a Gabin. Even his somewhat gross mouth, its worst
feature, can become sensitive, not with fancy make-up
and lighting but by the artist's method: imaginative
suggestion. His voice has been adequate to almost
everything he has asked of it. He has worked toward
more delicate vocal colors and his command constantly
increases.

Actors, even more than most artists, are restricted by their personalities, but Brando strives to
expand as far as possible, to use himself in playing
other people rather than to bring those people to
himself. In The Young Lions, for instance, we can see
at once that he has caught perfectly the stiff cordiality,
the slightly declamatory speech, the somewhat angular
movements, the charm and the consciousness of charm
that create another man--Diestl--for us. Yet, with
that paradox which is part of the fascination of acting,
he is also unmistakably Brando, not some flavorless
hack with wig and putty nose and laboriously disguised
voice.

Brando has evolved a personal style that relies
largely on understatement and the liberal use of pauses.
Often the effect is heartbreaking; remember the poignancy
he gave the vapid monosyllable "Wow" in On the Waterfront
when he realized that his brother was threatening his
life. Occasionally the style lapses out of meaning into
mannerism; some of Sayonara could have used compression.
But in essence he reflects in his style--as actors often
do--a prevalent artistic vein of his day. Kemble exem-
plified the classic, elegant eighteenth century, Kean
the wild, torrential romantics of the early nineteenth
century, Irving the elaborate majesty of the late Vic-
torians. I compare Brando with these luminaries only
to draw a parallel. He is a taciturn realist; an
epitome not of that joyous realistic revolution which
swept away the humbug that obscured the contours of the
world but of the generation born into realism which has
seen its world with harsh clarity, whose work is to
reconcile itself to that world's revealed boundaries and
to find its triumphs inwardly.[30]

---

[30]Stanley Kauffmann, A World on Film, pp. 33-34.

Reviews of subsequent Brando pictures merely reiterate Kauffmann's admiration--and prove again his ability to capture the vagaries of an acting performance in critical prose. But Kauffmann is just as articulate on other actors.

In reporting on <u>Some Like It Hot</u>, the Billy Wilder farce, the critic got to the heart of the Marilyn Monroe mystique, while making shrewd observations about the actress' talents and her shortcomings. He asserts that Monroe had few gifts as a comedienne.

> She is not nearly as good an actress, for instance, as her Continental counterpart, Miss Bardot; she lacks the French girl's voice, verve, moderate technical proficiency, and certainly lacks her range. But by now Miss Monroe and her advisers have learned where her strengths lie, and this role is superbly designed to conceal the weaknesses and display the strength--physical and personal. One aspect of her superiority over such pneumatic dummies as Jayne Mansfield, Anita Ekberg, and Diana Dors is that she has learned not to take sex seriously. As a performer she kids sex; and as a character, in this film, she is so humble about her attractiveness that her effect is equal parts sexual and endearing. It is rumpled, unpretentious, good-hearted sex.[31]

If this review hints that Kauffmann has a good critical eye, his review of the performers in <u>The Innocents</u> shows what a sharp ear he has. At one point in the critique, he elaborates on technical matters such as pacing and vocal mechanism:

> Deborah Kerr does her best, which is good, with the governess, and Megs Jenkins has warmth as Mrs. Grose, but [director Jack] Clayton's ear seems to have gone dull. He lets them play too slowly and, in many scenes, on the same vocal level, one of them entering on the note on which the other stopped.[32]

---

[31] Stanley Kauffmann, <u>A World on Film</u>, p. 148.

[32] <u>Ibid.</u>, p. 108.

Another acting critique which reveals Kauffmann as a careful observer

is his <u>New Republic</u> comment on <u>The Organizer</u>, directed by Mario Monicelli

and starring Marcello Mastroianni:

> [The movie] has several intrinsic virtues. First,
> Mastroianni's performance. With Toshiro Mifune and a
> few others, he is among those film stars who are also
> fine actors. Like Mifune, he displays versatility without
> depending on it; that is, he does not put on a different
> face, assume eccentric characteristics, and expect to
> be bemedaled merely for that, merely because a handsome
> sex star has consented to appear unpretty. He seeks
> internals and relevances, whatever the external form.
> When he tumbles off the freight train in this picture,
> he is a dirty, ragged, happy man pursued by the police
> and having the time of his life, conscious that he
> looks ridiculous (the man not the actor) but rich in
> sureties. The character grows: in iron, in guile, in
> the egotism required of zealots, in foible. It is a
> vivid portrait--unsmeared with third-class Moscow
> Art actorishness. There is also a scene which will
> comfort those who mourn that sustained acting is incon-
> ceivable in films. The speech in which Mastroianni
> rallies the wavering crowd to continue the strike is
> theatrical oratory at a high level, impossible without
> a sense of line, wtihout adequate voice and fire.[33]

Kauffmann's devotion to the art of acting is so genuine that, upon

occasion, he will recommend a stunning performance in an otherwise deficient

movie. Such was the case with Peter O'Toole in <u>Brotherly Love</u>:

> People won't go to see a fine performance in a
> poor film, as they did not go to see Richard Burton
> in <u>Staircase</u>, but it would be derelict not to notice
> fine work. <u>Brotherly Love</u> is a superfluous film. The
> director, J. Lee Thompson, is a pedestrian cinematic
> mind (though he evidently understands something about
> acting). . . .
>
> O'Toole has to survive some coarse incidents,
> like a tumble among garbage cans and chamber pots
> to prove how low he has fallen. But from his first
> appearance, there is conviction that a very difficult
> note has been struck <u>exactly</u>, with subtlety and fire.

---

[33]Stanley Kauffmann, <u>A World on Film</u>, pp. 341-342.

> Through all of this easily capsizable role, he balances
> pride and self-disgust, amusement and anguish. His
> voice is one of the best instruments among English-
> speaking actors, not big and boomy but delicately
> colored and strong. . . .
>
> O'Toole . . . is a romantic actor, in the largest
> sense of the term, caught in an age that has little use
> for that kind of romance. . . . It's a performance of an
> anachronistic character in what is perhaps becoming an
> anachronistic style, but it is splendid. Will anyone
> see it?[34]

Similarly, George C. Scott's enactment of the title role in Patton

was the ultimate reason for going to that picture--apart from, as Kauffmann

points out, a generally excellent screenplay. Kauffmann reserved his

praise for the actor, whom he considered

> truly commanding, fulfilling the hard, manic streak
> that was apparent years ago when he was playing Richard
> III and Jaques and Shylock for Joseph Papp in New York.
> Scott was never shy of self-confidence and now he has
> brought up additional power to support it. His voice
> has coarsened rather than mellowed through his career,
> but, in the latency of explosion with which an actor
> makes us pleasantly nervous, he is the most remarkable
> star since Brando.[35]

One more indication of Stanley Kauffmann's concern for good acting is

his career-long campaign for "whole actors"--meaning his plea for the sub-

titling, not dubbing, or foreign language films.[36] Again and again, the

critic has spoken out on how an actor, dubbed into English, is robbed of

a portion of his performance.

> If dubbing had been universally adopted when it
> was invented (1931), I would never have heard the voices
> of Vittorio De Sica in Bread, Love and Dreams, Françoise

---

[34]Stanley Kauffmann, Figures of Light, pp. 256-258.

[35]Ibid., p. 237.

[36]Stanley Kauffmann, A World on Film, pp. 64-69.

> Rosay in <u>Carnival in Flanders,</u> or Victor Sjöstrom
> in <u>Wild Strawberries,</u> to name three out of thousands.
> That is a quite genuinely dreadful thought to me and,
> surely, to others who esteem acting as a potent art.[37]

Kauffmann recognizes that actors in post-dubbing situations can never

supply the conviction of the real actor on the screen.

Because of his respect for the acting profession, Kauffmann is less

than gentle on performers who misuse their craft. At times, the critic

even resorts to indignation. In this arena, he is akin to that other master

of letters, John Simon; but Kauffmann gets his point across without resorting

to vulgar pranks like Simon. <u>The New Republic</u> critic has vented his anger

on Montgomery Clift, Burl Ives, and Jason Robards, among others; but the

reader suspects John Simon would have been far less humane under the same

circumstances.

On Montgomery Clift in <u>The Young Lions</u>:

> an unpleasant truth must be stated. Reportedly, Clift
> has recently had extensive plastic surgery performed on
> his face because of a motor accident. The change is
> startingly apparent, but what is worse, the surgery seems
> to have left much of his face immobilized. This is
> undoubtedly horrible for him, but it is not something
> that can be politely overlooked in a profession which
> consists principally of displaying your face and asking
> the audience to react to it.[38]

The same actor received a verbal slap for what Kauffmann considered his

non-performance in <u>Suddenly, Last Summer</u>:

> Montgomery Clift, as the doctor, is present a good
> deal of the time, but his contribution is small. Clift
> had, in earlier days, a certain fine-drawn tremulousness,
> limited but sometimes quite moving. It has gone; and his
> present effect, I'm afraid, is that of a husk that once
> contained a small kernel.[39]

---

[37] Stanley Kauffmann, <u>A World on Film</u>, p. 65.

[38] Ibid., pp. 31-32.

[39] Ibid., p. 82.

Thus, even when Kauffmann is panning an actor, he can be most descriptive. One of the critic's pet peeves is the proliferation of singers-turned-movie-actors of the Fifties and Sixties--Frank Sinatra, Dean Martin, Elvis Presley--a pattern established by Bing Crosby in the Forties. ("For many [Crosby] proved that he could act. For me he proved something quite different: that complete self-confidence and an acute sense of timing will see an experienced performer through a tailor-made part and will give him the gloss of having acted.")[40]

As for Burl Ives in Cat on a Hot Tin Roof:

> When Burl Ives played Big Daddy on Broadway, his widely hailed portrayal seemed to me merely the ingenious use of his presence by the director. From it, however, Ives has learned enough to make a career for himself; he is currently repeating that portrayal not only in this film but as a Texas beef baron in The Big Country and a Florida gang chief in Wind Across the Everglades, in each case a lusty, life-loving tyrant. May one suggest that three times is enough? Ives, to this viewer, is simply an outsize man with a moderately effectual personality, not an actor. Like Napoleon's army, he has traveled on his stomach. His performance, like his theatrical person and like Williams' play, is imposing bulk without much content.[41]

Kauffmann doesn't always reserve his dissatisfaction for men. Once in a great while, an actress suffers at his pen. Rita Tushingham and Siobhan McKenna are two examples. The reviewer's highly favorable comments for Richard Lester's The Knack were tempered by his lack of enchantment with the leading lady's looks:

> Rita Tushingham is reaping a reward that usually accrues to male actors: she gets overpraised because she is not good-looking. Virtues are read into her

---

[40]Stanley Kauffmann, A World on Film, p. 47.

[41]Ibid., p. 81.

acting on the assumption that a girl as plain as that
<u>must</u> be immensely talented in order to be in films at
all. She is spirited, convincing, and sometimes has a
comfy-slipper, rainy-day sex appeal; but, to me, there
is not much more.[42]

Perhaps for identical reasons, Kauffmann thinks Siobhan McKenna is

often overpraised. About her performance in the film version of <u>The</u>

<u>Playboy of the Western World</u>, he said this:

Siobhan McKenna is considered by some a great
actress; to me she is sometimes a satisfactory one.
Here she again leaves me unstirred, with her obvious
and somewhat labored effects, her heavy unexpressive
features. Additionally, Pegeen Mike is supposed to be
"a wild-looking but fine girl of about twenty." Miss
McKenna looks no more wild than, alas, she looks twenty;
she seems the coeval of the Widow Quin, which badly
unbalances the drama.[43]

And finally, Kauffmann on Jason Robards in Sam Peckinpah's <u>The Ballad</u>

<u>of Cable Hogue</u>:

Jason Robards is Hogue. From the first moment,
he is physically phony, because this grizzled desert
rat has a set of teeth that would be too white for
a TV denture-cleanser ad. On this initial phoniness,
Robards builds with empty gusto and stale actor's
rhetoric, and turns this intended folk ballad into a
ham salad.[44]

Again, beneath the bile, one senses care and involvement. Kauffmann

wants to like Robards. His lingering on an apparent triviality (the dentally

hygienic grizzled desert rat) is indicative of his insight. On this observable

matter, Kauffmann is, of course, exactly right: the actor's teeth are too

clean-looking, considering what his character has gone through. (The overall

---

[42]Stanley Kauffmann, <u>A World on Film</u>, p. 217.

[43]<u>Ibid.</u>, p. 219.

[44]Stanley Kauffmann, <u>Figures of Light</u>, p. 267.

failure of the performance, however, is matter for debate: Kauffmann's

judgment that Robards "builds with empty gusto and stale actor's rhetoric"[45]

is admittedly a case of subjective judgment. The point we are considering

is this: the critic is one who notices detail and mentions details in

print so that, in turn, his purely subjective pronouncements have some

foundation in observable behavior. There are no sweeping, unfounded judg-

ments here. Kauffmann is as removed as he can be from the band-wagon

journalism of Rex Reed, who strikes many of his colleagues as the epitome

of subjective wallowing.)

Another area of critical concern with Kauffmann is screenwriting. Obser-

vations about propriety, style, and content of screenplays can be found in

virtually every piece of criticism he writes. His review of John Huston's

The Misfits, from an original script by Arthur Miller, shows the critic

at his most meticulous:

> Miller has often had surprising lumps in his generally
> true dialogue. (In Death of a Salesman the vernacular
> Biff apologizes to his mother: "I've been remiss.")
> Here the mixture is as before. There is much acute and
> vivid writing; a phone call to his mother by Perce, the
> third man, is a brilliant character sketch. Then we get
> literary utterances like Guido's "We're all blind bom-
> bardiers. . . . Droppin' a bomb is like tellin' a lie--
> makes everything so quiet afterwards."[46]

Later in the same critique, after other dialogue samples, Kauffmann

expresses disapproval of the film's conclusion for its "fast, almost

synoptic talking-into-final-shape of the theme. The ending, after all the

candid confrontation of harsh facts . . . ., is as suddenly and incredibly

'up-beat' as anything by the late Oscar Hammerstein."[47]

---

[45] Stanley Kauffmann, Figures of Light, p. 267.

[46] Stanley Kauffmann, A World on Film, p. 101.

[47] Ibid., p. 101.

A literary man himself, Kauffmann cautions that "we mustn't be rigidly literary in our approach to film"[48] even though most films have their bases in the printed word, whether a novel, a playscript, or a scenario drawn up especially for the movie. His method allows him to sense the intrinsically filmic nature of movies and to offer reprimands to scenarists like Arthur Miller whose literariness sometimes obtrudes on common and/or cinematic sense.

Kauffmann is equally resourceful in describing the contributions of the film director. For example, his appraisal of John Schlesinger's _Midnight Cowboy_ is filled with specific directorial contributions. The tenor of the review is generally positive:

> Schlesinger's sense of pace is so fine that the whirling surface of the film is quite firm; and of course, part of the sense is knowing when to slow down, when to let a scene breathe. In his methods he has at least two hallmarks. One, which I noted in his first feature, _A Kind of Loving_ (1962), is the use of subsidiary action to keep a patch of dialogue from getting static. Example: Joe and his friend, Ratso, are talking at a luncheonette and, at the corner far behind them, a strident woman is telling someone an irrelevant story that we never quite hear but that contributes life to the scene. And Schlesinger likes to begin a sequence with a close-up of some oblique motion that slides up into the center. Example: we follow two drinks on a tray that end up on a sidewalk cafe table just as Joe and Ratso pass. And the very way that Ratso enters this film is an inspired touch. After the picture is well along, after we have actually forgotten that Dustin Hoffman is one of the stars, the camera slides down a crowded Broadway bar, until it reaches Joe. Then we realize that the person next to Joe is not one more extra, it is Hoffman as Ratso, who strikes up a conversation and launches himself into the story. It's not only a nice twist on Schlesinger's oblique device, it also, figuratively, binds the New York environment closer to Joe.
>
> Schlesinger, an ex-actor, is good with actors.[49]

---

[48]Stanley Kauffmann, _A World on Film_, p. 118.

[49]Stanley Kauffmann, _Figures of Light_, pp. 171-172.

What follows is a paragraph of praise for the principals, Hoffman
and Jon Voight, and how well Schlesinger uses them. But the director
doesn't receive total endorsement. Characteristically, Kauffmann notes
problem moments too:

> So much of this film is exceptionally good that its
> uneasy spots are especially troublesome. Ratso's fantasies,
> visualized for us, mar the viewpoint of the film, which
> is generally and rightly Joe's; and the fantasies themselves
> are trite. The Warhol-type party, with Warhol types, looks
> more like Schlesinger the tourist-shopper than the artist;
> anyway, can't we have an international statute against
> trying to depict decadence through wild parties? It never
> has worked, from Intolerance to La Dolce Vita to
> Schlesinger's own Darling. Enough, already.
>
> There are touches of overindulgence. A TV remote-
> control switch lies on the bed where Joe romps with the
> call girl, and the set switches dizzyingly, with heavy
> humor. The implied fellatio in a grind-movie balcony
> doesn't need the sci-fi missile on the screen to make
> its point. Nor do we need the shots of Joe straining
> in the sack to please a client. And there is some facile
> ugliness. Ever since his early documentary Terminus,
> Schlesinger has shown a weakness for the British Free
> Cinema fallacy; the belief that close-ups of a lot of
> ugly faces, particularly old ones, prove that (a) life
> is ugly and (b) film can tell the Truth about it.
>
> There are a few other flawed moments, like Joe's
> final brutality with a man whom he robs in order to
> get the ailing Ratso to Florida. The brutality is in
> the novel, but [author James Leo] Herlihy plays it in
> the key of Joe's motives, not as a flare of sadism. And
> the last shot--Joe arriving in Florida on a bus with the
> dead Ratso next to him, with the Miami skyline super-
> imposed--seems a clever substitute for the good last shot
> that Schlesinger couldn't think of.[50]

One of Kauffmann's trademarks, as demonstrated in the last two lengthy
quotes, is his astute selection of examples to make a point. After reading
those excerpts, one has no doubts about the virtues and shortcomings of
Midnight Cowboy, as seen from one perspective. The critic makes his assertion

---

[50]Stanley Kauffmann, Figures of Light, pp. 173-174.

(e.g., Schlesinger's fondness for "subsidiary action"), then methodically backs it up with an evocative illustration. It is difficult to imagine more provocative, insightful examples than those provided by Kauffmann. For anyone who has seen the film, these illustrations take on particular importance; the mind is flooded with Schlesinger's images.

That talent for summoning images from a film is not shared by many other film critics. As Lee Bobker has stated, even though many critics try to describe scenes from movies, Kauffmann is better than almost anyone in choosing examples to convince the reader.[51] The Midnight Cowboy critique is simply one of hundreds in which Kauffmann's delineations are nearly as forceful as the original image.

Aligned with Stanley Kauffmann's talent for description (acting, directorial, photographic) is his tireless effort to point out illogic ("inconsistencies and loose ends")[52] both in story line and in directorial and technical choices. The critic is constantly questioning moments in films that don't make sense. Ever the scholar, his reviews are dotted with rhetorical queries.

The film adaptation of The Sound and the Fury betrays a number of inconsistencies. Among the questions posed by Kauffmann at the end of his review are these:

> How does Jason, who boasts that he is the family mainstay, support them after he hits his employer Earl Snopes? What happened to Quentin's resentment of Caddy because of her mother's reluctance to defend her? Why did Jason tear furiously after the thieving Quentin and her lover only to tell her that she could do what she chose and then leave her?[53]

---

[51]Lee R. Bobker, Elements of Film, Harcourt, Brace & World, New York, 1969, p. 269.

[52]Stanley Kauffmann, A World on Film, p. 94.

[53]Ibid., p. 94.

There were also some questions of logic to be directed at the Delbert

Mann-Irwin Shaw film of O'Neill's Desire Under the Elms:

> the construction of the play after the baby's birth is
> so contrived that it draws attention to itself. Why
> should Eben immediately believe his father's story
> about Anna instead of her version? Why should she
> keep silent about her plan to murder the baby? Why,
> after being revolted by her crime, should Eben change
> so quickly and come back to accompany her to prison?[54]

Kauffmann also articulated some questions about Arthur Miller's screen-

play for The Misfits:

> The film moves with Roslyn, the girl: she is one
> of the two chief searchers for truth and she is the
> cause of the revelation of truth to Gay, her lover.
> But what does her search consist of? In the beginning
> we are shown a highly insecure, neurotic girl. . . .
> Then, although she has just told Gay she doesn't feel
> "that way" about him, she moves in with him; and the
> first time they are visited by their friends, one of them
> tells her "You found yourself, haven't you?" and the other
> says, "You have the gift of life." Where did she get it?
> . . . What produced this fantastic change? A few weeks
> of bliss with Gay? Can Miller seriously believe that?
>
> And how does she effect a resolution in Gay?[55]

Kauffmann's socratic method is a practice consistent with his scholarly

leanings. Constantly at the "why" of a subject, he represents a logical

approach not so conspicuous in his fellow critics (not present at all in

some of them). Even when he isn't issuing a paragraph of rhetorical questions,

he is probing for answers, as in this excerpt from a review of Lindsay

Anderson's This Sporting Life:

> Most of the weaknesses in script and execution
> are too commingled to be separable. The team backer,
> overplayed by Alan Badel with oily clichés, is intro-
> duced with suggestions of villainy, the criminal figure
> often hovering on the edges of commercialized sport.

---

[54]Stanley Kauffmann, A World on Film, p. 72.

[55]Ibid., p. 100.

> But no such thing: he turns out simply to be a busi-
> nessman who owns a piece of the team. The vicious and
> criminal implications are pointless, just trite hang-
> overs from past sport films. The old man who scouts
> for the team is drawn at length as a kind of shabby
> Fate (with a hint of homosexuality) who keeps materi-
> alizing out of the shadows. Toward the end of the
> film he disappears, unexplained, unfulfilled. The
> episode in which [Richard] Harris takes the widow out
> for the first time is a gauche scene instead of a scene
> of gaucherie. In a posh restaurant he puts his feet
> on a chair, insults other guests, chivvies the waiter--
> all quite unbelievable in view of the weeks it took him
> to get the widow to come out with him and his anxiety to
> please her. The woman walks out in understandable
> embarrassment; yet when he follows her home, she agrees
> to go to bed with him--an incredible ending to an
> incredible episode.[56]

Part of Kauffmann's careful scrutiny of films (and his ability to

elaborate with precision) is due to his habit of repeated viewing. Some-

times a return visit is to confirm an opinion. Sometimes it is to check

detail. In any case, when Kauffmann informs the reader he has seen a

film three times--as he has, to name two, La Notte and Red Desert[57]--he

admits to yet another practice not commonly followed in film criticism.

But no matter the reason for his return: the fact he does is evidence

again of his integrity and professional attitude, as well as his concern

for the sensations of film-viewing.

His attitude about the "feel" of cinema shimmers throughout his oeuvre,

and it evolves into an important statement in his essay, "The Necessary

Film." This brief credo is a public issuance of at least a portion of his

theoretical concepts. Whereas his scholarly criteria and his exploration

of aesthetic and social issues have long been a matter of record, here he

---

[56]Stanley Kauffmann, A World on Film, p. 211.

[57]Ibid., pp. 305 and 319.

reveals himself in a different (but not necessarily new) light. More

than ever before in his published critiques, he allies himself, Kael-like,

with the public at large, as he describes how movies "inescapably" touch

us:

> I suggest that the fundamental way, conscious or
> not, in which we determine the quality of a film is by
> the degree to which the re-experiencing of ourselves
> coincides with our pride, our shames, our hopes, our
> honor. Finally, distinctions among films arise from
> the way they please or displease us with ourselves:
> not whether they please or displease but how.[58]

Kauffmann hasn't yet evolved a formula (he isn't a monotonous writer),

but certain stylistic patterns recur often enough to merit attention. With

rare exceptions, one of the four methods outlined below is used at the

start of his reviews.

Kauffmann has a habit of synopsizing a film's plot in the second

paragraph of a critique. When the synopsis is delayed until the second

paragraph, the first is traditionally some form of background information.

The critic "eases" into his reviews in that manner. One typical beginning

is an account of previous work done by the director, his writer, or one of

the actors. The reviews for John Cassavetes' Faces[59] and Ingmar Bergman's

Hour of the Wolf[60] begin this way, as do a host of others.

An alternate opening is seen in this critique of Godard's innovative

Breathless:

> In addition to her function as aesthetic conscience
> of the Western world, France has always been a pioneer in
> morality. I don't mean matters like the so-called "French

---

[58]Stanley Kauffmann, Figures of Light, p. 282.

[59]Ibid., p. 120.

[60]Ibid., p. 62.

farce," which has as little relevance to French life as to anyone's; I mean, for instance, the fact that Madame Bovary was published in the same year as Little Dorrit and three years before The Marble Faun. The French continue to explore in both areas. Much of the result can be written off as mere excursion, still they do it.[61]

This sort of approach, repeated in notices for Bonnie and Clyde[62] and Joseph Strick's Ulysses,[63] places the film in a cultural and social context. It is a practice which, at least in the Breathless review, makes for a tidy resolution: in a postscript to that critique, Kauffmann ends as he began, with literary references (this time Shaw and Camus).[64]

A third common opening for a Kauffmann column occurs when an adaptation is under examination. The critic, in the first or second paragraph, explains how the film treatment diverges from the original. Several examples of this technique are reprinted earlier in this chapter.

A fourth method, and the final one listed here, is the use of background material on a movie's production or its première. Karel Reisz' The Loves of Isadora inspired Kauffmann to write this preface:

> Karel Reisz's film about Isadora Duncan, originally called Isadora, opened in Los Angeles in December, to qualify for an Academy Award nomination, with a running time of about three hours and with an intermission. After some adverse notice, it was cut to 150 minutes without intermission. It is now released in a 130-minute version. . . .[65]

---

[61]Stanley Kauffmann, A World on Film, p. 238.

[62]Stanley Kauffmann, Figures of Light, p. 18.

[63]Ibid., p. 25.

[64]Stanley Kauffmann, A World on Film, p. 240.

[65]Stanley Kauffmann, Figures of Light, p. 164.

A "serious" filmgoer or one who likes to be surprised clearly would
not want to make a habit of reading Kauffmann before going to a movie.
The critic's detailed plot synopses can rob the viewer of part of his
experience. (Remember that his review of Midnight Cowboy gave away Ratso's
death and described in full the fade-out shot.) Many critics, Judith Crist
for one, hedge on revealing important story developments, but not Kauffmann.
The schism between these two critical choices recalls Walter Kerr's distinction between reviewers and critics:[66] the former is more valuable before
and the latter after the experience of viewing the movie for oneself.
Kauffmann is distinctly more valuable afterwards. Like all good critics,
he then becomes a sounding board much in the manner of a good friend. His
readers no doubt look on him as Kerr might suggest: as an equal with whom
one wants to be embroiled in a lively discussion.

Kauffmann's movie criticism, it has been noted, "belongs to a tradition
that has taken its terminology and outlook from the examination of . . . the
drama and the novel."[67] That he upholds this tradition isn't so surprising,
considering his education and his literature and publishing background. Yet
Kauffmann does not falter when applying the tradition to the cinema, mainly
because he has a grasp of film's visual form and what connects that form to
the content of the piece. In proof of his knowledge are his reviews for Z,
A View from the Bridge, Billy Budd, and Spirits of the Dead. Let us examine
each of these in turn:

Kauffmann's criticism of Z, the Costa-Gavras political thriller, was
an occasion for the writer to express himself in a moderately technical

---

[66]See Andrew Sarris, The American Cinema, E. P. Dutton, New York,
1968, p. 34.

[67]Harris Dienstfrey, Book Week, June 12, 1966, p. 10.

way. He began by describing sensations, then moved to an analysis of
camera mechanics:

> The physical impression that this film gives is
> that it is hurrying to record certain facts before
> they are covered over. Motion is of the essence.
> Costa-Gavras' camera tracks and dollies almost con-
> stantly, yet without dizzying us (unlike a recent
> Czech fiasco called Sign of the Virgin), because
> all the motions are tightly linked to the impulses
> of the characters or of the audience. We insist that
> the camera moves as it does, so the tracking both
> feeds and stimulates our concern. It looks as if
> [director of photography Raoul] Coutard has used
> long-focus lenses for much of his close work,
> particularly outdoors, which gives many of the
> close-ups and two-shots a grainy, unglamorous,
> almost journalistic feeling. . . .[68]

Kauffmann, in his pan of A View from the Bridge, derides director
Sidney Lumet as a man who uses his technical skill for "excessive clever-
ness":

> He can make a film move swiftly, but when he comes
> to important points he hammers them. . . . When Eddie
> and his wife discuss their marital rift in their bed-
> room, we see them in a mirror, and on the dressing table
> before them is their wedding picture. The camera holds
> and holds and holds on it. What might have been a subtle,
> telling point is destroyed because Lumet has fastened
> his teeth in it. When Marco gets revenge on Eddie, by
> lifting a chair from floor level, we know how he feels,
> how Eddie feels; but Lumet has to insert a reverse shot
> from high above, looking down over the chair to Eddie's
> face--to spoil [Raymond] Pellegrin's acting with a
> camera caper.[69]

Poor editing was Kauffmann's concern when he wrote this passage in
his column about Peter Ustinov's production of Billy Budd: "The picture
is paced too slowly, is overemphatic in holding reactions (and the editing

---

[68]Stanley Kauffmann, Figures of Light, p. 217.

[69]Stanley Kauffmann, A World on Film, p. 105.

returns us unnecessarily to Face 1 after Face 2 has reacted to something
Face 1 said). . . ."[70]

Spirits of the Dead is an Edgar Allan Poe trilogy film, one-third of
which was directed by Federico Fellini. The Italian filmmaker shot Toby
Dammit, adapted from Poe's "Never Bet the Devil Your Head," and here are
Kauffmann's insights on the lighting:

> One point about Fellini's lighting is specially
> interesting. In his recent films the lighting has
> been much more theatrical than realistic: low angles,
> profiles cut out of the dark, the frequent recurrence
> of silhouettes, and the changes of light during a
> shot. In Toby Dammit an additional theatricality is
> clear. Often, but especially in the TV interview and
> in the award ceremony, scenes are lighted like stages
> and are surrounded by dark, the location in the world
> is treated like a setting in a theater, and we get the
> feeling that these lives--by implication, our lives--
> are being enacted before an unseen audience.[71]

The reviewer's comments demonstrate that he has a highly refined film
sense. When a technical discussion arises he has shown that he must bow
to no man: he comes armed with a vocabulary to deal precisely with the
dynamics of the art form. The excerpts above reveal his understanding of
the two-shot, the reverse shot, tracking, the long-focus lens, and so on.
Especially notable is Kauffmann's ascribing some kind of meaning to each
of the technical considerations--the darkness/theatre metaphor in Fellini,
for example.

A final passage of scholarly elucidation in Kauffmann is worthy of
inclusion. In 1969, the critic posted his objection to Max Ophuls' neglected

---

[70]Stanley Kauffmann, A World on Film, p. 117.

[71]Stanley Kauffmann, Figures of Light, p. 197.

classic, Lola Montès. To Kauffmann, the film suffered gravely on two points: (a) mediocre-to-bad acting and (b) a "teary," whore-with-a-heart-of-gold script.[72] The critic, while noting the film's virtues, objected principally on these grounds, fully recognizing that other critics revered the work as one of the finest in all cinema. (Andrew Sarris considers Lola Montès "the greatest film of all times.")[73]

Kauffmann's review plainly reveals his sensibilities. In the critique, he differentiates his criteria from those of other critics, those who

> subscribe, with passionate and unquestionable conviction, to a theory of the hierarchy of film values. They believe in selecting and exalting sheerly cinematic values . . . and in subordinating or discounting such matters as those I objected to. To them, this is exultation in the true glory of cinema.
>
> To me, it is a derogation and patronization of cinema. To me, this hierarchy says: "This is what film can do and we mustn't really expect it to do more, mustn't be disappointed if this is all it does."[74]

Above all, Kauffmann is interested in, fascinated by, what film can do (i.e., the diversity it can attain). He looks with chagrin upon critics who write as if cinema had restrictions and prescriptions. In 1966, he published an essay entitled "The Film Generation," in which he spoke with admiration for that generation, calling it "the most cheering circumstance in contemporary American art."[75] The young people who composed that film

---

[72]Stanley Kauffmann, Figures of Light, pp. 162-163.

[73]Andrew Sarris, "Whatever 'Lola' Has, Sarris Wants," The New York Times, April 20, 1969, p. D-15.

[74]Stanley Kauffmann, Figures of Light, p. 163.

[75]Stanley Kauffmann, A World on Film, p. 428.

generation found film the most important of the arts, an art form without

limits. Kauffmann even then must have sensed they were in diametrical

opposition to the narrow-minded movie critics he deplored.

In a follow-up article in 1970, Kauffmann added this footnote to his

previous essay: "I also hoped [in 1966] that the Film Generation would

make some demands. It has, and now it is in control."[76]

Elsewhere, Kauffmann has written:

> Certainly no one needs to prove the high degree
> of interest in film. Although the audience is smaller
> than it was twenty-five years ago, there are plentiful
> reasons to believe that qualitatively it is stratospheres
> beyond the pre-World War II audience that went to film
> theaters once or twice a week like automobiles to
> filling stations. Today's audience has much more knowl-
> edge about its enthusiasm.[77]

One person supremely happy about the preeminence of film in the Sixties

and Seventies is Stanley Kauffmann. He remains, in 1974, both a dedicated

scholar writing an ongoing film history and a student ever open to new forms.

In the words of one critic, Kauffmann is "neither blinded by technique

nor alienated by innovation."[78] His collections (comprising film notes from

1958 to 1970) and his subsequent criticism for The New Republic reveal film

as an emerging, maturing art form.

In the rarefied atmosphere that sometimes surrounds film reviewing,

writers occasionally become elitist and effete. No such flaws mar Kauffmann's

criticism. His scholarship and his inherent pleasure in what he is writing

---

[76]Stanley Kauffmann, Figures of Light, p. 279.

[77]Stanley Kauffmann, "Film Negatives," Saturday Review, March 1973, p. 37.

[78]Laurence Goldstein, The New York Times Book Review, May 15, 1966, p. 6.

about lend a note of individuality to his work. Writing about films has
been a near-life-long labor of love for Kauffmann, and to that field of
dramatic criticism he has made, and continues to make, a lasting contribution.

V. ANDREW SARRIS

> Most cultivated people know what they like and what
> is art in acting and writing, but direction is a rela-
> tively mysterious, not to say mystical, concept of
> creation. Indeed, it is not creation at all, but rather
> a very strenuous form of contemplation. The director
> is both the least necessary and the most important
> component in film-making. . . . He would not be worth
> bothering with if he were not capable now and then of
> a sublimity of expression almost miraculously extracted
> from his money-oriented environment.[1]

Thus Andrew Sarris characterizes the motion picture director. To the

general public, the film director is a mystery man and a mountebank, if he

is not, in the first place, a complete anonymity. But not many moviemakers

have remained anonymous to Andrew Sarris, film critic and movie editor for

The Village Voice. An investigator and historian at heart, Sarris has an

overriding concern with the mystery that is film directing. That single

concern leads to the core of his movie criticism.

Andrew George Sarris was born in Brooklyn, of Greek parents, in 1928.

His immigrant mother and father doubtless had something to do with the

boy's early-induced mania for movies: the elder Sarrises actually learned

English by reading the title cards of silent films.[2] Their moviegoing

habit endured in the sound era, and Andrew accompanied them. For young

Sarris, as for many other moviegoers of the Depression and the war years,

---

[1] Andrew Sarris, The American Cinema, E. P. Dutton, New York, 1968,
p. 37.

[2] Andrew Sarris, The Primal Screen, Simon and Schuster, New York,
1973, p. 126.

movies provided an escape, a dream world excursion. Hollywood was manu-
facturing its most memorable fantasies in the Thirties and Forties, and
Sarris, for ten cents a ticket, bought the magical dreams of Frank Capra,
John Ford, Cecil B. DeMille, George Cukor, Howard Hawks, and Busby Berkeley.

Sarris was educated in Brooklyn and Queens. After graduating from
secondary school, he enrolled at Columbia University, where he received
his bachelor's degree in 1951. Although Sarris had written about film
during his undergraduate days, he didn't look upon film criticism as a
viable career until after graduation. Like Pauline Kael and others, his
student years were highlighted by non-stop moviegoing, but the fantasies
of writing professionally about films were fulfilled later on. Sarris'
paychecks started rolling in during the Fifties, thanks to freelancing
work for esoteric magazines like Film Culture, for which he eventually
became associate editor.

In August 1960, he published his first review for The Village Voice.
Since that critique--of Hitchcock's Psycho--Sarris has been the Voice's
first-string film critic. The Psycho review, an affirmative notice which
brought angry letters, inaugurated a controversial career. From 1965 to
1967, Sarris extended his journalism efforts as editor-in-chief of the
English language edition of Cahiers du Cinéma. In 1969 he married Molly
Haskell, also a film critic and historian. She joined her husband on the
Voice staff. Now both contribute weekly columns. At present, Sarris is
an associate profesor of cinema at Columbia. In the interim, as time
allowed from 1960 to the present, Sarris spent a year abroad studying film,
principally in Paris; he taught film at Yale and New York University; and

he has been a frequent campus and community-interest-group lecturer,
popular because of the principles he expounds in his many books about
cinema: The Films of Josef von Sternberg (1966); The American Cinema
(1968), a reference volume dealing with the careers of two hundred directors;
and two collections of criticism--The Confessions of a Cultist (1970) and
The Primal Screen (1973). Besides authoring these works, Sarris has
edited Interviews With Film Directors (1967) and co-edited Film 68/69
(1969).

His active career as lecturer-critic-editor aside, Sarris is chiefly
known as the principal American exponent of the seminal auteur theory. It
is this notorious Franco-American concept of criticism, honoring the director
as the predominant artist of the cinema, that earmarks the Voice critic.
He has studied the works of every major filmmaker from Griffith and Chaplin
to Mike Nichols and Stanley Kubrick. His years of devotion and research,
coupled with his implementation of the auteur theory, resulted in 1968 in
his encyclopedic catalogue called The American Cinema.[3] In it, Sarris
traces the history of the film director and explains his use of the auteur
vision. In the process, the author ranks filmmakers according to their
achievements and places them in categories based on their rights to
auteurship.

Before exploring Sarris further, it seems sensible to present a
background of the auteur theory, the philosophy from which everything else
in his writing emerges. Because of the sheer bulk of his compilations,

---

[3]The account is actually more extensive than its misleading title suggests; the author considers not just American, but all English-speaking,
cinema, including, for further amplification, a section on Antonioni, Buñuel,
Claude Chabrol, René Clair, René Clément, Eisenstein, Pabst, Polanski,
Truffaut, and Visconti. Bergman and Godard are conspicuous omissions.

Sarris' name has become linked with that of _auteur_, so much so that casual readers might mistakenly presume him to be the originator of the concept.

Actually, the _auteur_ theory was first promulgated in the school of criticism spawned by Alexandre Astruc, André Bazin, and other French essayists. The first polemical statement, however, was issued in 1954 in the writings of an aspiring filmmaker named François Truffaut. The young Truffaut, then a critic for the _avant-garde_ journal edited by Bazin, _Cahiers du Cinéma_, was a persistent opponent of the status quo in French cinema.

His articles for _Cahiers du Cinéma_ (and the French weekly _Arts_) often contained virulent attacks on the old guard. Truffaut complained bitterly about studio practices and the antiquated film techniques in general use. Specific targets of Truffaut's wrath were the lack of opportunities for young French moviemakers; the enormous budgets to which film productions had soared; the practice of constantly employing over-priced stars; and the over-use of studio sound stages, to the total exclusion of location photography. Truffaut deplored all these practices. And he was not alone. He shared his staff position at _Cahiers_ and his ideals with other soon-to-be-famous personages: Jean-Luc Godard, Claude Chabrol, Jacques Rivette, and Eric Rohmer.[4]

Eventually, Truffaut's intelligent and incisive attacks, bolstered by the equally vociferous criticism of his _Cahiers_ colleagues, brought about sweeping changes in the French film industry. _Auteur_ criticism burst forth conjointly with the _nouvelle vague_, or "New Wave"--what the resultant

---

[4]Jean-Luc Godard's journalistic attacks of French cinema tradition were even more venomous than Truffaut's.

onrush of tradition-breaking films came to be called. Actually, the
"Wave" was, "like the British Angry Young Man movement . . . less a movement than a useful journalistic catchphrase. . . ."[5]

The nouvelle vague was spearheaded, not so surprisingly, by the
writers of Cahiers du Cinéma, who had turned to filmmaking for themselves.
Between 1958 and 1959, all the magazine's erstwhile critics made their
first feature-length films: Breathless, which Godard shot for less than
$90,000; The Four-Hundred Blows (Truffaut); Le Beau Serge (Chabrol);
Paris Belongs to Us (Rivette); and the first of Rohmer's "Six Moral Tales."
In an amazingly rapid transformation, five exciting writers became heralds
and chief practitioners of their own theory.

Although this explosion of activity began in 1958, the groundwork had
been laid several years before. It was Truffaut's seminal manifesto, entitled
"Politique des Auteurs" ("The Mark of Authors" or "The Auteur Policy") and
published in the January 1954 issue of Cahiers, which established the
guidelines for the auteur approach. In brief, Truffaut declared that,
popular opinion to the contrary, movies were not a group art. His associates

---

[5]Peter Graham, The New Wave, Doubleday & Company, Garden City, New
York, 1968, p. 7. What made the "New Wave" new? Wolf Rilla, a successful
film scenarist and director in his own right, devotes a chapter of his
A-Z of Moviemaking to that consideration. According to Rilla, the
nouvelle vague films were united by (a) their rebellion against highly
glossy, mechanically (technically) perfect, expensive studio projects;
(b) their lack of resources and shortage of film stock (there was actually
less footage shot); (c) their occasional (and assumptively deliberate)
technical incompetence: wobbly cameras, shoddy sets, uncertain focus,
patchy lighting; (d) their reliance on improvisation--of actors, directors,
and crews; and (e) their substitution of one "time passage" technique
for another: opticals (fades, dissolves, montages)--until then one of
the basic "rules" of film grammar to denote lapses of time and distance--
were replaced by jump cuts, a practice which came into being originally
because money wasn't available for the expensive process of having opticals
made; in the Sixties jump cuts in themselves became an enduring part of
film grammar. See Wolf Rilla, A-Z of Moviemaking. The Viking Press:
New York, 1970.

gleefully seconded him on this point. (Godard: "The cinema is not a trade. It isn't teamwork. One is always alone while shooting, as though facing a blank page.")[6]

Cinema, along with the stage, has long had the mark of illegitimacy associated with it because of the numerous individuals involved in the creative process. Therefore, many theorists held (and perhaps still hold) that movies cannot be a true art form. Truffaut's intent was to dispel this notion. According to the Frenchman's precepts, film is like any other work of art: its totality is "shaped by, and totally obligated to, the unique personality of its creator."[7] This then becomes one of the basic tenets of the auteur theory: no matter how many disparate elements a movie contains--acting, story, dialogue, photography, set decoration, et al--"a film should . . . be viewed as a single formal entity . . . unified by the personality of the artist--in this case, the director."[8]

Upon this foundation has risen an abiding and much-debated method for appraising films. In terms of promoting his newly voiced convictions, Truffaut with his mutual elevation of the director and condemnation of the movie writer did the trick. Andrew Sarris has written about this phenomenon,

> If Truffaut's "Politique des auteurs" signaled a break with anything, it was with a certain segment of the French cinema that was dominated (in Truffaut's view) by a handful of scriptwriters. The target was the well-upholstered, well-acted, carefully motivated

[6]Pauline Kael, I Lost It At the Movies, Little, Brown and Company, Boston, 1965, p. 119.

[7]Marion Magid, "Observations: Auteur! Auteur!," Commentary, March 1964, p. 70.

[8]Ibid., p. 70.

"Tradition of Quality" represented by Claude Autant-Lara, Marcel Carné, René Clair, René Clément, Henri Clouzot, André Cayatte, Jean Delannoy, Marcel Pagliero, and a host of even lesser figures. This "Old Guard" was responsible for films like <u>Devil in the Flesh</u>, <u>The Red and the Black</u>, <u>Forbidden Games</u>, <u>Gervaise</u>, <u>Wages of Fear</u>, <u>Diabolique</u>, <u>Justice Is Done</u>, and <u>Symphonie Pastorale</u>, in short, what American reviewers considered the class of French filmmaking into the late fifties.[9]

The furor, as one might suspect, was enormous. For a young upstart to take the French literary tradition to task was considered gross bad taste. Particularly repugnant to Truffaut were the screenwriters who were adapting celebrated French classics; he maintained that the directors should write, or at the very least conceive, their own scripts. Perhaps the most succinct example of this critical ideology at work is the Andrew Sarris critique of <u>The Night of the Hunter</u>, the only film Charles Laughton ever directed:

> Rumor has it that the final shooting script of <u>The Night of the Hunter</u> was one-third Laughton, one-third James Agee, and one-third Davis Grubb. Be that what it may, <u>The Night of the Hunter</u> displays a striking visual style, almost semi-Germanic Griffith, which is completely lacking in the Huston-Agee-Forester <u>The African Queen</u> and the Windust-Agee-Crane <u>The Bride Came to Yellow Sky</u>. Moral: Directors, not writers, are the ultimate auteurs of the cinema, at least of cinema that has any visual meaning and merit.[10]

In 1954, it was somewhat earth-shattering to hear the director being spoken of as an <u>auteur</u>. Cinema circles were instantly abuzz. Today we are a bit more accustomed to talk of directorial esteem. Names such as Bergman, Fellini, and Antonioni fall easily from people's lips, and

---

[9]Andrew Sarris, <u>The American Cinema</u>, p. 28.

[10]<u>Ibid.</u>, p. 215.

besides achieving acclaim, these men are now revered as _auteurs_, _registi_, and, thanks to Joseph Gelmis' anthology of interviews, "superstars."[11]

The postulations of Truffaut and his fellows, although innovative and rebellious, might have been regarded, even grudgingly accepted, as a quaint and forgettable French curio. (In truth, not that many people read _Cahiers du Cinéma_; although a prestigious and influential journal, it is unlikely, as Marion Magid suggests, that readership is anywhere in the vicinity of the number of people who quote from it.)[12] The _auteur_ policy, however, did _not_ remain a quaint curio due primarily to two factors: (1) influential men in the film industry began taking a look at the principal credo--director as _auteur_--and some of the secondary and tertiary premises; and (2) _Cahiers du Cinéma_ began publication of an English-language edition, first in London then in New York. It is essential to look at each of these phenomena in turn.

In 1958, Marcel Carné, one of the lingering veteran directors, dared to heed the _Cahiers_ crowd; his experimental _The Cheaters_, with a cast of unknown actors, was a box-office smash. The receipts from _The Cheaters_ encouraged producers and other directors to listen to Truffaut, Godard, Chabrol, and Rohmer. When their own films were released, these critics-turned-filmmakers became almost overnight sensations. (At the Cannes Eleventh International Film Festival in 1959, the press labeled the youthful directors the "New Wave" and the tag stuck. The previous year Truffaut's journalistic protests had caused him to be barred from the festival, but

[11] Joseph Gelmis, _The Film Director as Superstar_, Doubleday & Company, Garden City, New York, 1970.

[12] Stuart Rosenthal, "The Terse, Sardonic, Pragmatic Loner in Donald Siegel's Unacclaimed Films," _St. Louis Post-Dispatch_, May 2, 1971, p. 5-C.

in 1959 he was tapped as best director for The Four-Hundred Blows. His comrades didn't fare badly either: Roger Vadim, Claude Chabrol, and Alain Resnais--all under thirty--shared headlines with Truffaut, while producers from the world's movie production centers were busily outbidding one another for distribution rights to the festival's small budget, small cast, "personalized" films.) In due time, the new directors moved into universal limelight. The "New Wave" was surging forth; and so was the auteur theory.

By 1960, it had crossed the English channel and from there it made its way across the Atlantic. On both shores it was wholeheartedly adopted by a coterie of critics and movie addicts. In 1965 the English language version of Cahiers became available in America, and Andrew Sarris was its editor-in-chief. Truffaut's decade-old credo was capturing even more attention, and, in certain circles, inspiring even more outrage.

Easily enough understood, if not accepted, is Truffaut's hypothesis that the director is the solitary creator of his film. Not so easy to comprehend, or perhaps accept, is the further postulate that "a film should be judged in the context of the rest of the artist's output."[13] This conviction can be seen as a logical development of the director-as-auteur philosophy: the most worthwhile films, it was submitted, would be those marked indelibly by the personalities of the director--an extension of beliefs in the other arts. For instance, masterpieces by Picasso, Rembrandt, and Shakespeare are held in esteem frequently because the creators' names

---

[13]Stuart Rosenthal, "The Terse, Sardonic, Pragmatic Loner in Donald Siegel's Unacclaimed Films," St. Louis Post-Dispatch, May 2, 1971, p. 5-C.

immediately suggest quality; why then, the critics reasoned, should not film _auteurs_ be awarded the same respect? In that manner, each film becomes, in essence, an evolving personal statement from its creator.

By now a prevailing question might be: What are the requisites for becoming an _auteur_? To help answer that question, to establish from the outset which movie men deserved the ultimate veneration of _auteur_, the _Cahiers_ critics supplied a "pantheon" of the cinema's great directors. These avowed masters typify all the best qualities at work, not the least of which is longevity, sheer endurance throughout the years. But, as Andrew Sarris emphasized when he entered the _auteur_ game, the "ranking of directors is based on total rather than occasional achievement."[14] (Whether or not current superstars like William Friedkin, Peter Bogdanovich, Mike Nichols, and Robert Altman will attain the pantheon remains to be seen.)

The entire policy, in effect, places certain established masters, like Hitchcock and Ford, beyond reproach. Other directors, as Sarris indicates here, do not weather so well:

> There were (and are) weak and strong directors as
> there were weak and strong kings, but film history,
> like royal history, concerns those who merely reign
> as well as those who actually rule. Indeed, the strength
> of a John Ford is a function of the weakness of a Robert
> Z. Leonard just as the strength of a Louis XIV is a
> function of the weakness of a Louis XVI. The strong
> director imposes his own personality on a film; the
> weak director allows the personalities of others to
> run rampant. But a movie is a movie, and if by chance
> Robert Z. Leonard should reign over a respectable
> production like Pride and Prejudice, its merits are
> found elsewhere than in the director's personality,
> let us say in Jane Austen, Aldous Huxley, Laurence

---

[14]Andrew Sarris, The American Cinema, p. 27.

> Olivier, Greer Garson, and a certain tradition of gentility
> at Metro-Goldwyn-Mayer. Obviously, the auteur theory cannot
> possibly cover every vagrant charm of the cinema. Nonethe-
> less, the listing of films by directors remains the most
> reliable index of quality available to us short of the
> microscopic evaluation of every film ever made.[15]

To put it plainly, the non-_auteur_ directors don't stand a ghost of a chance

in the environs where an _auteur_ critic holds sway. If a director's per-

sonality isn't boldly stamped on his picture, he will never make the _auteur_

list.

The French critics were the ones who initiated the list-making mania.

In the pages of _Cahiers du Cinéma_, they periodically issued supplements

to their original "pantheon." As a result, the listing was augmented con-

siderably. By the time Andrew Sarris stepped into the picture, it was of

mammoth proportions.

Taking his cue from the French school, Sarris, in his reviews, began

to focus on filmmakers and their personal, distinctive stamp. He began

to clarify the premises of _auteurisme_ for American readers. As he

"clarified," so did he append. That's when the real furor began.

Sarris on the _auteur_ aesthetic:

> . . . the first premise of the _auteur_ theory is the
> technical competence of a director as a criterion
> of value. . . . The second premise of the _auteur_
> theory is the distinguishable personality of the
> director as a criterion of value. . . . The third
> and ultimate premise of the _auteur_ theory is con-
> cerned with interior meaning, the ultimate glory
> of the cinema as an art. Interior meaning is
> extrapolated from the tension between a director's
> personality and his material. . . .[16]

---

[15] Andrew Sarris, _The American Cinema_, pp. 30-31.

[16] Andrew Sarris, "Notes on the Auteur Theory in 1962," _Film Culture_,
Winter 1962-1963.

His first premise is self-explanatory, his second a repetition of Truffaut. It is the "third and ultimate premise" which finally divided American film critics into opposing camps and created a schism that remains unbridged to this day. Sarris views "tension" as a prime requirement for auteurship. His adversaries see it as plainly ridiculous, a feeble method of explaining away bad movies.

It is Sarris' contention that form and content are not conjunctive, but rather disjunctive. When style (the director's personality) and content (the director's material) clash, and the director resolves the conflict by rising above his material--all the better. Then we are in the presence of an auteur. This formulation certainly goes against the Western tradition of ensemble, of a work of art being of one piece.

And this is a peculiar paradox of the auteur philosophy. Opponents indicate that Sarris and his French mentors labor under misconceptions when ranking directors of the Hollywood system. Most American directors, they state, have been "mere foremen, called in for the job after the laborers--including the actors--were hired by the studio."[17] Auteur proponents willingly accept the fact, indeed revel in it.

With a derisive smirk, Pauline Kael has characterized the auteur ideal as a director who

> signs a long-term contact, directs any script that's handed to him, and expresses himself by shoving bits of style up the crevasses of the plots. If his "style" is in conflict with the story line or subject matter, so much the better--more chance for tension.[18]

To Sarris, this tension is one of the inherent glories of film.

---

[17]"Cinema: The Film Maker as Ascendant Star," Time, July 4, 1969, p. 46.

[18]Pauline Kael, I Lost It At the Movies, p. 273.

Reasoning of this kind allows for _auteur_ inspiration in movies as diverse as top-budget musicals and poverty-row "B" features of the gangster and Western genres. Needless to say, it is infuriating enough for a conventional critic to hear Sarris laud every musical comedy Minnelli did for Metro; but when the _auteur_ fraternity begins hailing "the thousand beauties of Nicholas Ray's _Party Girl_," or "the exquisite tensions deployed in _Crimson Kimono_ . . ."[19] or the "breathtaking pace" of _Duel at Silver Creek_ or the "dynamic element" of _Invasion of the Body Snatchers_,[20] some of the stalwarts are thrown into trauma. One of the veterans most sorely beset was former _Esquire_ critic Dwight Macdonald. The deliberation between Sarris and Macdonald passed beyond the realm of academic debate long ago; niceties were dispensed with almost at once, with Macdonald suggesting his fellow-critic's bold _arriviste_ qualities--a "Godzilla monster" who had "come clambering up from the primordial swamps."[21] Sarris countered in his _Voice_ column by "casting aspersions on Macdonald's political past, as well as on his eyesight."[22] Most critics tend to dismiss as hurriedly as possible a movie with a title like _Invasion of the Body Snatchers_, if they ever acknowledge its existence to begin with. _Auteur_ critics happily juxtapose such films alongside the recognized works of Griffith, Welles, and von

---

[19]Marion Magid, "Observations: Auteur! Auteur!," p. 70.

[20]Stuart Rosenthal, "The Terse, Sardonic, Pragmatic Loner," p. 5-C.

[21]Marion Magid, "Observations: Auteur! Auteur!," p. 70.

[22]_Ibid._, p. 70.

Stroheim.[23] It little matters that the Hollywood contract directors were
often assigned bad scripts and pathetic shooting schedules; to Sarris
and his companions, the "tension" between artist and material could often
produce praiseworthy, sometimes "pantheon"-worthy, results. After all,
movies are seen as an anti-literary medium, with the scriptwriters coming
off second or third best; therefore, the inclusion of literary values can
only serve to hamper the filmic ones. The auteur scribes seems unanimous
on this point.

Andrew Sarris' direct connection with the politique began in the
spring of 1961. At that time he attended the Cannes Film Festival, where
the New Wave was still surging. When the festival drew to a close, he journeyed
to Paris, where he proceeded to spend a year.[24] By the graces of Henri
Langlois and the archives and facilities of the Cinémathèque Française,
Sarris passed his year by screening foreign language films and in experiencing
for the first time or rediscovering pre-1955 (subtitled) American films.
Godard and Antonioni were shown side by side with Ford, Hawks, and Hitchcock.

Viewed in the climate of the Cinémathèque's basement projection room,
these movies took on a special quality. Confronted with alien languages,
Sarris began to concentrate on the visuals, the technique, and to identify
styles. Before long, he duplicated this procedure for film-watching even
when seeing pictures spoken in his native tongue, focusing not on what was
said, but rather how the director, his photographer, his set decorator,
his costume designer, and his editor communicated visually. Patterns began

---

[23]The young French writers were the ones who first advertised their lack
of selectivity. They watched and wrote policy papers on all kinds of films.
It was revealed that their free time was spent in the basement projection room
at the Cinémathèque Française, where they applauded the inanities of the grade-B
programmers of the Thirties and Forties. See Marion Magid, loc. cit., p. 71.

[24]Andrew Sarris, "Sixties Cinema," Rolling Stone, November 22, 1973, p. 45.

to emerge. And Sarris' aesthetic principles for cinema were born.

This orientation toward looking at more than listening to a movie has

marked the critic's writing from 1961 to the present.

No other American critic devotes as much space to the look of a film.

His reviews are punctuated by minutiae about montage, process shots,

camera movement (tracking, panning, crane shots), and mise en scène (the

director's staging of scenes and his working as much as possible within

the frame without cutting). Sarris senses the need to be armed with a

critical vocabulary to deal with the dynamics of the motion picture art.

The following excerpts show the critic's facility with discussing cinema

technique.

In a tribute to Jean-Luc Godard's pyrotechnics, Sarris wrote that

the filmmaker had been

> audacious in breaking every possible rule imposed upon
> a director by producers and aestheticians. If Godard
> has been abused for his impudence, Federico Fellini
> (8½), Richard Lester (A Hard Day's Night), and Tony
> Richardson (Tom Jones) have struck a post-Breathless
> bonanza by exploiting Godard's gimmicks to the hilt.
> The meaning of all the freezes, jump cuts, and zany
> camera speeds of the Sixties is simply that directors
> have found the courage at long last to call attention
> to their techniques and their personalities.[25]

As part of a conjoined review for James William Guercio's Electra

Glide in Blue and Arthur Barron's Jeremy, Sarris wrote with disfavor about

trends in the musical sound tracks of recent pictures:

> I am getting a little tired of second-string rock
> concerts masquerading as movies. . . .

---

[25]Andrew Sarris, Interviews with Film Directors, The Bobbs-Merrill
Company, Indianapolis, 1967, p. ix.

Also, with so much pop philosophy emanating from
rock lyrics these days, I am never quite sure to what
extent the songs are intended to supplement the script.
Occasionally, there are outright contradictions between
what a song is saying and what the screen is showing.
For example, the Simon and Garfunkel "Mrs. Robinson"
has always struck me as the generous tribute of a young
man to an older woman. Unfortunately, there was no such
generosity shown to Anne Bancroft's "Mrs. Robinson" in
"The Graduate," with the result that the film took credit
from the soundtrack for feelings it repudiated on the
screen. By the same token, Alan Price's Threepennyoperatics
in "O Lucky Man!" result in lyrics which are too light for
thought and too heavy for song.[26]

In reevaluating Luis Buñuel's _Viridiana_, Sarris observed that

Buñuel stays at a middle distance. He doesn't
show a great concern for actors. . . . Buñuel has
always been somewhat cold. . . .

Neither Buñuel nor Ophuls uses the close-up.
Close-up equals warmth, equals identification, equals
whatever. Close-up is also a fundamental element of
montage; close-up has a rhetorical place in the alter-
nation of shots. . . . It's always something we say
when we are reviewing, but what does "close-up" really
mean? Is it an observation? . . . So what if Buñuel _had_
used close-ups? . . . Maybe there's just some accidental
reason for shot choices.

First of all, Buñuel's been completely deaf for
many years. This partly explains the effect of a
Buñuel film: it's so vivid, so forceful. Partly
due to the deafness, you get the visual equivalent
of a silent movie. And in silent movie drama, the
long shot is more crucial than in the talkies. In
silent movies you have to have a razor-sharp visual
sensibility in order to really communicate. And so,
while everything is sharp and vivid, you also need a
certain distance.[27]

One of Sarris' early statements on the career of Jean-Luc Godard

commences this way:

[26]Andrew Sarris, "Films in Focus: Lost Tracks, Found Trends,"
The Village Voice, August 30, 1973, p. 57.

[27]Gerald R. Barrett, "Andrew Sarris Interview: October 16, 1972,"
Literature/Film Quarterly, July 1973, pp. 202-203.

> Although Godard is the most self-conscious film-
> maker in the world, the most addicted to inside jokes
> for the initiates and to internal aesthetic judgments
> for himself, he is also in many ways the most realistic
> director of all time. . . . We are all familiar with
> some of the mannerisms of realism. No background. Un-
> professional actors. Bad sound recording. An emphasis
> on exteriors. . . . Black and white, small screen and
> oodles of montage.[28]

In his review of Robert Altman's The Long Goodbye, Sarris reflected

on an earlier film based on a Raymond Chandler novel, Howard Hawks' The

Big Sleep:

> The crackling dialogue is still divided somewhat
> mysteriously between Hawks, Chandler, Brackett, Furthman,
> [and] Faulkner, but the mood is decisively Hawksian, estab-
> lished perhaps in that one labyrinthine tracking shot of
> Bogart in the drug-drenched house with the fringe curtains.
> . . . Suddenly, Bogart snaps his fingers, and reason reigns
> in the house of evil and chaos and mystery.[29]

On Peter Hall's film adaptation of Harold Pinter's The Homecoming:

> What holds "The Homecoming" together on the screen
> is Hall's very artful framing of his characters against
> expressive patches of their fragmented environment in
> the background. The Pinteresque pauses are thus covered
> by the very studiousness of the camera set-ups. Hall's
> precise cutting and framing thus provide a visual cor-
> relative for Pinter's verbal wit. However, Hall pays
> a price for analyzing the relationships in terms of a
> shifting point of view. We lose the voyeuristic perch
> which we take so much for granted in the theatre and
> we become too subjectively involved with the individual
> characters to re-experience the shock of the total spec-
> tacle on the stage. Hence, Sam's near-fatal heart-attack
> and flop on the floor were gruesomely funny on the stage
> because everyone else stood around with varying degrees of
> indifference and insensitivity, and we could see all the
> unmoved characters out of the corners of our eyes. By

---

[28]Andrew Sarris, Interviews with Film Directors, p. 166.

[29]Andrew Sarris, "Films in Focus: Living the Private Eye Genre,"
The Village Voice, November 8, 1973, p. 94.

emphasizing a subjective camera movement from Sam's
suddenly vertiginous point of view, Hall breaks the
fall and muffles the thud.[30]

Sarris once dubbed <u>Lola Montès</u> the greatest film of all time. After
a fifteenth viewing of Max Ophuls' classic, he had this to say:

> To be moved by <u>Lola Montès</u> is to feel the emotion
> in motion itself as an expression of a director's delirium,
> and this is not an easy task for the conceptualized vision
> of the average viewer, conditioned for years to frame-by-
> frame pictorialism by which every shot is milked for all
> it's worth. What makes <u>Lola</u> even more difficult to
> appreciate is its refusal to conform to the standard
> look of what most people tend to demand of a great film.
> <u>Lola</u> sins first and foremost by being photographed in
> garish color rather than in virtuous black-and-white
> and across a screen more wide than square. It is romantic
> rather than realistic, sensuous rather than severe. It
> glories less in the simplification of its style than in
> its elaboration as it glides and strides and turns and
> tracks across a fluid screen in the most dazzling display
> of baroque camera movement in the history of the cinema.[31]

The critic was even more specific about John Ford's directing choices
in <u>The Man Who Shot Liberty Valance</u>:

> The opening sequences are edited with the familiar
> incisiveness of a director who cuts in the camera and
> hence in the mind. James Stewart and Vera Miles descend
> from a train which has barely puffed its way into the
> twentieth century. Their powdered make-up suggests
> that all the meaningful action of their lives is past.
> The town is too placid, the flow of movement too stately
> and the sunlight bleaches the screen with an intimation
> ot impending nostalgia. An incredibly aged Andy Devine
> is framed against a slightly tilted building which is
> too high and too fully constructed to accommodate the
> violent expectations of the genre. The remarkable aus-
> terity of the production is immediately evident. . . .
>
> Stewart is concluding his interview in the newspaper
> office when, through the window, the buckboard enters the
> frame of the film. We have returned to the classic economy

---

[30]Andrew Sarris, "Films in Focus: Muffled Comings, Jagged Goings,"
<u>The Village Voice</u>, November 29, 1973, p. 81.

[31]Andrew Sarris, <u>The Primal Screen</u>, p. 153.

of Stroheim's silent cinema where the action invaded
the rigid frame and detail montage took it from there.
. . .

At a nod from his wife, Stewart walks into the
next room away from the mourners, away from the present
into the past. Just as Vera Miles begins to open her
hat box, there is a cut to Stewart introducing the
flashback by placing his hand on a historical prop, a
dismantled, dust-ridden stagecoach. From the cut from
the hat box to that climactic moment nearly two hours
later when we see a cactus rose on the coffin, the
cinema of John Ford intersects the cinema of Orson
Welles. . . .

The first sequence of the flashback is photographed
against a studio-enclosed skyscape far from the scenic
temptations of the great outdoors. A stagecoach is held
up almost entirely in close-up. . . .

Godard's neo-classical political collage in Le
Petit Soldat is matched by Ford in a schoolroom scene
where Stewart is framed against a picture of Washington
and Woody Strode against a picture of Lincoln. Ford's
obviousness transcends the obvious in the context of
his career. . . .

The shooting of Liberty Valance is shown twice from
two different points of view. Even Kurosawa can be
superficially clever with this sort of subjective maneuver.
Ford's juxtaposition of an action and its consequences from
two different points of view is far more profound when
the psychological chronology is properly assembled in the
spectator's mind. The heroic postures of Wayne, Stewart
and Marvin form a triangle in time. The conflicting
angles, the contrasting plays of light and shadow, the
unified rituals of gestures and movements and, above all,
Ford's gift of sustained contemplation produce intellectual
repercussions backward and forward in filmic time until,
on a second viewing, the entire film, the entire world of
John Ford, in fact, is concentrated into the first
anguishing expression of Vera Miles as she steps off the
train at the beginning of the film, and everything that
Ford has ever thought or felt is compressed into one shot
of a cactus rose on a coffin photographed, needless to say,
from the only possible angle.[32]

[32]Andrew Sarris, The Primal Screen, pp. 147-151.

These excerpts represent Andrew Sarris' recognition of the importance of a "film language" for describing the art form--terms for the visual, aural, and editing dynamics in movies. Yet he also recognizes the difficulty stemming from the necessity for terminology because, in his words,

> cinema, unlike painting and sculpture, is only partly visual. Like music, cinema exists in time, but only partly. Like literature, it is locked in language, but only partly. It is like photography, but only partly.[33]

Sarris has little patience with those who deify European film at the expense of American cinema. Elitists denigrate the apparent absence of style in our movies; but Sarris avows that Americans are blind to the styles in English language films because they are too busy listening. They are oblivious to many native directors' visual artistry, an artistry just as bold as Antonioni's, Fellini's, Kurosawa's, or Renoir's. In a recent interview, Sarris complained of this insensitivity on the part of audiences:

> I saw Vertigo the same year I saw Last Year at Marienbad and they were identical. Everybody was talking about Last Year at Marienbad. "Ah, tracks." They'd never seen tracks before. People just didn't analyze American films stylistically. I'm not knocking the verbal thing; I'm not saying that isn't an element, but I'm merely saying you should look at the movie too, and while you're looking at it . . . you would notice style. To say that John Ford doesn't have a style . . . for critics to rave over Kurosawa who's been imitating John Ford all these years . . . the point is that it's silly to say that American directors like Ford, Hawks, Hitchcock, Sternberg, Lubitsch (in the American period), Lang did not have . . . vivid, brilliant, visual styles. . . .[34]

---

[33]Andrew Sarris, ed., The Film, The Bobbs-Merrill Company, Indianapolis, 1968, p. 5.

[34]F. Anthony Macklin, "Everyone Is An Auteurist Now, More or Less; An Interview With Andrew Sarris," Film Heritage, Summer 1973, pp. 34-35.

These expressions relate quite directly to Sarris' feelings about the importance, perhaps dominance, in film of the visual aspect. Whatever literary quality is present is purely secondary. Such has been Sarris' orientation since that year in the screening rooms of the Cinémathèque.

Unfortunately, the critic's reasoning can sometimes be quite naive. When he complains about the "literary critics," he sets them up as straw men, misrepresenting their demands of the medium so he can elevate his point of view. Witness this misguided condemnation:

> All the films we like--if we try to analyze what they're about, what they contribute to our knowledge, it's rather slight. Even Citizen Kane or Children of Paradise--what do they say that is so illuminating as far as content goes, as far as information is concerned? I think the cinema is more a medium of incantation than information; it's more a medium of emotion than intellect. . . . If I had to limit myself to what I knew from what I'd seen in movies, I'd really be very stupid, very uninformed. I don't understand this attitude--I don't understand people like Dwight Macdonald and Stanley Kauffmann and John Simon pretending the task of film is to educate. I think that's a condescending view. . . . Movies somehow heighten, sharpen, focus things; they don't originate things. You don't go to movies to get a whole new philosophical or sociological orientation on life.[35]

Predictably, for a man who uttered the words above, Sarris took pains to see Franklin Schaffner's Papillon not on the fashionable East Side but in Times Square--"in its proper habitat. Movies are best enjoyed in a climate of minimal expectation."[36] Though they differ in other respects, Sarris and Pauline Kael share one philosophy: they insist movies are what they are because of the fun, not the intelligence involved.

---

[35] F. Anthony Macklin, "Everyone is an Auteurist," pp. 31-32.

[36] Andrew Sarris, "Films in Focus: The Perils of Papillon," The Village Voice, January 10, 1974, p. 57. Sarris' expectations may have been mininal for Papillon, but even so he disliked the film intensely.

> At least as far as movies are concerned, what we
> like is not always art. I suppose every critic has an
> unrecorded shame list of bad films he secretly enjoys
> along with a recorded pride list of serious films he
> secretly loathes. If the gap between what a critic really
> likes and what he officially admires is too great, he
> may overcompensate for his aesthetic guilt by exaggerating
> the gulf between art and entertainment in the cinema.
> Worse still, he may suggest to his readers that pleasure
> is a response to bad art.[37]

It was Andrew Sarris, not Pauline Kael, who wrote these words.

Sarris has proved that even scholarship can be fun. Research conditions
were especially ideal for him: the vaults of the Cinémathèque Française
aren't lacking many prints, so his Paris education was reasonably compre-
hensive. The critic's research and evaluation didn't stop when he returned
to home shores. In New York, he continued ranking filmmakers on the basis
of the cumulative output, placing only secondary emphasis on the quality
of any single work. (Much of Sarris' ranking of directors for The American
Cinema was executed with the collaboration of the late Eugene Archer, who
worked on The Times as one of Bosley Crowther's backup critics from 1960
to 1965, after which he turned to screenwriting.)[38]

During the evolution period for the politique, Sarris issued weekly
accounts of the Manhattan movie scene. Ultimately, filmmakers were pigeon-
holed under these superscriptions (which became, in turn, chapter heads in
The American Cinema): "Pantheon Directors" (those at the top of the heap--
Chaplin, Ford, Griffith, Hitchcock, Lang, Welles, and a few others); on a
slightly lower plateau, "The Far Side of Paradise"; down to "Expressive

---

[37]Andrew Sarris, The Primal Screen, p. 30.

[38]Gerald R. Barrett, "Andrew Sarris Interview," p. 199.

Esoterica"; on down to "Fringe Benefits"; next to "Less Than Meets the
Eye"; then to "Lightly Likable"; and finally to "Strained Seriousness."[39]
Every film director, in time, was slotted into one of those categories.

Dutifully, despite his passion for auteur aestheticism, Sarris admits
several shortcomings of the practice. To begin with, "the _auteur_ theory
cannot possibly cover every vagrant charm of the cinema."[40] Some rather
gratifying films, he contends, actually come off as undirected, direction-
less in several senses. Sarris cites Marlon Brando's _One-Eyed Jacks_ as one
of his examples:

> Indeed, _One-Eyed Jacks_ is more entertaining than
> many films with directors. A director-conscious critic
> would find it difficult to say anything good or bad about
> direction that is nonexistent. One can talk here about
> photography, editing, acting but not direction. The film
> even has personality, but like _The Longest Day_ and _Mutiny
> on the Bounty_, it is a cipher directorially.[41]

Thus the _auteur_ theory cannot be applied all-inclusively.

Another shortcoming has to do with the matter of esoterica. As
Sarris explains,

> _Auteurists_ as well as others who write seriously
> about films do tend to get cryptic. . . . Who cares
> that . . . Robert Florey in 1937 had a tracking shot
> that was something out of "Life and Death of a Holly-
> wood Extra" that represents "a supreme moment in the
> history of the moving camera"?[42]

---

[39]Because of the unavailability of material on certain directors or the
scarcity of prints, Sarris concluded _The American Cinema_ with several miscel-
laneous categories: "Oddities, One-Shots, and Newcomers," "Subjects for Further
Research," "Make Way for the Clowns!" and, inevitably, "Miscellany," a catch-
all of second-raters and/or early film men with gravely uneven careers.

[40]Andrew Sarris, _The Primal Screen_, p. 50.

[41]_Ibid._, p. 50.

[42]Gerald R. Barrett, "Andrew Sarris Interview," pp. 203-204.

Anti-_politique_ critics gravitate to this very argument in their con-
demnations. One admires Sarris' candor in voicing his opponents' most
fervent battle cry.

Even so, the critic staunchly retains his _auteur_ stance. Those draw-
backs notwithstanding, the policy, he insists, has a flexibility that keeps
it practicable. Not every film by every _auteur_ will be championed across
the board by every _auteur_ critic. As for Sarris, he has admitted he prefers
Mervyn LeRoy's _Waterloo Bridge_ to his beloved Fritz Lang's _The Return of_
Jesse James "even though LeRoy cannot begin to fit into Fritz Lang's shadow."[43]
That confession comes as a shock considering Lang is one of Sarris' revered
"Pantheon" directors and LeRoy is merely in the "Lightly Likable" division.

Asked whether or not he could pan a film made by an _auteur_--Hitchcock,
for example--Sarris side-stepped the issue somewhat by elaborating on this
matter of flexibility. He replied,

> Everyone's movies vary. . . . Hitchcock has made
> some unsuccessful movies. There are some I don't like
> much--but this is the problem with criticism. Pauline
> Kael and I reviewed _Topaz_. Pauline doesn't like Hitch-
> cock; I do. She and I liked exactly the same things
> in the movie. But she started her review with the
> things she didn't like. I started with the things I
> did like. Very often, the difference between a favorable
> review with reservations and an unfavorable review with
> reservations is very slim.[44]

With revelations of this nature, Sarris modifies, but doesn't quite
invalidate, the accusations against him that he doesn't ever see a movie,
that he is too hung up on the name of Howard Hawks, for example, to faith-

---

[43] Andrew Sarris, _The Primal Screen_, p. 29.

[44] Harvey Aronson, "Movies and Their Critics--Whoops, We Mean Reviewers,"
Cosmopolitan, August 1972, p. 137.

fully experience what Hawks is executing. It is true that Sarris'
reviews occasionally reflect not what is up on the screen, but rather
the critic's predispositions toward a director, actor, scenarist, or genre
upon entering the theatre. To re-read Sarris' critique of The Man Who
Shot Liberty Valance in this light is to observe some of these predispositions in operation. Despite the rigorous recording of details from
that film, one wonders if Sarris isn't shaping the picture to fit his concept
of John Ford's oeuvre. What, ultimately, must one make of his opening
remarks?

> The Man Who Shot Liberty Valance is a political
> western, a psychological murder mystery and John Ford's
> confrontation of the past--personal, professional and
> historical. The title itself suggests a multiplicity
> of functions. "The man who" marks the traditional
> peroration of American nominating conventions and has
> been used in the titles of more than fifty American
> films. In addition to evoking past time, "shot" may
> imply a duel, a murder or an assassination. "Liberty
> Valance" suggests an element of symbolic ambiguity.
> This is all a priori. After the film has unfolded,
> the title is reconstituted as bitter irony. The man
> who apparently shot Liberty Valance is not the man who
> really shot Liberty Valance. Appearance and reality?
> Legend and fact? There is that and more although it
> takes at least two viewings of the film to confirm
> Ford's intentions and at least a minimal awareness of
> a career ranging over 122 films in nearly half a century
> to detect the reverberations of his personality.[45]

Further, how does one react to this later proposition?

> Whatever one thinks of the auteur theory, the
> individual films of John Ford are inextricably
> linked in an awesome network of meanings and associ-
> ations. When we realize that the man in the coffin
> is John Wayne, the John Wayne of Stagecoach, The Long
> Voyage Home, They Were Expendable, Fort Apache, She
> Wore a Yellow Ribbon, Rio Grande, Three Godfathers,
> The Quiet Man, The Searchers and Wings of Eagles, the

---

[45]Andrew Sarris, The Primal Screen, p. 147.

> one-at-a-time reviewer's contention that Wayne is a bit
> old for an action plot becomes absurdly superficial.
> The Man Who Shot Liberty Valance can never be fully
> appreciated except as a memory film, the last of its
> kind, perhaps, from one of the screen's old masters.[46]

Sarris lingers long to provide testimony to Ford's "growth." Perhaps that

kind of reasoning is fallible and superficial, as faulty as the conventional

critics Sarris complains about. Then again, perhaps not. Whatever one's

opinions, Sarris' rationale is unquestionably in direct response to his

auteur education. He is simply applying what he has learned.

To the end, he trumpets the politique. In every interview he grants

(and he is certainly more generous with his time than most other film

critics), he emphasizes that the auteur theory really isn't a theory at all.

It is more correctly what the original French word suggests: a policy, a

decision to promote directors. In America, the politique was directed

specifically against daily reviewers like Bosley Crowther who were con-

stantly minimizing or ignoring directorial contributions.[47] Since 1960,

through sheer attrition, the fortresses of the conventional critics have

been worn down. The battle between the auteurists and their foes is not

yet over; but some ground has been won. Above all, Sarris remains proud

of the eye-opening contributions of the policy. Because he has researched

so many directors and spent so many hours in screening rooms, he has had

the rare advantage of looking from an historical perspective--and sharing

that with others. Utilizing the politique, Sarris and his colleagues have

discovered or re-discovered numerous talents. The auteurists have assessed

---

[46] Andrew Sarris, The Primal Screen, p. 149.

[47] Gerald R. Barrett, "Andrew Sarris Interview," p. 197.

and subsequently resuscitated the reputations of filmmakers formerly

looked upon as hacks; in addition, they brought recognition to former

luminaries whose films had been forgotten or mistakenly considered dated.

> I would look at reviews in the Times of John Ford
> movies where the director would not even be mentioned
> in the entire review, and I thought this is ridiculous--
> people like Ford and Fritz Lang not being mentioned at
> all; the whole thing being treated like the emanation
> from a national industry or studio or a writer. Until
> auteurism came along--you can check this out--in the
> New York Times official credits, the writers always
> preceded the director. You can look in Variety still--
> the director is way down at the bottom. Look at the Times
> today--the director is on top; look at Cue--the director
> is listed. And Cue, you know, is anti-auteurist. So
> we made people aware of direction; they had to start[48]
> thinking about it. This was a kind of shock tactic.

If other critics have seen the politique as an eye-opener, it has been

tantamount to a religious experience for Sarris himself. The revelations

of auteurism are far too numerous to publish here, so one instance must

suffice:

> Sometimes a great deal of corn must be husked to
> yield a few kernels of interior meaning. I recently
> saw Every Night at Eight, one of the many maddeningly
> routine films Raoul Walsh has directed in his long
> career. This 1935 effort featured George Raft, Alice
> Faye, Frances Langford, and Patsy Kelly in one of those
> familiar plots about radio shows of the period. The
> film keeps moving along in the pleasantly unpretentious
> manner one would expect of Walsh until one incongruously
> intense scene with George Raft thrashing about in his
> sleep, revealing his inner fears in mumbling dream talk.
> The girl he loves comes into the room in the midst of
> his unconscious avowals of feeling and listens sympa-
> thetically. This unusual scene was later amplified in
> High Sierra with Humphrey Bogart and Ida Lupino. The
> point is that one of the screen's most virile directors
> employed an essentially feminine narrative device to
> dramatize the emotional vulnerability of his heroes.

---

[48]F. Anthony Macklin, "Everyone Is An Auteurist Now," p. 30.

> If I had not been aware of Walsh in <u>Every Night at Eight</u>
> the crucial link to <u>High Sierra</u> would have passed
> unnoticed. Such are the joys of the <u>auteur</u> theory. [49]

Characteristically, Sarris dedicated his recent <u>The Primal Screen</u> "to all

the <u>auteur</u>ists in Creation."[50]

Often a romantic and an idealist, Sarris can often reveal a pragmatic

streak too. Asked if he would like to experience movies as he did when he

was a boy, he responded:

> I enjoy movies now more than I ever did when I
> was a child, because now I know that what's happening
> on the screen is not pure. The more I find out what
> a mess production is, how awful people are who make
> movies, how trivial and petty and disgusting they are,
> all of those awful production stories that people tell
> me, the more I admire what finally comes out. Out of
> all this confusion, the clashing of egos, the commercial
> calculations, so much of value comes out. That is the
> final feeling, the discovery that out of this complex
> situation something clear and beautiful results. That's
> really a great thrill![51]

Childhood and innocence are gone for Sarris, yet what remains is a stead-

fast belief that the more knowledge one has about films the more pleasure

there is to be derived. One might think a postulate would be: the more

one knows, the more insightful and articulate he can be.

The gift of being articulate, however, is not Andrew Sarris' cachet.

Sadly, the writer lapses upon occasion into ambiguity and esoterica. (We

have previously seen examples of the latter.) As media critic Richard

Corliss has observed, Sarris plays with words, occasionally to his discredit.[52]

---

[49]Andrew Sarris, <u>The Primal Screen</u>, p. 53.

[50]<u>Ibid.</u>, p. 7.

[51]Gerald R. Barrett, "Andrew Sarris Interview," p. 205.

[52]Richard Corliss, "Perils of Renata, Pearls of Pauline," <u>National
Review</u>, April 7, 1970, p. 369.

He is facile with words, words that sometimes aren't very meaningful. One method Sarris practices is to employ opaque phrases, then let them lie, wanting further qualification. For the critic, Richard Brooks' "sub-Proustian visualization in Sweet Bird of Youth and his facile Freudianizing for In Cold Blood are particularly damning proofs of an imagination more shallow than fallow."[53] "Facile Freudianizing" is plain enough, but what, one wonders, is a "sub-Proustian visualization"?

Often this glibness of Sarris' culminates in sentences of increasingly turgid syntax:

> Fortunately (for my viewing purposes), the complete print of Once Upon a Time in the West is still circulating in Europe though dubbed into French, Italian and who knows what else, the catch being that Once Upon a Time in the West is basically an English-language production, perhaps too basically English and not as nuanced and idiosyncratic in its dialogue as it might be, but I don't think even a Buck Henry-Terry Southern script would make Sergio Leone's westerns fashionable in New York, a city so feminized in its tastes that the only cowboys that make money are those who ride at midnight far from the lone prairie.[54]

John Simon, as is his wont, spotted the worst of Sarris. Grammarian that he is, Simon balked at Sarris' "steady stew of tromedy" accolade for Godard's Masculine-Feminine. The quote, and Simon's rebuff, are reprinted in the John Simon chapter. Noteworthily, the Voice reviewer's more recent criticism has tended toward a grammatical precision not often evident in earlier writings. Readers can only speculate whether or not John Simon's public reprimands brought about the change.

---

[53] Andrew Sarris, The American Cinema, p. 190.

[54] Andrew Sarris, The Primal Screen, p. 204.

It must be stressed that Sarris, whatever his vices, is a perceptive self-critic. Answering a request for guidelines to good criticism, he stated,

> A critic needs three things: he needs intellect, he needs intuition, and he needs intelligibility. Some people are more developed in one of those areas than in the others. My weak area has always been intelligibility. I don't communicate very well. I guess it's because, basically, I'm more interested in getting ideas than in elaborating or persuading or making a beautiful object of my own. I feel that the subject is so large. My bad habit is a tendency to be too concise. Sometimes I have trouble writing anything at all![55]

In his sentiment about disinterest in creating "a beautiful object" with his writing, he once more confronts the doctrine of John Simon. Two men could hardly be more radically separated on an issue. The latter, you will recall, wants his essays to be works of art.

Sarris' strain of pragmatism emerges again in his perception of his profession. In a survey-interview of film critics, he was asked about the goals and utility of his job. As opposed to Simon, who "writes for history, not just for the moment," the Voice columnist viewed his purpose as "consumer cost consultant," directing the public toward good wares and away from risks.[56] Nonetheless, he added that he and his colleagues wrote with multiple goals beyond that principal one: "We're partly reviewers, partly critics; we're dealing with the immediate reaction, and we're also trying to deal with historical perspective."[57] Perhaps Sarris would want

---

[55]Gerald R. Barrett, "Andrew Sarris Interview," pp. 203-204.

[56]Harvey Aronson, "Movies And Their Critics," p. 136.

[57]Ibid., p. 136.

to be remembered for this typically humble admission: "I never have the idea that any piece of criticism I do is the last word on the subject."[58]

Andrew Sarris has his faults as a critic, yes; but he has great virtues as well, and virtues in addition to his honesty and invariably candid admissions. Because of his overview, because of his method of describing individual films as evolving statements of their makers, he is in a unique position in the American critical confraternity. Most other regularly published critics regard a picture as a single product. Although they may refer to other works of the filmmaker, Sarris' colleagues rarely utilize their columns to scrutinize thematic or stylistic parallels in a director's work. But since the movie director is Sarris' prime focus, he does all these things. In this sense then, because he traces evolution and development, Sarris has had more of an impact as film historian and theorist than as critic.

Sarris' significance derives from his import into this country of the auteur policy, audacious in the late Fifties and early Sixties, but now more generally accepted. Today, even more traditional critics (among them, some, like Pauline Kael, who attacked it at the beginning) are accepting it to a degree. Sarris views the original debate with amusement and the wisdom of hindsight:

> It is a generally overlooked paradox of the famous auteurist controversy that though my debate with Pauline Kael in Film Quarterly attracted a great deal of attention as a squabble between two schools of thought, it served also to propel two obscure polemicists from the little film magazine backwaters into the mainstream of the critical establishment.[59]

---

[58] Harvey Aronson, "Movies And Their Critics," p. 163.

[59] Andrew Sarris, "Sixties Cinema," Rolling Stone, November 22, 1973, p. 46.

For that _auteur_ debate, then, we can be truly thankful. If nothing else, in catapulting Kael and Sarris to fame, it infinitely enriched the state of American film criticism.

VI. JUDITH CRIST

In her eleven-year career as a movie reviewer, Judith Crist has thrived on controversy. She has emerged unscathed from clashes with Hollywood studio magnates, bouts with other critics, and tons of hate-mail. A representative correspondent, anonymous, once wrote Ms. Crist: "You'd probably drop dead if you saw a movie you liked. I know I'd drop dead if I ever read a kind word about a movie from you."[1]

It's true the critic has been notoriously unkind to some films, among them a number of public favorites. Within her first month of reviewing for the New York Herald Tribune, Ms. Crist responded negatively to two major studio productions: Spencer's Mountain and Cleopatra. Her critiques, and the ensuing furor from Warner Brothers and Twentieth Century-Fox, thrust Ms. Crist stage center.

In a 1972 interview, she recalled those early days:

> When I rapped Cleopatra, all of Twentieth yelled
> at my boss, Jock Whitney [the Tribune's publisher]. By
> then I was also doing the "Today" show, and Darryl Zanuck
> had a vicious correspondence with Al Morgan, who was
> producing the show. This was over the show's request
> for stills of the film. "Why help that woman?" Zanuck
> wrote. We finally got one still that Twentieth had sent
> by mistake to the Trib. After a while, Al Morgan began
> returning Zanuck's letters stamping them "Bullshit."
> That Christmas, Al gave me a "Bullshit" stamp as a
> present. The interesting thing is that the two times
> studios reacted that way, they made my career. Absolutely.

---

[1]Judith Crist, "What Good Is a Movie Critic?: A Critic's Credo," TV Guide, August 29, 1970, pp. 6-7.

> I was known as the critic who didn't like
> Cleopatra.[2]

With the publication of her Cleopatra pan, Crist dove into the
mainstream of film criticism. She has been there ever since.

Like other critics in this study--Stanley Kauffmann, Andrew Sarris,
and Vincent Canby--Judith Crist, née Klein, is a native New Yorker. An
alumna of Hunter College (A.B., 1941) and the Columbia University School
of Journalism (M.S., 1945), she joined the Herald Tribune in 1945. At
the Tribune, she started as a general-assignment reporter, then graduated
to arts editor. (The Tribune's "Lively Arts" section was the forerunner
for the now-independent New York magazine, where Crist and John Simon are
contributing editors.) In 1957, she was named the paper's associate
drama critic, second string to Walter Kerr.

In 1963, she became a film critic. As noted, her reputation was born
almost instantly. Crist has said, "All I know is I had fifteen years of
page-one bylines . . . without attracting a lot of attention . . . but the
minute I wrote my first movie review the whole world knew me. . . ."[3] One
of the first reviews was of the aforementioned Spencer's Mountain. Her
notice, pointing to the film's "smirking sexuality, its glorification of
the vulgar, its patronizing tone toward the humble, its mealymouthed
piety . . .",[4] cost the Tribune a quarter of a million dollars' worth of
advertising by Warners and Radio City Music Hall, where Spencer's Mountain

---

[2]Harvey Aronson, "Movies and Their Critics--Whoops, We Mean Reviewers,"
Cosmopolitan, August 1972, p. 136.

[3]Ibid., p. 136.

[4]Judith Crist, The Private Eye, the Cowboy and the Very Naked Girl:
Movies From Cleo to Clyde, Holt, Rinehart, and Winston, Chicago, 1968, p. 3.

premièred. ("The _Trib_ wrote an editorial saying how childish that sort
of thing was . . . and that I was the paper's critic, right or wrong. And
both Warners and the Music Hall came back to the fold eventually.")[5]

After the demise of the _Herald Tribune_, Crist continued with its short-
lived successor, _World Journal Tribune_. When it folded in 1967, she
transfered, with many other WJT staffers, to the paper's offshoot magazine,
New York. Her film columns through 1967 were collected in a 1968 volume
entitled _The Private Eye, the Cowboy and the Very Naked Girl_. The title
indicates the same thematic concerns as Pauline Kael's _Kiss Kiss Bang Bang_,
published the same year. Since April 1968, _New York_ has been Judith Crist's
chief base of operations, for in her weekly column she inspects every major
film that arrives in Manhattan. This is a task unequalled by any of her
colleagues. To illustrate: Crist reported on 164 movies in 1973; by
contrast, Kauffmann reviewed eighty-five in _The New Republic_ and Kael, with
half-year status at _The New Yorker_, forty-seven. Only trade papers like
Variety print more reviews than Crist and, at the trades, duties are
divided among many staff writers.

Ms. Crist has frequently taken on other assignments to augment those
already listed. For a while in 1966 and 1967, she was critic-at-large for
Ladies' Home Journal, and from 1963 to 1973 she appeared regularly on NBC's
Today with summaries of current films and Broadway shows. (She originated
the now-popular TV critic phenomenon during New York's 1962-63 newspaper
strike.) Since 1965 she has been the weekly critic of movies on television
for _TV Guide_. In addition, Ms. Crist is a colleague of Andrew Sarris at

---

[5]Harvey Aronson, "Movies and Their Critics," p. 136.

Columbia University, where she teaches a graduate workshop in critical
writing for the School of Journalism. Even when away from her writing
desk and her classroom, she keeps busy--talking about film. Each year
she reserves space on her calendar for periodic guest-shots on the television talk shows hosted by Dick Cavett and Mike Douglas and additional
space for approximately twenty dates on the campus-film-society and
community-service lecture circuit.

As much as any critic, Ms. Crist has devoted her adult life to movies.
As an ultimate testament to her passion, she now hosts "film weekends"
at the Tarrytown Conference Center, the former Mary Duke Biddle estate.
Guests from all walks of life share (for eighty dollars) two days of marathon
moviegoing, presided over by Ms. Crist and a film celebrity. (Robert Redford,
Alan Bates, Peter O'Toole, Paddy Chayefsky, Robert Altman, and Frank Perry
have appeared.) The Judith Crist Film Weekend series is now in its third
season.

"I am of the post-nickelodian pre-television generation," the critic
quips, "the children of Loew's Paradise."[6] Always a cinéaste, her dedication
to film remained, perhaps strengthened, when she turned from mere moviegoer
to serious critic. "I'm a movie nut," she explains;[7] but that was a foregone
conclusion, with her viewing of two-hundred theatrical movies a year (four-
hundred in 1969, three-hundred in 1970, and nearly three-hundred in 1972)
and reporting on almost as many. Some critics are not movie nuts. Dwight
Macdonald once remarked, "One of the advantages of this job [reviewing for

[6]Judith Crist, The Private Eye, the Cowboy and the Very Naked Girl, p. xi.

[7]Pamela Susskind, "Critic Around the Clock," Newsweek, March 27, 1967, p. 95.

the once-a-month Esquire] is that I don't have to see many movies."[8]

That is a sentiment not shared by the six critics in this study, least

of all Judith Crist.

But in her love affair with cinema, Ms. Crist is not just a buff

writing esoterica for specialty magazines. She reaches a large audience

through TV Guide and New York (not as wide as the one she had before

departing the Today program, but still a considerable number). In conse-

quence, her reviews are primarily directed at the general reader, not the

literati who comprise Kauffmann's and Simon's readership, not the industryite

who follows Kael, not the Village Voice subscriber who reads Sarris. The

fact that Crist writes for the public-at-large is nothing to be ashamed of:

"Critics may be born," she has written;

> for public and professional purposes they are made by
> being given their voice. The voice I . . . sought was
> in the mass media. I am, I suppose, a teacher and
> preacher at heart and I am not interested in converting
> the converted, in chatting with fellow specialists and
> intellectuals via the high-of-brow and low-of-circulation
> "little" publication or an esoteric FM station. I'd
> long discarded the notion that popularity indicates
> middle-brow status or that anything that is good, let
> alone great, must of necessity appeal only to a chosen
> few. . . . And it is the simple logical progression for
> the passionate reformer (the teacher-preacher bit) to
> choose to speak to the millions, in the hopes of being
> heard by hundreds of thousands and listened to by
> tens of thousands, rather than to the thousands among
> whom there are hundreds who've either heard it all
> before or could speak it out for themselves. In short,
> I am a journalistic critic with no pretensions to
> esoterica. . . .[9]

---

[8]Dwight Macdonald, On Movies, Prentice-Hall, Inc., Englewood Cliffs, New Jersey, 1969, p. 299.

[9]Judith Crist, The Private Eye, the Cowboy and the Very Naked Girl, pp. xiv-xv.

These revelations open up several subject areas that mark Crist's style: her journalistic training and writing style, her mass audience orientation, and her self-admitted status as preacher-teacher.

No doubt a reflection of her _Tribune_ experience, Crist's writing is characterized by sprightly journalese. Her diction is frequently a display of hip terminology, embedded information, and reportorial action verbs (avoiding, wherever possible, the form "to be"). _Variety_, the show business journal, is renowned for having coined theatrical and cinematic jargon. Crist, in true journalistic fashion, keeping abreast, is quick to adopt the new words. No stranger to slang, she was one of the first critics to popularize such _Variety_-inspired word-compounds as "sexploitation" and "blaxploitation"[10] and among the first to popularize trade names like "spaghetti western" (for western shot in Italy), "quickie-flick" (for made-for-TV movies), and "chop-socky" (for Chinese kung-fu movies).[11] Additional _Varietyese_ like "oater" (for western), "actioner" (for action melodrama)[12] and the ubiquitous "wow" ("_Blacula_ Wow 27G")[13] creeps into her columns from time to time.

Arthur Cooper, of _Newsweek_, has declared that Ms. Crist expresses herself in "a strenuously hip prose, like a square dancer practicing the boogaloo in a hayloft" and he labels her style "inappropriate," considering

---

[10]Judith Crist, "Sic Transit Gloria Mundi, West," _New York_, May 22, 1972, p. 75.

[11]Judith Crist, "This Week's Movies," _TV Guide_, March 16, 1974, p. A-7.

[12]Judith Crist, "Movies: Pure Honey," _New York_, December 31, 1973, p. 77.

[13]_Variety_, August 15, 1973, p. 10.

her "medium-middle-central" taste.[14] Whether all this is an accurate representation or not, it seems clear that Crist keeps attuned to trends in the film industry and that her prose reflects contemporary usage. True, there are contradictions in her style, elements alien to her mass-audience frame of mind, but they are few and far between. These exceptions will be discussed later.

Apart from her facility with current vernacular, Judith Crist's journalism training is mirrored in her habit of embedding within sentences and paragraphs information that is not essential to the main drift. This process is one of the salient features of her writing style, for she is past and present mistress of the interrupted sentence, whether by dash, a series of commas, parenthetical interpolations, or elliptical constructions. This excerpt of Crist's review of Peter Bogdanovich's The Last Picture Show represents a moderate usage of the interrupted sentence, in this case to embed the actors' previous credits.

> Timothy Bottoms, who made his debut in Johnny Got His Gun, looking very much like a young Howard Duff, emerges as a remarkably aware actor with his portrait of the protagonist, Sonny, a high school senior. Jeff Bridges, Lloyd's younger son, fulfills the promise he showed in Halls of Anger, as Duane, Sonny's jock type buddy. The casting of the film, and the director's penetration of his actors, is nothing short of brilliant, with Ben Johnson, a veteran of Hawks and Ford westerns, as the last frontiersman and the focal figure in town; Eileen Brennan, of Little Mary Sunshine fame, as the worn waitress who inherits Johnson's cafe (Sonny is deeded his pool hall). . . .[15]

---

[14]Arthur Cooper, "Critic as Superstar," Newsweek, December 24, 1973, p. 97.

[15]Judith Crist, "Movies: The Movies Didn't Get Bigger, the Festival Got Smaller," New York, October 4, 1971.

The construction is slightly more complex in her review of the Renée

Taylor-Joseph Bologna film, Made for Each Other:

> The original screenplay was written by Renée Taylor
> and Joseph Bologna, the husband-and-wife acting-writing
> team that wrote Lovers and Other Strangers (then four
> one-act plays, with Miss Taylor appearing in one) for
> Broadway and collaborated with Cy Howard and David Z.
> Goodman in bringing it to the screen. Much of the
> flavor (and some of the characteristics) of that work
> is carried over in their new film. . . .[16]

Sometimes, Crist's embedding can be drawn to excessive lengths, as

in these passages from critiques for Bob Fosse's Cabaret and Ernest Lehman's

film of Portnoy's Complaint:

> The international cast [in Cabaret]--the European
> performers were found in various countries, as were the
> locales that blend for a striking feel of time and
> place--is excellent.[17]

> Lehman--and we shall honor him for his original
> novelette, The Sweet Smell of Success, whose screen-
> play he co-authored, and some of his screen adaptations--
> has certainly provided a handsome cast amid, at very
> least, authentic settings.[18]

It is doubtful that the ordinary copy writer would separate the

subject and predicate quite so far. News stories, famous for their inter-

polations, rarely push the interpolations to the extremes demonstrated

in these two examples. It is when Crist is compelled by excesses such as

these that the veteran newspaperwoman in her strikes out in a style all

her own. In evolving a transition in one of her columns that dealt with

several black films, she wrote:

---

[16]Judith Crist, "Movies: Reupholstery," New York, December 11, 1971,
p. 78.

[17]Judith Crist, "Movies: Best of Both Worlds," New York, February 21,
1972, p. 61.

[18]Judith Crist, "Movies: Grounds for Complaint," New York, July 3, 1972,
p. 52.

> That this "burn, baby, burn" scurrility [of The
> Spook Who Sat By the Door] is out of date even for the
> blacks (albeit its appeal to the know-nothings is all
> too obvious) is attested to by the documentary Save
> the Children, another black-made film that I hope will
> transcend its possibly misleading title.[19]

At times, the critic's prose reaches a state of almost constant

embedding. Perhaps her rave notice for Robert Altman's Images demonstrates

this practice best. Virtually every sentence of the concluding paragraphs

is an interrupted one.

> The cast is impeccable, Miss York has never been
> better; René Auberjonois, an Altman veteran (his
> M*A*S*H chaplain, Brewster [McCloud] bird-lecturer;
> McCabe [and Mrs. Miller] saloonkeeper), Tony Winner for
> Coco and most recently the best Malvolio of my
> experience in a Lincoln Center Twelfth Night, is
> superb as the unreachable husband, quip on the lips
> and hands gloved; [Marcel] Bozuffi, best remembered
> perhaps as the killer of Z and The French Connection,
> brings virility to Gallic romance, and [Hugh] Millais
> makes his artist-lover a fanny-pinching vulgarian.
> And Cathryn Harrison, Rex Harrison's granddaughter
> via his son Noel, proves that at twelve she has a
> firm hold on the family talent.

> Images is, above all, a film of sensation, one
> to be felt--and that you will feel. Both in its
> advanced techniques (Altman continues his breakaway
> from traditional soundtrack) and its understandings,
> it honors its creators.[20]

Sometimes one gets the impression Judith Crist's reviews are jigsaw

puzzles built of words, and that the reader must assemble the pieces. The

critic's practice of embedding is not random or occasional either. It is

an intrinsic characteristic of her style. Kurt Vonnegut's Slaughterhouse-

Five was filmed in 1972, and Crist's review of it provides the quintessential

illustration of her style. Here is an excerpt:

------

[19]Judith Crist, "Movies: Seasonal Slurp," New York, September 24, 1973,
p. 90.

[20]Judith Crist, "Movies: Some for the Cachet, Others for the Cash,"
New York, October 9, 1972, pp. 72-73.

That the heart of the matter that matters to Vonnegut has come to the screen with a throbbing cinematic
pulse of its own should be credited to the screenplay
of Stephen Geller (whose novel, She Let Him Continue,
became the on-screen Pretty Poison) and, above all, the
direction of George Roy Hill. With the incomparable
Dede Allen as his editor, Hill once again, as in The
World of Henry Orient and Butch Cassidy and the Sundance
Kid, shows his tenderness and fondness for the humanity
beneath the grotesque. The great accomplishment here
is his own ability to time-trip, to blend the past, the
fleeting present and the endless future without a moment's
confusion and with full appreciation of the elements
of each scene. Unlike Catch-22, of which this film
will inevitably remind you in its essential statement,
there is a caring for the specific and there is none
of the snickering retrospection tinged with either
scorn or sentiment that is too often used to view the
innocence that was once sincerely ours. Hill's is a
fascinating film, a human comedy whose blackness is in
the nouveau-cynical eye of the beholder.

As an added richness, Prague was chosen as the
location to duplicate pre-war Dresden and it was at
the Barandox studios there that the fine Czech cine-
matographer, Miroslav Ondriček (Loves of a Blonde,
The Firemen's Ball, If. . . ., Intimate Lighting) was
brought to the project. And not least, the music,
composed by that often misused and abused J. S. Bach,
was scored and performed by Glenn Gould, providing
superb accompaniment to a masterly film.[21]

Inevitably, embedding and interruptions of this quantity equal con-

volutions. Some of Crist's convolutions are easy to work out of. Some

are not. At times, the convolutions are problematical because they seem

to wrest control from their creator. Like the Frankenstein monster,

they take on a life of their own.

As if in acknowledgment of her occasionally congested writing style,

Ms. Crist has confessed to "an inescapable infatuation with the sight of

---

[21]Judith Crist, "Movies: Billy Pilgrim's Progress," New York,
April 3, 1972, p. 59.

[her] own words. . . ."[22] In her infatuation with words, the critic doesn't always remain with native ones. Foreign languages, particularly French and Latin, sometimes invade Ms. Crist's work. For instance, she labels Demy's Umbrellas of Cherbourg not soap opera but opéra de savon;[23] Louis Malle's The Thief of Paris concerns, she says, the haute bourgeoisie and the characters wear fin de siècle fashions;[24] her pan of Godard's Contempt winds up "Chacun à son goût, as we Russians like to say."[25] These are quirky and inexplicable exceptions to the generalization made earlier: that Crist is a non-esoteric writer for the masses.

Other examples: "Those who go to see [Bergman's] The Silence with prurient interest are in for a disappointment; those who find its sexuality offensive are suffering from a major case of honi scit."[26] [Movie producers] are "turning to drug addiction with, of course, the usual pro bono publico pretensions."[27] "Support your local critic, of course--but who can expect him to serve in loco parentis?"[28] "François Truffaut's Fahrenheit 451 is . . . [a] pedestrian reductio ad nihil foray into Ray Bradbury's realm. . . ."[29]

As for René Clément's Is Paris Burning?,

---

[22]Judith Crist, The Private Eye, the Cowboy and the Very Naked Girl, p. xix.

[23]Ibid., p. 85.

[24]Ibid., pp. 241-242.

[25]Ibid., p. 86.

[26]Ibid., p. 46.

[27]Judith Crist, "Movies: Dick and Jane Shoot Up," New York, July 19, 1971, p. 58.

[28]Judith Crist, "Movies: Dial R for Rotten," New York, June 7, 1971, p. 58.

[29]Judith Crist, The Private Eye, the Cowboy and the Very Naked Girl, p. 210.

> Everybody was there except Quasimodo. It was one
> of those "Hey there!" occasions--hey there, it's Kirk
> Douglas--and hey there, it's Glenn Ford and Jean-Paul
> (Belmondo, you shnook--you were expecting maybe Sartre?
> And come to think of it, why not?) and Simone and Yves
> and, hey there, Tony Perkins and, cheri, Charles Boyer
> and Alain of the pouty mouth Delon and your favorite
> Untouchable and Deanna Durbin's, Robert Stack--and
> dahling chubby Orson Welles. What an occasion--and
> Quasimodo, poor petit hunchback, he miss it all--quel
> dommage! . . .

> The director was French, but the money for the
> film American. And for American money you got to have
> box-office appeal, nicht wahr?[30]

Conjoined with the foreign phrases in this last passage is Ms. Crist's

affinity for cute colloquialisms, informalities, and "in" references, like

the one to Deanna Durbin. Robert Stack, star of TV's The Untouchables,

honored Ms. Durbin with her first screen kiss in 1939's First Love. That's

fine for readers who catch the reference. For those who don't, it comes

off as disturbingly arcane and/or cliquish.

This particular custom has emerged in Crist seemingly as an effort

to align herself more closely with her readers--what she might think of

as placing them on a level of equality. In the excerpt above she introduces

a chatty informality (the Belmondo-Sartre confusion, the parodies of

affected chit-chat with "cheri" and the re-spelled "dahling," the pointed

use of the second person, presumably as if drawing the reader into a

dialogue), and that informality ranks as a secondary hallmark of her work.

Time and again her reviews are given over to these elements, akin to

the hip jargon examined earlier. In her Cabaret review, she declares

that the original, non-musical picture (I Am a Camera) was considered

---

[30]Judith Crist, The Private Eye, the Cowboy and the Very Naked Girl,
pp. 197-198.

"immoral and refused a Motion Picture seal of approval, no less, because Sally was, er, promiscuous."[31] It is that editorial "er" which signals this as a Crist statement. Placing Living Free, the Born Free sequel, on a year-end worst list, she ridicules the film as "icky-poo pablum."[32] Rejoicing over the announced TV presentation of a favorite movie, she bubbles "Golly, mums, one network has acquired 'West Side Story' for next season. . . ."[33]

From the journalistic prose, the colloquialism, and the obscure allusions emerges a tone which individualizes Crist's style. It is a tone of breezy familiarity, of smart cocktail chatter, of sophisticated (but reliably informed) topicality. To Arthur Cooper the tone is "inappropriate," yet it appeals to hordes of people. (New York's circulation is 1,500,000, TV Guide's is 19,000,000.)

Still, despite the apparent power she wields, Judith Crist has not lost perspective. She realizes the impact her word has but rejects the role of the tyrant-critic. The film critic, she has declared, "is not out to rule the world, egomaniac though he must seem by his choice of profession."[34] Importantly, she has also admitted the subjectivity involved in film reviewing.

> Critics are people; their opinions are personal.
> But their subjectivity is, hopefully, tempered by a
> background, an experience, a knowledge that broadens
> the value of their viewpoint. . . .

---

[31] Judith Crist, "Movies: Best of Both Worlds," New York, February 21, 1972, p. 60.

[32] Judith Crist, "Movies: The Year of Something for Everyone," New York, January 1, 1973, p. 53.

[33] Judith Crist, "What Good Is a Movie Critic?: A Critic's Credo," TV Guide, August 29, 1970, p. 9.

[34] Ibid., p. 8.

> I think only the pretentious among us would lay
> claim to trying to "elevate the public taste." I have
> a sneaking suspicion that the public can elevate its
> own taste, given half a chance; that anyone will enjoy
> a good movie more than a bad one, let a fine actor
> affect him more deeply than a ham can, see that a great
> director has more to tell him than a hack has.[35]

In short, Crist places a good deal of confidence in public opinion.
(No wonder the press has dubbed her the "people's critic," the critic of
the common man.)[36] Her trust in the perfectability of public taste is
likely rejected by many of her associates, John Simon foremost among them.

Crist is on hand to remind her readers in a non-imperious way that
certain films are just a matter of taste. She recognizes that her own
taste is somewhat eccentric and, now and again, she acknowledges those
eccentricities. The practice accounts for these rather frank admissions:
"The films of Robert Bresson require a special taste which I recognize
and appreciate but have not yet acquired for my own."[37] Appreciation of
The Grande Bouffe depends upon "your personal taste--and 'taste' is used
in all its various meanings. . . . [It] is, I must insist, a matter of
taste. And it is to mine. . . ."[38] Ms. Crist's 1972 movie best-list,
as with most of her lists, was preceded by a "traditional warning that
this is, of course, a personal-preference listing."[39] Her recognition
and forthright declaration of film criticism's subjectivity is remarkable.

---

[35]Judith Crist, "What Good Is a Movie Critic?," p. 81.

[36]Harvey Aronson, "Movies and Their Critics," p. 135.

[37]Judith Crist, "Movies: Bang! Bang! You're Dead," New York,
November 27, 1972, p. 83.

[38]Judith Crist, "Movies: Seasonal Slurp," New York, September 24,
1973, p. 91.

[39]Judith Crist, "Movies: The Year of Something for Everyone,"
New York, January 1, 1973, p. 51.

Not surprisingly, it is no secret that Crist has certain genre preferences. Among her favorite films are mystery thrillers. ("My mother used to warn me that two things in particular were a complete waste of a young girl's time--going to movies and reading detective stories. Now one is my profession and the other my avocation.")[40]

Statistically, a large proportion of Crist's most generous praise is lavished upon detective and mystery films. We have observed that she reports on more films than almost any other critic. Of those hundreds of features, a large percentage are in the action vein; and while Crist cracks down hard on gratuitous violence and exploitations of sex, she readily delivers bravos to the thrillers which eschew those points. Recent examples of the genre which were well-received by the critic are Get Carter, The House That Dripped Blood, Shaft, When Eight Bells Toll, Gumshoe, Without Apparent Motive, The Cop, Detective Belli, Pulp, The Long Goodbye, The Laughing Policeman, Man on a Swing, The Black Windmill, and The Midnight Man. Such films are not always so favorably regarded by her colleagues, few of whom place thrillers on their year-end best-lists, as Crist does: Mafioso (1964), Harper (1966), Our Man Flint (1966), In the Heat of the Night (1967), This Man Must Die (1970), Sleuth (1972), and The Long Goodbye (1973). No other genre, as a whole, seems quite so appealing to her taste.

Crist, who avers that the function of the critic is "to act as an advance agent, as the previewer who has been there and hands on an opinion to a friend," sees a way out of the problem over critical taste: "No need, of course, to follow a friend's advice blindly. You learn, after a while,

---

[40]Bruce Williamson, "Judith Crist's Magical Mystery Tour," Saturday Review, March 1973, p. 8.

what your friend's hangups and tastes are--and you act accordingly."[41]
In some respects, Crist's work, like Kael's, resembles that of James Agee.
All three have seen movies as principally entertainment, secondarily art,
thirdly an industry, an industry where mass production and distribution
play an immense part. Crist has explained, "I never arrived at film with
the notion that, wow, it's an art form."[42]

Instead she insists that she has a moderately rigid standard for
evaluating movies. Her standard

> requires that the movie fulfill its aspiration and that
> in the course of that fulfillment it illuminate some
> facet of experience for me, provide some sort of emo-
> tional empathy or tell me about somebody or something.
> A film might aspire to do nothing but make one realize
> that people are funny or life is a ball or that surfing
> is exciting--or it might strive to encapsulate the fate
> of man in the story of a cowboy encountering civilization,
> or a philosophy of life in a family relationship. If
> the aspiration is honest, a film has virtue even if it
> does not quite succeed. I think honesty of approach,
> an assumption that the audience has intelligence, a
> dash of inspiration and a bit of style are the least
> I demand of a film. If one gets more than that--hallelujah.
> I don't think anyone who is willing to devote his time
> to watching should settle for less--and he has not only
> the right but also the duty to demand more.[43]

Despite the ambiguity of some of her terms ("honesty of approach,"
for example), Crist assembles a reasonably precise catalogue of her expectations for films. In publicly outlining a credo, she makes explicit the
implications of all her years of reviewing. Although some reviewers,
namely Kael and Simon, would quibble with her demand that a movie should
fulfill its aspirations, Crist at least has set up criteria. Many critics
have failed to do even that, let alone abide by a set of standards. Crist

---

[42] Arthur Cooper, "Critic as Superstar," p. 97.

[43] Judith Crist, "What Good Is a Movie Critic?: A Critic's Credo,"
TV Guide, August 29, 1970, pp. 8-9.

<u>does</u> adhere to her standards, and because of that dedication she has
gained the reputation to which she clings.

> I am, admittedly, a severe critic ("severe" is
> the polite word that has been applied to me; "acerbic"
> is the usual one, and a triple-S rating, as a "snide,
> sarcastic, supercilious bitch," is the most glorious
> epithet I've gotten from an industry man).[44]

In one of her most severe and/or acerbic and/or triple-S moments,
Crist dealt a blow to Otto Preminger's <u>Hurry Sundown</u>. Preminger has never
been a favorite of this critic, and her eleven years in journalistic criticism are peppered with pans of his productions; most Preminger films, from
<u>In Harm's Way</u>, through <u>Sundown</u> and <u>Skidoo</u> to <u>Such Good Friends</u>, contend
for Crist's "worst movie of the year" prize. She condemned <u>Hurry Sundown</u>,
as she had previously done <u>Cleopatra</u> and <u>Spencer's Mountain</u>, with a combination of bile and good humor. Here in its entirety is that March 27,
1967 review:

> Gather roun' chillun, while dem banjos is strummin'
> out <u>Hurry Sundown</u> an' ole Marse Preminger gwine tell us
> all about de South.
>
> Tain't de Deep South, or de ante- or post-bellum
> South. It's de Stereotype South dat you and me done
> love since ole Massas Caldwell and Faulkner done see
> all dat decay down yonder past de ole cotton fields.
> Dere's dem decayin' rich white folks up in de big
> house, afussin' an' afornicatin' (an' usin' saxa-
> phones as high-larious sex symbols) an' betrayin'
> deir old mammies an' tryin' to cheat poor folk out
> of deir land. And dere's dem decayin' un-rich white
> trash down in de town, cheatin' poor folk an' social
> climbin' all over an' jest markin' time from one
> lynchin' bee to de next.

---

[44]Judith Crist, <u>The Private Eye, the Cowboy and the Very Naked Girl</u>,
p. xv.

De rich whites dey got marital problems an' retarded
children; de white trash dey got red necks an' bratty
children--but all God's chillun--hell, baby, dey already
got shoes, so now dey got college degrees an' land-ownin'
ambitions an' Jim Backus to represent them in court an' a
banjo handy so that when that lynchin' party is en route
they can all gather roun' like de Hall Johnson Choir and
sing dat hallelujah title song. Lawsy, chillun, dey
ain't been so perspicacious a study of Southern problems
since ex-Governor Wallace's last speech on civil rights.

The road to this disaster is, we hasten to note, paved
with good intentions (after all, being pro-civil rights
is safe box office these days) as well as with tasteless
sensationalism and plain and fancy foolishness. Otto
Preminger has provided us not only with soap-opera
plotting but also with cartoon characters and patronage
of Negroes that are incredible in 1967. The whole melange
would be offensive were it not simply ludicrous.

For villainy there's Michael Caine, speaking a dialect
that out-Remuses the old Uncle himself, as a sort of sax
player by avocation who has married above his station,
given his son mental retardation by leaving him alone in a
hotel room for a day, and dodged the draft. It's post-
World War II in Georgia, and Caine needs two small farms
belonging to brave veterans for a big land deal. One
farm is owned by a distant relative who has an unretarded
son Caine covets, the other by Caine's high-class wife's
old mammy and her uppity son, who has a sort of going
romance with a schoolteacher who is even uppitier because
she's been living in Harlem.

Well, Jane Fonda, Caine's wife, is a good kid, fond
of her mammy and really pro-Negro and devoted to her
retarded son. But she's hung up on Caine, a real love
captive melting at his touch, getting all boozed up and
stuff--you know how these decadent high-class Southern
gals are. So she goes along with his attempts to get
the veterans' farms with tactics that make Simon Legree
look like the soul of subtlety. But then Diahann Carroll,
that uppity Harlem gal, corners Jane in the ladies' room
for some girl talk and sets her straight.

It's a new Jane, who doesn't even melt when Caine
grabs her by the breast and who sets out for the Men-
ninger Clinic to get her son unretarded. Caine, pro-
testing that "It can't end like this" (and indeed only
115 of the film's 146 minutes have droned by), sets out
for a last-ditch dynamiting attempt with his redneck

chums. And don't think we don't wind up with title-
song harmony in the dawn's early light as all God's
chillun come marching across the fields to rebuild
their white friend's demolished homestead and signify
that any small troubles in the South are easy
mended--albeit by slickness, soap and slobbery.

This elliptic synopsis doesn't take note of the
bigoted old judge, the Negro-loving lecherous sheriff,
the dying cotton-wool-headed mammy who asks deathbed
forgiveness for being "a white folks nigger," the
husband back from the wars with a nightie "from
Paris France," the small boy who denounces Daddy
as a "nigger lover." They're all there but, shucks,
you got to hear Jane Fonda say "Mind if I crochet
while we talk?" to get the flavor.

Those involved in this film deserve better than
having their names repeated here. For to say that
Hurry Sundown is the worst film of the still-young
year is to belittle it. It stands with the worst
films of any number of years.[45]

For this review, Ms. Crist won her third "Front Page" award for

criticism from the New York Newspaperwomen's Club. When the prize was

presented, she received this telegram from Otto Preminger: "Congratulations

on your award from the man without whom it would not have been possible."[46]

Crist's formidable prose style and her "severity" don't force her

into primness and priggishness. As we have seen, she deals in informality

too; her reviews are liberally spiked with colloquialisms and, as evidenced

by her sarcastic dismissal of Hurry Sundown, she is not lacking in wit.

Quips abound in her work. On occasion, her witticisms stand with the

best of Alexander Woollcott and Dorothy Parker.

A year-end survey of bad movies warned readers that Michael Ritchie's

Prime Cut "exemplifies the gangster movie gone bananas--or frankfurters,

---

[45]Judith Crist, The Private Eye, the Cowboy and the Very Naked Girl
pp. 232-233.

[46]Harvey Aronson, "Movies and Their Critics," p. 137.

since the opening sequences involve the chopping up of a mobster into a string of hot dogs, thereby achieving the food turnoff of the year."[47] When the movie version of Jonathan Livingston Seagull opened in 1973, Crist joined the legion of media observers who found more to jest at than praise. A portion of her critique contained an uncharacteristic slam at mass taste.

> For wallowing there's Jonathan Livingston Seagull,
> which might better be termed "Jesus Christ Supergull
> Scientist," a seemingly endless soppy stream of scenery,
> seagulls, and religiosity. . . . In preparation for the
> film, I finally got around to reading the 93-page
> lavishly illustrated book that has been purchased by
> or for some 10 million readers and been a top seller
> for 70 weeks. You can get through the book in about
> 30 minutes--which makes it superior to the movie right
> off the bat. . . .
>
> [The theme] is, of course, a case of mind over
> matter. And we ought to mind and it ought to matter
> that this pap is the popular placebo of people
> advanced enough to read. It's the sort of garbage
> only a seagull could love.[48]

Of the stolid musical remake of Lost Horizon by Ross Hunter (Imitation of Life, Madame X), Crist concluded "only Ross Hunter, in this whole wide world, would make a 1937 movie into a 1932 one."[49]

Nor were there any kind words for John Guillermin's airborne melodrama, Skyjacked, starring Charlton Heston:

> It is a libel on all airlines, what with the pilots
> humping the hostesses, the passengers in "economy" class
> packaged in like coolies in steerage, and the conditions
> even in first class such that when the plane changes

[47] Judith Crist, "Movies: The Year of Something for Everyone," New York, January 1, 1973, p. 53.

[48] Judith Crist, "Movies: Current Shock," New York, October 29, 1973, pp. 80-83.

[49] Judith Crist, "Movies: Shangri-La-De-Da," New York, March 19, 1973, p. 71.

course the passengers are hurled from their seats to
bounce like popping corn amid a hail of coats and
pillows and hand baggage.

What with Huston at the controls and Yvette
Mimieux as the most humped hostess, we get further
originals via Walter Pidgeon as a Senator and Jeanne
Crain as a businessman's wife ("You'll like Minnea-
polis, Harold" is her comeback line, for starters);
there's a sort of hippie girl who is all but humping
the Senator's nubile son by takeoff, a pregnant woman
who will obviously give birth in flight, a black
cellist (presumably the prop department couldn't
come up with a banjo) named "Mr. Brown" in the sort
of bigoted thinking that jams an Italian-jabbering
couple and their three kids into steerage and has
Leslie Uggams, that accomplished black performer,
be the stewardess to say "screw you" to the hijacker.
As to him--if you haven't got him spotted by his
twitches and tics by the time he gets to his seat--
you deserve everything you get thereafter. Welcome
to it.[50]

Crist's humor can contain a touch of the sardonic, and her sarcasm

reigns supreme when she is dealing with either institutional-administrative

ignorance or one of her pet peeves: excessive violence and the Motion

Picture Code.

In April 1973, the controversial Costa-Gavras film State of Siege

was cancelled two days before its scheduled showing at the newly opened

American Film Institute Theatre at the Kennedy Center. George Stevens, Jr.,

director of the Institute, announced that the picture's theme made its

showing "inappropriate" to the occasion--and this decision immediately after

The New York Times had quoted Stevens' declaration that a film's controversy

would never eliminate it from presentation at the Center. Stevens read

the film, correctly, as critical of U. S. foreign policy, and he didn't want

---

[50]Judith Crist, "Movies: Good 'Egg,'" New York, June 5, 1972, p. 62.

to risk offending President Nixon, the man whose personal nomination
for 1972 best-film Oscar was <u>Skyjacked</u>.[51] Crist retaliated in this
manner:

> What an April fool poor George Stevens Jr. has been
> made to look--and by the good gray <u>Times</u>, no less, courtesy
> of the early deadline for its Sunday Arts and Leisure
> section! . . .
>
> <u>State of Siege</u> . . . does not, as Stevens seemed to
> think, "rationalize an act of political assassination."
> The plot hinges on that, because once again Costa-Gavras
> has built two levels, one of thriller and the other of
> political probe and revelation--but in fact the very
> futility of political assassination is realized by both
> the victim and the assassins. . . .[52]

In short, Ms. Crist, along with other journalists, among whom Rex Reed
was most outspoken, felt the American Film Institute's actions unjustified.
Admittedly, the critic's furor was simply a matter of principle. Denied
a showing at the Institute's small 224-seat theatre, <u>State of Siege</u> opened
commercially the very same week, and to big box-office. Crist's rationale
(and the rationale of her colleagues), however, was to advertise the
Institute's act of censorship.

A gadfly, and not one to let issues lie dormant, Judith Crist the
week following her <u>State of Siege</u> review wrote a scathing critique of
<u>Soylent Green</u>, a science fiction film with Charlton Heston.

> Heston's a cop investigating a murder. . . . Anyway,
> as in <u>Skyjacked</u>, [he] winds up bloody and heroic trying
> to save us from ourselves. Better he should concentrate
> on the goings-on at the American Film Institute.[53]

---

[51]Judith Crist, "Movies: The Year of Something for Everyone," p. 53.

[52]Judith Crist, "Movies: Production Politic," <u>New York</u>, April 16,
1973, p. 86.

[53]Judith Crist, "Movies: This Crow Ain't Fit For Eatin'," <u>New York</u>,
April 23, 1973, p. 75.

Charlton Heston, it should be explained, was the chairman of the
board at the American Film Institute, and he kept notoriously close-mouthed
on the State of Siege controversy. Significantly, there is not a single
reference to that fact in Crist's column, nor is there a prior mention,
in that issue, about the controversy. Readers either appreciate the jest
or don't depending upon their knowledge, from elsewhere, since Crist doesn't
tell them, of Heston's A. F. I. connections, and their having read Crist's
previous column. The critic's manner of attack in this case recalls John
Simon's tactics: a single, swift lambast in a final sentence, then immediate
departure. It is characteristic of Crist that her extra-critical functions
be embedded as they are. Her political bias surfaces the same way: an
occasional swipe at President Nixon is usually buried in this fashion--for
example, reiterating the President's admiration for Skyjacked or Broadway's
Irene, both of which she and most of her critical confraternity detested.

Other objects of detestation are her enduring pet peeves, mentioned
above. The first of these is violence. Frequently, in denigrating on-
screen blood-letting, mutilation, and mayhem, Crist gets a bit violent
herself. Just as frequently, the object of her attack is made to seem
ridiculous by way of her witty put-downs.

> The current sampling of the new pornography
> (i.e., emphasizing blood and gore and psychotic sex
> rather than sexual activity) is The Beguiled, a foul
> film produced and directed by Donald Siegel, noted
> primarily for B-level films of violence. This film,
> derived from a novel by Thomas Cullinan, is tailored
> exclusively for sadists and women-haters; its high-spot
> is the on-camera amputation of Clint Eastwood's leg by
> Geraldine Page with razor and hack-saw, with not a cut
> of flesh, gush of blood or grinding of bone omitted;
> and its thesis is that females will calmly kill any
> man who denies them sexual satisfaction. . . .

This excrescence is rated R, so that the family that
likes to vomit together can do it at the movies. That
grand amputation scene certainly proves that Lenny Bruce
was underestimating public taste when he predicted only
that we'd pay admission to see small children get run
over by automobiles.[54]

Crist was not ecstatic about Straw Dogs either.

If the first month of the year has contributed
anything to our movie experience, it is at least proof
positive of the moronic aspects of the rating system.
Anyone under eighteen is forbidden to see the best
film of 1971, Stanley Kubrick's masterly A Clockwork
Orange, X-rated because there is nudity and a murder
(although we do not see the actual deed or the corpse)
by a blow with a large erotic sculpture. But you may
take your young to the worst movie of 1971, Sam
Peckinpah's R-rated Straw Dogs. After all, they won't
see pubic hair--just a gang of mental defectives
slaughtering each other and raping a very rapable girl
in a vast variety of blood-soaked sadistic and perverse
ways, without pause and without purpose. . . .

[The] Peckinpah film, like his The Wild Bunch, is
pure inspiration, telling us, wonder of wonders, that
evil lurks in the hearts of men--as de Shadow done know from
way back--and proceeding to show it by way of an incredible
and unoriginal "realism" (three parts a Hardy-country
version of Tobacco Road, one part Of Mice and Men, six
parts pure De Sade). It is one of the trash-series of
films we've endured (all parts pure von Sacher-Masoch)
in recent years that tell us that violence and/or war
are not nice and wallow in the unniceties for hours. . . .

Peckinpah's contempt for intelligence (in his hero
as well as his audience) and his obvious preference for
the fighter-fornicator (as in The Wild Bunch) is the
director's hang-up. What is truly contemptible is the
suggestion by his admirers that non-machismo-minded
men will get a vicarious release from the desperation
of their own days by seeing the bookish worm turn.
(All anyone with an I.Q. of 70-plus can get out of
this film is a case of the heaves.)[55]

[54]Judith Crist, "Movies: Archy Redivivus," New York, April 12, 1971,
p. 63.

[55]Judith Crist, "Movies: 'X' Should Be for Execrable," New York,
January 24, 1973, p. 64.

Once and for all time Ms. Crist clarifies she is no fan of protracted and pointless violence. Ever the crusader against bloodshed in films, she nonetheless is not a purist: her violent opposition to the Motion Picture Association of America (MPAA) and its rating code makes that clear. Ever since that organization began its practice of rating movies (the industry's attempt at self-censorship so that governmental censorship would not be imposed), Crist has been its chief faultfinder. One fault she alludes to in the excerpt immediately above: A Clockwork Orange, a film with its share of violence, was given an X-rating and Straw Dogs, which she considers infinitely inferior on any number of counts, was granted a more lenient R.

Crist has written tirelessly of the ambiguities and double standards of the rating system--which currently lists films as either G (open to all ages, "general audiences"), PG ("parental guidance" suggested), R ("restricted"), and X (no one under seventeen admitted). The debatable factor is the content of the film, because the rating board determines its letter evaluation solely on the basis of what can be seen on the screen; therefore, implicit or suggested sexual activity and violence are acceptable (and are passed with a PG or R), at least so goes the official MPAA doctrine. And Crist goes up in arms every time this doctrine is violated. (In addition, with the MPAA, quality is not a condition: Midnight Cowboy, critically favored and a multiple award winner, was branded X, while every Disney studio product, no matter how insulting, insipid, sexist, or racist, is automatically granted a G.)

Ms. Crist's accusations evolve from these dichotomies, coupled with the age-old complaint of Who's-to-decide-what-my-child-can-and-cannot-see?

One movie week out of three finds the critic musing about the mentality
of the MPAA rating board: "It not only shatters your alphabetical trust
but also makes one wonder just what moralities and minds are allocating
those letters."[56]

If Judith Crist can be said to have a "cause," it involves the topics
just discussed: faltering corporate-administrative judgment, excessive
violence, and the rating code. Get rid of them all, she would say. Since
those excesses and injustices are still with us, Crist is still polemicizing
against them.

Judith Crist is inarguably a "people's critic." Her reviews, directed
primarily at the general audience, are often criticized for this very reason.
Detractors dwell on her "low-brow" aims. In so doing, they lose sight of
the admirable job she does in supplying information to the serious film
student. Earlier in this chapter, excerpts from Crist demonstrated how
her critiques spill over with parenthetical data. She invariably lists
the previous credits of the major contributors to a film. In addition,
she is constantly exhibiting her movie-history knowledge (or taking
advantage of her cross-reference files), attempting to place films in some
kind of perspective. She is one of the most helpful critics in terms of
providing the reader with background information on a picture, such as
the change from source to screenplay, the director's stylistic habits,
behind-the-scenes occurrences during shooting, and problems of editing,
distribution and legalities. Writing about such topics, the erstwhile
reporter in Crist emerges.

---

[56]Judith Crist, "Movies: Dial R for Rotten," New York, June 7, 1971,
p. 58.

In reporting on John Avildsen's <u>Guess What!?!</u>, the critic reserved one paragraph to disseminate this background story:

> The year's delay is another bit of the good fortune that seems to be hounding the young men of The Cannon Group Inc. Produced by David Gil and directed, photographed and edited by John G. Avildsen, producer and director of <u>Joe</u>, the movie was completed early in 1970 for about $200,000. The two men went on to <u>Joe</u>, whose release last summer was a triumph of topicality. <u>Guess What!?!</u>, however, was pounced upon by a would-be distributor who wanted it as the lead film for a theater-franchise operation he was planning. Cannon sold it to him for $400,000 (thereby rewarding its investors handsomely) with the contract specifying that the film had to be in general release within six months. The distributor's plans came to naught; the movie reverted to Cannon, which now can offer its pre-profited-by film to the public with the not quite accurate (time-wise) ad line of "<u>Guess What!?!</u> the producer and the director of <u>Joe</u> have done now."[57]

Crist established herself as something of an investigative reporter in 1971 when she described the studio post-production machinations on <u>They Might be Giants</u>, starring George C. Scott and Joanne Woodward.

> The politics of movie-making are, of course, part of the eternal Hollywood; leave it to the men at the top to corrupt the intention and art of the creators, all in the name of pandering to that perpetually underestimated public intelligence. Writer James Goldman and director Anthony Harvey are so well established (even as money-makers, as <u>The Lion in Winter</u> should testify) that one would think their work unassailable. Their newest collaboration, alas, has been mangled by the ham hands, with cutting and the insertion of simple-minded prologue and epilogue done after the completion of <u>They Might be Giants</u>. For testament of what we might have received, I urge you to read the screenplay, published in paperback by Lancer Books.

---

[57] Judith Crist, "Movies: The Tempora, or Maybe the Mores, Are Out of Joint," <u>New York</u>, May 10, 1971, p. 71.

> But I urge you too to see the film, for the major
> cut is toward the end--and what comes before is indeed
> the work of giants. . . .
>
> A pity that Messrs. Goldman and Harvey had to have
> their own climactic view deleted; it's been replaced by
> someone's epilogue that "the heart knows things that
> the mind does not begin to understand." And in your
> heart you know Hollywood has had the last word.[58]

Censorship is always a bugaboo for a practicing journalist, and Crist,

like so many of her colleagues, is quick to leap to the defense of an

oppressed artist--as was the case with Marcel Ophuls and his The Sorrow

and the Pity.

> To each nation its own moral prophylaxis. For us
> it is the fiction, as in "Let's Not Be Nasty to the
> Mafia" (at least not by name), or in turning The Damned
> into "The Darned" when it is bowdlerized for television.
> For the French it is the documented fact that must be
> kept from the "masses."
>
> In France, television wants no part of The Sorrow
> and the Pity, an extraordinary documentary about Nazi-
> occupied France written by Marcel Ophuls and Andre
> Harris and directed by Ophuls, the son of the late
> great Max. The two worked on it as reporters for
> government-sponsored television but were dismissed
> after the strike and student riots in 1968. They
> finished the film in 1970--but French television
> refused to run it and it was only through the reported
> intervention of François Truffaut that they were able
> to find a small offbeat theater in which to show it.
> The film was an instant popular success and moved on
> to several Parisian theaters; it was bought for showing
> on Swiss, German, Dutch, Belgian, Hungarian, and Swedish
> television and shown at the last New York Film Festival.
> Now, through Cinema V, it is available to us--and must
> be seen.[59]

More recently, the reviewer chronicled the production story of The

Autobiography of Miss Jane Pittman, shown on television in this country,

but released theatrically abroad.

---

[58]Judith Crist, "Movies: Of Cops and Copouts," New York, May 31, 1971,
pp. 60-61.

[59]Judith Crist, "Movies: Truth Unvarnished, Guilt Ungilded," New York,
March 20, 1972, p. 68.

Set aside the evening of January 31 for watching The Autobiography of Miss Jane Pittman on CBS and then pause to ponder the implications and the generalizations to be drawn from the background and making of this movie. They will, I suspect, provide more than a clue as to why, just as much of the theater's talent has been diverted to movies, much of the fresh creativity in theatrical film is now being diverted to television. Two tyro producers, Bob Christiansen and Rick Rosenberg, brought forth their first film in 1970, Adam at 6 a.m. It opened here at the end of the year and there were other critics who, like me, found it a fine work indeed. . . . But its admirers proved a minority in that year of the youth-weltschmerz craze; Mr. Rosenberg estimates that about a dozen people went to see the movie. And then came nine months of unemployment. Another film project started, fizzled, and finally came to flower under television auspicies as one of those quickie-flicks. It was Suddenly Single, with Hal Holbrook, and its success was followed by their producing Truman Capote's The Glass House and, most recently, A Brand New Life, both of which garnered Emmys.

They had acquired the screen rights to Ernest J. Gaines's novel, The Autobiography of Miss Jane Pittman, the life story of a fictional 110-year-old former slave, spanning the century from the Civil War to the beginning of the civil rights movement in 1962. They attempted to set it up theatrically, but, meeting indifference from film companies, turned to television. The memory of Adam at 6 a.m. rankled--the eighteen months devoted to the project, the handful who saw the film--all this in contrast to the short-term intensity of a production for television and, perhaps above all, the fact that a minimum of 20 million viewers would see the finished work on that one evening. Rosenberg is the first to concede that there are still subjects that television won't touch. But it was television that came to the aid of Miss Jane Pittman, with CBS adding $650,000 to the producers' $250,000 and agreeing to let it run as a special 105-minute film in a two-hour slot (in contrast to the usual 72-minute quickie flick in a 90-minute allotment).

Tracy Keenan Wynn, Ed's grandson and Keenan's son, who had won an Emmy for his adaptation of The Glass House, wrote the screenplay. For director--and another moral's to be drawn here--they chose John Korty, that original and gifted young filmmaker who made a remarkable debut in 1966 with Crazy Quilt and followed it with the delicious

> Funnyman and then the lyrical riverrun. There hadn't
> been a box-office smash among them, and so the movie
> companies weren't propositioning Korty; in the last
> three years he has made three television films. And
> for star--anybody here remember Cicely Tyson, that
> always exquisite actress who appeared on the large
> screen most recently as the mother in Sounder and won
> our vote, and that of the National Society of Film
> Critics, as best actress of 1972? But she'd been
> bested in the Oscar race by Liza Minnelli--and certainly
> no movie company has been pounding on her door with
> any role to compare with that of Miss Jane. And so
> producers, director, and star, all of whom had their
> roots (and presumably hearts) in movies, joined in
> an enterprise for television, a movie made for the
> small screen at a final cost of about $950,000 (about
> thrice the price of the average TV flick), shot in 30
> days on location in and around Baton Rouge, made under
> the production banner of Tomorrow Entertainment, Inc.,
> to be telecast under the sponsorship of Xerox. . . .[60]

Crist makes her mark when she delves so thoroughly into these special

areas. Apparently, no other critic feels compelled to; but surely students

and scholars should be thankful to her for adding to the behind-the-scenes

fund of knowledge. What distinguishes the critic from the run-of-the-mill

entertainment page reporter is that she unites her reportage with her

criticism; she makes the former an integral part of the latter.

Even with her expertise, Crist is not immune to mistakes. No doubt

owing to her increasingly voluminous output (and the ever-present deadline),

she has made more than one factual error.

In her review of The Godfather, she listed director Francis Ford

Coppola's earlier films out of sequence: the filmmaker, she said, "rose

above the disastrous Finian's Rainbow with You're a Big Boy Now. . . ."[61]

---

[60]Judith Crist, "Movies: To Set the Tube Aglow," New York, February 28,
1974, p. 58.

[61]Judith Crist, "Movies: Truth Unvarnished, Guilt Ungilded," New York,
March 20, 1972, p. 69.

Crist implies that Finian's Rainbow was produced before You're A Big Boy Now. Just the reverse is true. Another error that slipped by Crist's editor occurred in her evaluation of Red Sky at Morning; the critic praised "Jean Simmons' portrait of the Navy officer's wife. . . ."[62] Certainly Ms. Crist was chagrined to realize that Jean Simmons does not appear in Red Sky at Morning, even if a look-alike does: Claire Bloom has the role of the Navy officer's wife. Previewing the film Luther for her readers, Crist spoke of Albert Finney's title role performance, when, in fact, Stacy Keach has the part.[63] (The critic was presumably recalling Finney in the Broadway production of John Osborne's script.)

As counterbalance to these oversights, Ms. Crist has at least one admirable trait. She, more than any other critic in this study, writes re-evaluations, suggesting how her opinions on particular movies have changed. These admissions have not become regular practice in her columns; they crop up without notice, but their very appearance attests to the fact that Crist doesn't sense herself as all-powerful, as the final word on what must be said about a film. In her retrospection, she has gone on record declaring Howard Hawks' Bringing Up Baby "less hilarious at each revival"[64] and noting that Mike Nichols' personal achievement with The Graduate diminishes over the years ("who among us might not seriously re-evaluate The Graduate, were the independently popular Simon & Garfunkel songs that glued it together deleted?")[65]

---

[62]Judith Crist, "Movies: Crime Doesn't Pay--or Does It?" New York, May 17, 1971, p. 61.

[63]Judith Crist, "Movies: Below Zero," New York, February 4, 1974, p. 57.

[64]Judith Crist, "Movies: You Can Go Home Again, If You Know the Way," New York, March 27, 1972, p. 74.

[65]Judith Crist, "Movies: Uneasy Rider," New York, October 11, 1971, p. 66.

These reassessments are a final guidepost to Judith Crist's style. If nothing more, they show the critic's passion for seeing and re-seeing movies. And it is a passion this self-confessed "movie nut" has verbalized many times. ("Movies are where the action is. . . . The young, exciting talent is being drained off into films and into television.")[66]

Asked about the possibility of retirement in the near or distant future, Ms. Crist gave this stouthearted response: "Retire? No. I want to keep teaching and preaching. . . ."[67] Judging from past experience, she will continue to do just that. Both in person and in print, she has just concluded eleven years of teaching and preaching about film. It's a profession that seems to suit her well.

With her news reporter orientation, her frequent personal appearances, her support of mass taste while denigrating cultists and esoterica, and her highly individual and readily identifiable writing style, Judith Crist has proven a formidable force in contemporary American film criticism.

---

[66]Pamela Susskind, "Critic Around the Clock," Newsweek, March 27, 1967, p. 95.

[67]Barbaralee Diamonstein, Open Secrets: Ninety-four Women in Touch With Our Time, The Viking Press, New York, 1972, p. 77.

VII. VINCENT CANBY

Vincent Canby's movie reviews reflect an acute awareness of his film-going readers. His columns for The New York Times sometimes belie his official statement that "You can't think about the public's likes and dislikes; the purpose [of film criticism] is to explore your own reactions in an honest way."[1] When it comes to aesthetic considerations, Canby may be his own man; but his explorations of his private reactions are almost always supplemented by discussions about mass taste, conformity or disjunction of opinion, and the failure of this or that movie to attract an audience.

The reviewer's interest in the consumer angle might best be demonstrated in this extract from an editorial he taped for the Times' radio station, WQXR:

> A lot of what's wrong with movies has nothing to do with movies themselves--but with the ordeal of going to them. In summer, theatres are so frigid with air-conditioning that I've often felt like doing weather reports instead of reviews. In winter, they're just as cold in the morning--then overheated by nightfall.
>
> If the movie is any good, you have to stand in line--at least on weekends. When you get to the ticket window, there's another shock--the price. $3.50 a seat in the evening at most first-run theatres. Soon they'll be charging $5 a seat for "Last Tango in Paris"-- which is a lot of loot for a non-musical film, even one that's been compared to Stravinsky's "Rites of Spring."

---

[1] Harvey Aronson, "Movies and Their Critics--Whoops, We Mean Reviewers," Cosmopolitan, August 1972, p. 135.

> Food prices have skyrocketed. For reasons of
> avarice, theatres stock only those candy bars big
> enough to feed a family of four. Though every member
> of a family of four wants his own--at 50¢ each. It's
> axiomatic that one out of every four persons will
> leave the <u>uneaten</u> portion of the candy bar on the
> seat--so that the next customer can sit on it. With
> problems like these--who has time to think about the
> movies?[2]

More directly than almost any other critic, Canby stands for the

consumer (in print, as well as in this uncommon excursion onto radio).

Canby, at least, acknowledges that there exist workaday moviegoers who

must be bothered with mundane matters of uncomfortable theatres, long

lines, exorbitant ticket prices, babysitter fees, and on and on. When

other critics admit the existence of a moviegoing public, the occasion is

more often one of derision rather than sympathy (see, in particular, John

Simon's estimation of the masses). Not coincidentally, Renata Adler,

Canby's immediate predecessor, sympathized with the plight of the moviegoer

too. This attitude, probably indigenous to the <u>Times</u>, is one of those

distinctions between Canby and his colleagues to be explored in this chapter.

Canby stands apart from his contemporaries in more ways than one.

Unlike the covey of journalistic celebrities bred by the electronic media

in the last five years or so, he virtually shuns publicity. He has chosen

to restrict his opinions to the arts and leisure section of the <u>Times</u>,

without resorting to the airwaves. His WQXR editorial was a rarity. So

are his television appearances. (One of his few TV exposures was a 1974

PBS panel discussion, on <u>Black Journal</u>, of the emergence of black films.)

----

[2]"Canby: 'Movie Going An Ordeal,'" <u>Variety</u>, January 24, 1973, p. 5.

Forays into the broadcasting medium are not for Vincent Canby. One
never finds his name on lecture series either. A low-keyed, mild-
mannered individual, Canby once asserted rather firmly that "the idea
of critics as celebrities is kind of sick."[3] The ever-present Simon,
Kael, Sarris, and Crist (and among critics not analyzed here, Rex Reed)
would seem to disagree. Of the others represented in this study, only
Stanley Kauffmann approaches Canby's seclusion; and Canby is even more a
mystery figure than his New Republic counterpart. Regrettably, his official
biography is skimpy. We can learn bare facts of his professional experience--
dates and duration of assignments--but little else. Details about his
career are simply not supplied. Neither Canby nor any of the traditional
biographical listing sources has bothered to augment the data. We can
only guess whether this decision is Canby's personal one or a matter of
his not being asked to supply information. The former reason appears some-
how more likely than the latter, however. Every journalist-turned-Times-
critic preceding Canby received a healthy dose of promotion: upon their
installments, we were given a generous resume of the personal and private
lives of, for example, Renata Adler, Stanley Kauffmann, Clive Barnes, Walter
Kerr, Lawrence van Gelder, and Russell Baker. The same routine treatment
would seem to be in order for Canby, but for one reason or another, it
appears that he has chosen to remain just outside the limelight. Both
his words (regarding critics as celebrities) and his actions betoken a
desire to guard his private life--rather a refreshing gesture in view of
the highly public nature of his ubiquitous associates, but disappointing
for a researcher trying to document Canby's pre-Times existence.

----

[3]Harvey Aronson, "Movies and Their Critics," p. 136.

What do we know about those years? Only this: During the Forties,
Canby was a student at Dartmouth, where, predictably following the pattern,
he began writing movie reviews. The Fifties are a gap; but we do know
that Canby spent more than six years (1959 to 1965) at _Variety_ before
moving to the _Times_. While at _Variety_, Canby (based in New York City)
signed all his reviews "Anby," continuing the four-letter tradition of
identification begun by Sime Silverman when he founded the trade journal
in 1905 and required his vaudeville reporters to label themselves in
that cryptic fashion.[4] As "Anby," he covered the Manhattan preview and
première beat.

In December 1965, Canby received his first byline for a _Times_ review.
Doubtless, he was pleased at working under his full name. Meanwhile, the
Times editors presumably sensed potential in him; so four-letter code
signatures became a thing of the past. He started writing regularly for
the paper in 1966, working in Bosley Crowther's shadow. At that time, other
backup critics for Crowther included Howard Thompson and A. H. Weiler. The
three of them reviewed the programmers: horror double bills, westerns,
crime dramas, and war pictures. Rarely were they assigned an A film. In
1968, upon Crowther's retirement, Renata Adler was shifted into first-
string position. Canby became senior film reviewer when she vacated the
position in February 1969. He has manned the post ever since.

Bits and pieces of autobiography land in his columns from time to
time; but official sources divulge no more than is recorded above. Only
Harvey Aronson, in his survey of film critics, dislodged two other revealing

---

[4]Robert J. Landry, "Variety's Four-Letter Signatures, the Dog-Tags
of Its Critics," _Variety_, January 9, 1974, p. 26.

pieces of information about Canby: for relaxation, he normally spends six weeks a year in Saint Martin, fishing and skin-diving; and he hopes one day to write a novel.[5] Perhaps these two activities take precedence over radio broadcasts, talk-show telecasts, and public appearances.

Aronson's survey-and-interview article was commissioned in 1972. One of his aims was to determine the power and influence of film critics. As part of his research, he interviewed, in addition to the critics themselves, motion picture studio executives, advertising and publicity employees, distribution heads, and screening room officials. The consensus within this cross-section was that Judith Crist, then a regular on Today, was the most influential reviewer; Canby was runner-up.[6] Now, since Crist has lost her television post, Canby may well be in the top spot in terms of reaching a national audience. It must be remembered that although Canby's paper has an enviable circulation, many of its readers are not avid film-goers. (This same survey is the one which suggested that, percentage-wise, Pauline Kael is the most influential critic. More of her readers seem to have the movie habit.)

Nonetheless, Canby can be considered one of the leading tastemakers among movie critics. Probably his principal importance lies in the fact that he writes for the newspaper of record. His prose is marked for posterity if only by virtue of the vaults of microform in every college, university, and public library. A Times review is, therefore, a prestige item. Excerpts from it look impressive for marquee quotes, in newspaper

---

[5]Harvey Aronson, "Movies and Their Critics," p. 136.

[6]Ibid., p. 137.

ads, and for lobby displays. While industry observers agree that a negative film review from the Times won't, of its own, kill box office (as it is believed Clive Barnes' reviews can destroy a play's chances for survival) the Canby opinion is, nonetheless, a potent one.[7]

In an analysis of the movie criticism being done at the Times, Roger Ebert, of the Chicago Sun-Times proposed that what the New York paper requires is somebody "who would just tell people whether they should go out and go to the movies."[8] Vincent Canby is that man. Quite often, in his role as consumer affairs person, he seems to be telling his readers just that. Roger Greenspun, one of Canby's second-stringers until his dismissal in August 1973, fell into editorial disfavor because his reviews didn't follow the advise-the-public pattern. His notices were becoming very specialized. Greenspun was accused of being too intellectual--"rarefied" and "esoteric" were the condemnatory adjectives.[9] Ebert's explanation for Canby's longevity at the Times is that he eschews (either spontaneously or with calculation) rarefied, esoteric criticism. Canby's notices are never too particularized for the general reader. The reviewer speaks in nonspecialized diction, using far less cinematic jargon than the five critics discussed earlier.

Ebert complains that Canby, like Barnes, is best at writing consumer reports: "giving the reader some notion of whether a given movie or play

---

[7]Harvey Aronson, "Movies and Their Critics," pp. 134-135.

[8]Roger Ebert, "Movie Critics' Role: What Does It Demand?," The Denver Post, "Roundup," February 10, 1974.

[9]Ibid., p. 39.

is worth the money."[10] Ebert's premise is well-founded. In fact, this consumer-reports orientation can be expanded into a hypothesis to explain why Canby was employed by the _Times_ in the first place and why he has lasted so long.

The consumer point-of-view can be accounted for through what little we know of Canby's previous experience. Certainly, if the _Times_ was in need of a consumer expert, they did well to engage the services of a former _Variety_ journalist. Canby's experience for the trade newspaper was an important prelude to his current chores, for _Variety_ staffers are hired strictly as reporters, not necessarily for their critical faculties.[11] Reviewers there appraise films from the standpoint of box-office potential and exploitation possibilities; aesthetic estimations come second, or not at all. At _Variety_ the aim is to let readers (principally, distributors and exhibitors) know the drawing power of a given movie. These brief excerpts from several of Canby's _Variety_ notices demonstrate several things: the kind of evaluations he would make, the journalistic shorthand he practiced, and the relative accuracy of his predictions about a film's popular "consumption."

Praising Akira Kurosawa's _The Men Who Tread on the Tiger's Tail_, Canby noted

> This is the kind of picture that needs quite a few program notes to give it meaning, but if the art house exhibitor goes to the trouble, his efforts will not be wasted. Discriminating audiences, properly briefed, should find much of interest in this re-working of an

[10]Roger Ebert, "Movie Critics' Role," p. 39.

[11]Robert J. Landry, "Variety's Four-Letter Signatures," p. 26.

old Kabuki tale, banned first by the Japanese war
government in 1945 and then again by the Occupation
powers in 1946. . . .

Production values and camera work are not spec-
tacular, but quite adequate, especially considering
the fact that when film was in production almost all
of the Japanese homeland was being subjected to a
daily drubbing by the U. S. Air Force.[12]

He wrote this notice for Crack in the Mirror:

Producer Darryl F. Zanuck and director Richard
Fleischer, who collaborated so effectively on "Com-
pulsion," have turned out another vivid melodrama
in "Crack in the Mirror," beautifully acted by Orson
Welles, Juliette Greco, and Bradford Dillman, each
of whom plays two roles. As a promotion gimmick and
as an opportunity to let the stars show their stuff,
the dual-role bit is a great idea. However, it also
tends to belabor the film's small point and to dis-
tract audience interest from any central situation.
. . .

Another problem is that about halfway through,
the film's focal point switches from the working
class triangle to the problems of the upperclass
trio, with the result that audience interest and
emotional involvement are put to a severe test. . . .

"Mirror" is an intriguing film, but ultimately,
like its central characters, unappealing, not likely
to stir wide b.o. sympathy without some hard
exploitation sell.[13]

Upon the re-release, in 1960, of G. W. Pabst's 1931 The Threepenny

Opera, Canby wrote in Variety that

Despite the tremendous general popularity of film's
"Mack the Knife" theme, which might be expected to
interest many filmgoers who do not ordinarily seek
out the esoteric, picture will be most appreciated
by art house audiences and, particularly, by cinema
buffs interested in film techniques. . . .

---

[12]Vincent Canby, "The Men Who Tread on the Tiger's Tail," Variety,
January 27, 1960, p. 6.

[13]Vincent Canby, "Crack in the Mirror," Variety, May 11, 1960, p. 6.

> While the film is chiefly interesting as a museum
> piece, it is an often lively one that stands to attract
> a lot of interest in "selected" dates.[14]

George Cukor's Let's Make Love brought forth this response from Canby:

> With Marilyn Monroe and Yves Montand to ride the
> top of the marquee, producer Jerry Wald has what
> stands to be one of the box-office smashes of the
> year in "Let's Make Love," a cheerful lightweight
> comedy-with-music very familiar in form but still
> delightful in execution. Picture is overly long
> and has its dull patches, but those facts may be
> of interest only to academicians, not to the fans.
> . . .[15]

As for End of Innocence, from Argentine filmmaker Leopold Torre-Nilsson:

> Here is a fascinating film worthy of the best
> playing time which discriminating art house exhibs
> can give it. "End of Innocence" (original title
> in Spanish: "House of the Angel") serves to
> introduce U. S. audiences to the fact that the
> Argentine film industry, almost unknown Stateside,
> can turn out pictures of firstrate quality, both
> technically and artistically. And, being the
> first such in this market, "Innocence" should create
> business-building interest and excitement among
> artie patrons on the lookout for the new and
> different.[16]

"Anby" used further Variety journalese to describe the impact of

Federico Fellini's Juliet of the Spirits. According to the reporter, the

picture "first dazzles--and then boggles--the eye, but on the strength of

the Fellini name as well as the comment it is bound to create, it shapes

up as a big grosser in key situations."[17] This was Canby's final Variety

critique before moving to The New York Times. From first (a report on Pretty

[14]Vincent Canby, "Threepenny Opera," Variety, July 13, 1960, p. 6.

[15]Vincent Canby, "Let's Make Love," Variety, August 24, 1960, p. 6.

[16]Vincent Canby, "End of Innocence," Variety, September 7, 1960, p. 16.

[17]Vincent Canby, "Giulietta de gli Spiriti," Variety, November 3, 1965,
p. 6.

Boy Floyd) to last (Juliet of the Spirits) at Variety, Canby proved himself a consumer analyst, forever weighing a movie's "draw" (its appeal to the masses) and its potential b.o. (box-office take). He was, in a sense, a public servant, at least for those who followed the trades. In turn, this capacity led to frequent implicit alignment with mass taste: his rapturous comments about Let's Make Love make that clear. Ingratiatingly, he states, for one example, how the "dull patches" of the film are of interest only to academicians, not the fans.

Variety, therefore, was a good training ground for Canby. His outlook as a film reporter not primarily a film critic, and his association with popular taste made him a reasonable choice as top movie man for the Times.

This particular approach to film reporting persists in Canby's present-day critiques, and that perhaps explains why there is nothing overwhelmingly unique about his writing style. He writes standard, clear, literate English, but with no individualizing quirks. (Gone too is the former Varietyese and it has not been replaced by any clearly defined stylistic choices; there is nothing in Canby to match the rampant embedding of Crist or the calculated use of the unfamiliar by Simon.) Roger Ebert contends that what is missing from Canby is a "personal voice; we don't get the notion of a unique intelligence being engaged by a work of art."[18] Instead, the critic continues in the Variety vein with statements like "be advised to go see 'A Funny Thing Happened on the Way to the Forum'. . . . Here, at last, is a motion picture spectacle for old men of all ages."[19] As for Jules Dassin's black

---

[18] Roger Ebert, "Movie Critics' Role," p. 39.

[19] The New York Times Film Reviews (1959-1968), Arno Press, New York, p. 3642.

film <u>Up Tight</u>: "Even though Sidney Poitier is not in it, this movie is obviously going to talk to a large audience."[20]

The latent reporter emerges in Canby quite frequently. Here in a review of Freddie Francis' <u>Torture Garden</u>, Canby is more thorough about the conditions of the moviegoing than he is about the film itself:

> The melodrama, starring Jack Palance and Burgess Meredith, opened yesterday at the 42nd Street New Amsterdam Theater, and other neighborhood houses, with all of the ritual required on such occasions--and that I find irresistible. Among other things, the newspaper ads promised patrons free packages of "Fright Seeds for your own Torture Garden."
>
> (A request for a package elicited a certain amount of surprise from the New Amsterdam ticket-taker yesterday morning, although he eventually obliged. According to a Columbia Pictures botanist, the seeds are for timothy grass, which has long cylindrical spikes and is generally used for hay.)[21]

In similar fashion, a December 1968 review of Pinter's <u>The Birthday Party</u>, directed by William Friedkin, concluded this way:

> It opened yesterday.at the Coronet. Before going you might call the theater to ask what the weather's like. Yesterday afternoon it was just slightly warmer inside than it was outside.[22]

Canby may be a cut-and-dried journalist, one without any readily perceivable writing style, but that does not mean he is a dull writer. Quite the contrary. His <u>Variety</u> education prevents that. In addition, he harbors too many biases to be considered dull. His views have been the source of heated debate with readers and other critics alike. Occasional

---

[20] <u>The New York Times Film Reviews</u> (1959-1968), p. 3810.

[21] <u>Ibid</u>., p. 3773.

[22] <u>Ibid</u>., p. 3807.

letters to the Times' "Movie Mailbag" show disturbance over Canby's pro-

nouncements. One correspondent, an Edwin W. Schloss, wrote

> A man is entitled to his opinion, even if his opinion
> is a little out of touch with reality. That's how I
> felt after reading Vincent Canby's review of "A Touch
> of Class". . . .
>
> Canby's reasons for not liking the movie are so
> weak that you have to read his review again just to
> find out why he didn't like it. And even then I'm
> not sure. . . .[23]

Indeed, Canby's reasons, as expressed in his critique, _are_ weak.

In a nine-paragraph notice, he tells the reader only that the situations

in A Touch of Class are "downright dumb"--presumably because the film is

"a remodeled comedy out of the nineteen-forties, when it was written in

Hollywood . . . that adultery was tabu. Adultery must not be consummated,

but it was O.K. as long as it was being constantly interrupted."[24] True,

the adultery in A Touch of Class begins with interruptions, but before

long it is consummated. Canby's reasoning appears unsound on this point,

yet he presents no other views as to why the film displeased him. Mr. Schloss

had a point. Canby was vague.

As detailed in the Sarris chapter, Alfred Hitchcock is a director with

full status in the Sarris pantheon. Furthermore, he is something of a _cause_

célèbre in the _auteur_ world. Since the Fifties, the venerable "master of

suspense" has become a sort of proving ground for admirers of the _politique_.

Auteur adherents have a boundless admiration for his output, even for the

---

[23]"Movie Mailbag," The New York Times, July 29, 1973, p. D-8.

[24]Vincent Canby, "Segal and Jackson Star in 'A Touch of Class,'" The New York Times, June 21, 1973, p. 52.

post-_Psycho_ productions;[25] most critics find it difficult to share that

respect. One way or another, "a review of a new Hitchcock film is

invariably made the occasion for a larger ideological statement."[26]

After Sarris, Vincent Canby is probably the best-known critic in

the United States who employs _auteur_ strategy. If the latter does not

duplicate the unremitting _auteur_ passion of the former, he nonetheless

utilizes the _politique_ when confronting major filmmakers. Canby's review

of _Topaz_, Hitchcock's 1969 film and one panned by the critical majority,

serves to reveal Canby's true _auteur_ attitude. Beyond that, the review

stands in several ways, and one amusingly unintentional one, as an example

of the _politique_ in a nutshell (i.e., the director as supreme being). In

his report, Canby was pleased to record that

> Hitchcock, who can barely tolerate actors, has been self-
> indulgent in the casting of "Topaz." The film has no one
> on the order of James Stewart or Cary Grant on which to
> depend. . . . Most of its performers are, if not entirely
> unknown, so completely subordinate to their roles that
> they seem, perhaps unfairly, quite forgettable. . . .
> ["Topaz"] uses politics the way Hitchcock uses actors--
> for its own ends, without making any real commitments
> to it.[27]

---

[25]Truffaut, of course, did the famous series of interviews recorded in
Hitchcock. See François Truffaut, _Hitchcock_. Simon and Schuster: New York,
1967. (Originally published as _Le Cinéma Selon Hitchcock_. Robert Laffont:
Paris, 1966.) Claude Chabrol has been heavily influenced by the Briton;
critics point to specific Hitchcockean traces in Chabrol's _La Femme Infidèle_,
This Man Must Die, and _Le Boucher_. Truffaut also has paid dutiful _hommage_
in his films. His reverence even goes so far as to use Hitchcock's composer,
Bernard Herrmann, and to base two of his films on novels by William (_Rear
Window_) Irish: _The Bride Wore Black_ and _Mississippi Mermaid_. See Roy Armes,
French Film. Studio Vista/Dutton Paperback: London, 1970.

[26]Marion Magid, "Observations: Auteur! Auteur!," _Commentary_, March 1964,
p. 71.

[27]Vincent Canby, "Screen: Alfred Hitchcock At His Best," _The New
York Times_, December 20, 1969, p. 36.

The Times critic then proceeded to appraise the actors, beginning with the male lead, "John Stafford, who plays a Washington-based French intelligence man"[28]--all of which is well and good, except that the actor playing that role is Frederick Stafford. Auteurism in its extreme would seem to wipe out the actor altogether. Topaz, which Canby dubbed "virtuoso Hitchcock . . . pure Hitchcock,"[29] also made the reviewer's year-end ten-best list, while at The Village Voice it was similarly ten-bested by Andrew Sarris.

Canby's pro-Hitchcock bias is bolstered by prejudices for and against other directors. The fashionable year-end review of the best and worst films is an occasion to air these feelings. In his compilation of the ten worst movies of 1972, the critic admitted to nourishing certain biases: "It's never easy to compile a list of the 10 worst films of the year. There always are considerations. No movie directed by Billy Wilder will ever be allowed on the list, even if it seems as bitterly archaic as 'Avanti.'"[30]

Canby neglects to specify what qualities Wilder has given Avanti to balance its failings (i.e., its "bitterly archaic" nature). Nor is he any more specific about his aversion to Ken Russell or his excuse for the failures of Sam Peckinpah. Canby only states, and rather loftily, "No list of the most awful films of the year would be complete without something by Ken Russell, even a comparatively placid drama such as 'Savage Mes-

---

[28]Vincent Canby, "Screen: Alfred Hitchcock At His Best," p. 36.

[29]Ibid., p. 36.

[30]Vincent Canby, "The 10 Worst Movies of 1972," The New York Times, January 7, 1973, p. D-1.

siah'. . . ."[31] This statement comes in sharp contrast with his notion,
expressed in the same article, that "No matter how bad a film by Sam
Peckinpah is--and both 'Straw Dogs' and 'The Getaway' are pretty bad--you
simply cannot put a Peckinpah film on the list."[32] Such judgment appears
to be a clear instance of critical myopia. Why, one wonders, should Peckinpah be blameless when his films don't work, while Russell is roasted for
his direction of a "comparatively placid drama"? How is a Peckinpah film
redeemed just by being a Peckinpah film, and why is Savage Messiah tainted
simply by being a Russell film? The dilemma seems largely the case of a
film critic turning a deaf ear and a blind eye to the failures of favorite
directors. Canby doesn't supply answers. With his undefended assertions,
he only raises questions.

Canby, it appears, is generally reluctant to divulge any kind of
aesthetic demands he may have for motion pictures. His readers probably
do not discern any habitual or identifiable standards. He is remarkably
secretive with regard to what makes a film "work" for him. Occasionally,
a movie arrives on which he vents his rancor. Sometimes, in such an
instance, Canby makes a rare and uncharacteristic revelation, an extra-
critical explanation for his bias.

When The Trial of the Catonsville Nine premièred, Canby was one of
scores of reviewers to pan it. Most of the other critics, however, offered
precise accounts of the film's aesthetic failure. The Times writer, in
his brief column, took another approach. First he complained bitterly

---

[31] Vincent Canby, "The 10 Worst Movies of 1972," p. D-1.

[32] Ibid., p. D-1.

about the lionization of the fathers Berrigan, then pointed to the "self-defeating smugness" of the film, then concluded:

> I admit to a certain number of doubts about these
> doubts, which could be laid down to a conservative
> Protestant upbringing that always looked askance
> at the kind of razzle-dazzle fundamental religion--
> depending on first-rate public relations to spread
> the word of commitment--practiced by the Berrigans.[33]

His admission of that "conservative Protestant upbringing" is tantamount to disclosure of a state secret. Canby's prose is normally spare and rarely overlaps into autobiography. Here he relaxes his restraint and levels with his readers. As a confession of personal inadequacy or inherent disposition, it is to be admired. In those rare moments when Canby is frank about himself, he is mercilessly frank. Probably foremost among Canby's revelations is his plain-spoken admission that many of his favorite films have "appealed to [him] for reasons that often had nothing to do with their esthetic and historical values."[34]

Canby, however, does not discuss some of his shortcomings. Perhaps he is not aware of them. Perhaps he doesn't view them as shortcomings. The critic is less thorough than any other writer in this study. His criticism of the elements of film is habitually in less detail. Sometimes, when he doesn't think the individual elements of a film are worthy of discussion, he omits them entirely. For his review of Ash Wednesday, a brief eight-paragraph summation, he omits any reference to the quality of performances (Elizabeth Taylor, Henry Fonda), direction (Larry Peerce), music (Maurice

---

[33] Vincent Canby, "'Catonsville Nine' Begins Run as Film," The New York Times, May 16, 1972, p. 48.

[34] The New York Times Film Reviews (1969-1970), Arno Press, New York, 1971, p. 262.

Jarre), editing (Marion Rothman), or cinematography (Ennio Guarnieri)--
choosing to state that Jean-Claude Tramont's script was written "with all
the fearlessness and perception demanded in the boiling of an egg."[35] The
remaining paragraphs are equally unhelpful in explaining why the film did
not meet with the critic's favor. Granted, Canby has to be succinct, since
he is writing for a daily newspaper--a newspaper, like all others, with
problems of space and deadline. Still, one wishes, given his deadlines,
he were a bit more judicious in his choice of precisely what to say in his
little space. Some reviews are little more than plot summary: three of
the six paragraphs devoted to West World outline the plot; an opening paragraph explains the medical and literary background of scenarist-director
Michael Crichton; the penultimate paragraph states that there is a degree
of illogic in the movie; and a final paragraph lists the three principal
actors: Richard Benjamin, Yul Brynner, and James Brolin.[36] This pattern
is repeated, with scant variation, again and again.

Throughout his years of reporting and criticism, from his earliest
Variety review to his most recent Times byline, Canby has displayed little
or no comprehension of acting. Certainly he cannot rate with Stanley Kauffmann, whose precise vocabulary denotes a critic that has studied the craft.
But Canby isn't even as articulate as, say, Pauline Kael or Judith Crist,
both of whom, without having studied acting, take pains at describing external
choices an actor makes. Kael, Crist, and most of their colleagues leave the
mechanics (specific descriptions of character motivation, etc.) to Kauffmann.

---

[35]Vincent Canby, "'Ash Wednesday' Opens," The New York Times, November 22,
1973, p. 50.

[36]Vincent Canby, "The Screen: 'West World,'" The New York Times,
November 22, 1973, p. 51.

Canby, by contrast, has no reserve of practical experience for expressing technically, and no apparent skill for expressing metaphorically, the quality of an actor's work. Nor is the critic adept at criticism of the filmmaker. If his daily reviews are indications (and, of course, they are the vehicles by which we judge the critic's credibility), Canby knows very little about directing. Acting and directing are rarely mentioned, and never at length, in his daily columns. An eleven-paragraph dismissal of The Paper Chase (largely plot synopsis) fails to mention the quality of any of the acting, except for an all-purpose "marvelously well-played" for John Houseman.[37] The contributions of director James Bridges are completely ignored. Similarly, the photographer in Don Siegel's Charley Varrick is "nicely played by Sheree North."[38] A comparable compliment is paid the leads of Martin Scorsese's Mean Streets: Robert De Niro "has an exceedingly flashy role and makes the most of it . . ." while Harvey Keitel "is equally effective. . . ."[39] Canby, in short, is not very exhaustive.

As with every sweeping generalization, there are occasional exceptions. Thus it is that the general rule about Canby's shallowness is excepted. One of the critic's most descriptive and profound weekday columns contained this negative notice for Under Milk Wood. Canby reiterated the radio origins of Dylan Thomas' script, then described it as "never quite as satisfactory" on stage because "the stage needs words and these Thomas provides-- by the bushel basket."

---

[37]Vincent Canby, "Screen: 'Paper Chase,'" The New York Times, October 17, 1973, p. 55.

[38]Vincent Canby, "The Screen: Robbers vs. Robbers," The New York Times, October 20, 1973, p. 27.

[39]Vincent Canby, "'Mean Streets' at Film Festival," The New York Times, October 3, 1973, p. 38.

Too many words, perhaps, for the stage. Too many
words, I'm convinced, for the screen. It's not simply
the quantity of words, though. It's also their ornate-
ness. They overflow the ears and get into the eyes. Great
clouds of them everywhere, like swarms of big soft gnats.
They won't stop, and they make the job of film adapter
almost impossible.

This business of finding screen images to match
those in Thomas's text can be, at best, redundant. At
worst, banal, misleading or wrong. "To begin at the
beginning," says the First Voice (Richard Burton), a
sort of composite narrator, guide and angel of death
who conducts our tour of Llaregub, "it is spring, moonless
night in the small town. . . ." What we see, however, is
night so awash in moonlight that we could, if we wanted,
read the small type that guarantees a vacuum cleaner
for a year. . . .

When Burton urges us, the members of the audience,
to look into "the blinded bedrooms" to see "the glasses
of teeth, Thou Shalt Not on the wall, and the yellowing
dickeybird-watching pictures of the dead," there's not
much for the camera to do but to try desperately to
keep up with the language--and the language wins. . . .

Burton's readings are fine, especially when you
close your eyes. Nothing that Andrew Sinclair, the
director, chooses to show us does more than complement
the text, which often means literalizing it, making
it seem smaller, less mysterious, more postcard-
picturesque than need be. When Burton tells us that
we can hear the dew falling, I had a small panic that
Sinclair would show us even that, though he doesn't.
. . .

Less successful, perhaps because he has to handle
so many words, is Peter O'Toole, ordinarily a fine
actor, as the old, blind Captain Cat. O'Toole's
readings are so perfectly rhythmical, his wind so
magnificently controlled for long eruptions of words
without pause, that he almost put me to sleep. . . .

Gone is any sense of discovery of language, which,
when Thomas was working well, could make one feel very
young again, almost drunk with surprise and pleasure.
The problem is all those pictures. In a way, Thomas
did to words what booze did to him. He shook them up,

> liberated them, twisted them around so that they took
> on, if only momentarily, a higher order of meaning.
> The camera has the presence of a sober-sided friend.
> It interrupts most of the poet's flights of fancy.[40]

In this critique, Canby traverses subject areas normally alien to him:

actors' line readings, directorial choices, and the process of adaptation

from one medium to another. For the most part, though, the reviewer's

daily work smacks of superficiality and hurried judgment. One imagines

these problems are a result of deadline pressure and publications of first

drafts which tend to come off the top of his head and seem a bit stream-of-

consciousness. It is reasonable to place some of the blame on deadlines

because Canby's Sunday follow-ups and special think-pieces are traditionally

more astute. More space is set aside for the Sunday essays, for one thing,

and presumably Canby has more time to compose them--although he is required

to work well ahead of time. (Renata Adler, when she was principal movie

critic at the _Times_, explained how the arts-and-leisure articles work and,

in so doing, provided insight into the rigors of deadline writing. During

her tenure, the deadline for the Sunday piece was the Tuesday morning before.

Presumably, Canby works under the same routine.)

As an essayist, Canby has proposed these questions: "Has Movie

Violence Gone Too Far?"[41] (just about was the answer); "Whatever Happened

to Richard Burton?"[42] (he became more a star, less an actor); and "Those

---

[40] Vincent Canby, "'Under Milk Wood' Arrives on Screen," _The New York Times_, January 22, 1973, p. 20.

[41] Vincent Canby, "Has Movie Violence Gone Too Far?," _The New York Times_, January 16, 1972, p. D-1.

[42] Vincent Canby, "Whatever Became of Burton?," _The New York Times_, June 13, 1971, p. D-1.

Fanatical Fans of Foreign Flicks--Where Are They Now?"[43] Each of these

Sunday pieces is a probing investigation of special problems and phenomena

in the film industry. Simply in terms of length they are weightier than

Canby's Monday-through-Saturday output, wherein he is limited to, at very

most, eight or nine paragraphs. The Sunday edition generally allows for

articles twice as long, sometimes more (the violence essay ran twenty-two

paragraphs, the foreign film analysis twenty-seven). More importantly,

however, these arts-and-leisure essays are weightier in quality. Canby

has time to develop his observations. Whether he is expanding on a film

review from the week before or establishing new discussion areas, he does

his best work here. In his Richard Burton essay, Canby makes some knowing

observations about the Welsh actor's decline. (To give a feel for the

flow, the opening statements are reprinted in their entirety.)

> In "Villain," his latest and least interesting
> bad movie, he makes a real old-fashioned Star
> Entrance: the camera first sees a figure in deep
> shadow lying on a bed. Someone knocks on the door
> and calls the man. He gets up, stumbles through
> the gloom into what turns out to be the loo, and
> turns on a switch by the medicine cabinet. There,
> suddenly, in the flat brilliance that is the peculiar
> dismal quality of fluorescent light, especially in a
> bathroom, staring back at himself in a mirror, is
> a face so blank that it appears to be almost feature-
> less. Oval, if a little heavy in the jowls below,
> with tiny eyes above, the hair a little too long,
> but not really in the style of today, nor in the
> style of the London hood he is playing, but in the
> style of someone relaxing at Downey's after the
> night's performance of Shakespeare-in-the-Park.
> The star has made his entrance, the actor has arrived,
> but a character never shows up.

---

[43]Vincent Canby, "Those Fanatical Fans of Foreign Flicks--Where Are
They Now?," The New York Times, February 17, 1974, pp. D-1 and D-12.

There are some who say that Richard Burton peaked
on the British stage before he ever became heavily
committed to motion pictures. There are others who
think they see glimmers of talent in just about everything he does--as I do. John Gielgud, who directed
him in his New York stage appearance in "Hamlet" in
1964, shook his head about the Electronovision film version of that performance and was very sad about all of
Burton's "Shropshire Lad" mannerisms that he (Gielgud)
had not been on hand to check. It used to be that
Burton was never uninteresting, even when he wasn't
good--for performances mistakenly conceived, but
foolishly and consistently pursued, can be interesting.
Now he's just drab. In "Villain," he comes close to
being ludicrous as the sadistic, homosexual, underworld
boss whom he plays from time to time, when he becomes
momentarily interested in the part, like early James
Cagney, as Cagney might be parodied by a clever East
End mimic.[44]

In January 1974, the American Film Theatre was at the halfway point
in its first subscription season. The AFT was designed, as Canby summed
it up, "to bring culture to the otherwise depressed, that is, the American
moviegoer."[45] The critic then initiated a scathing dissection of the organi-
zation--its goals and its practices.

Because the AFT is apparently a financial success,
despite early ticket problems when a computer system
broke down, and because it is apparently going into
a second season in the fall, it is fair, I think, to
assess what has been accomplished so far. . . .

With the exception of Peter Hall's fine production
of "The Homecoming," which works so well as a film
that you don't pay any attention to its theatrical
seams, the AFT looks to be producing a new type of
film--one that may not ultimately be in the greatest
demand. The AFT is manufacturing the Coffee Table

[44]Vincent Canby, "Whatever Became of Burton?," The New York Times,
June 13, 1971, p. D-1.

[45]Vincent Canby, "When Is a 'Rhinoceros' a Turkey?," The New York Times,
January 27, 1974, p. D-1.

Movie, something that is supposed to establish one's
intellectual credentials by physical association.
Purchase tickets but give them to your friends.

I don't mean to sound furious about what the AFT
is up to. These films won't harm you. They'll bore
quite a few and perhaps make a lot of other people
feel as if they've taken their culture vitamins for
the year. The disappointing thing about the project
to date is the smallness of the thinking, which, I'm
afraid, accurately represents the extent of the so-
called arts explosion in the United States. . . .[46]

At this juncture, Canby launches into a play-by-play account of the

films presented. Then he closes:

Plays aren't films and films aren't plays, and
three of the four AFT productions to date have landed
in a no man's land between theater and film. With the
exception of "The Homecoming," they do not record for
posterity great theatrical performances, and they do
not add anything to one's cinematic experience. Almost
any five-minute segment of Robert Altman's "The Long
Goodbye" is a greater artistic experience (pardon my
language) than any 60-minute segment of the AFT's
"Iceman," "A Delicate Balance," or "Rhinoceros". . . .

The AFT seems bent on preserving, not really accurately,
plays that either have already been better preserved by
others, or plays that reflect not the vitality of living
theater but the poverty that is contributing to its decline.
With its intermissions, its Playbill-like programs, its
piety about great works of theater and consummate artists,
the AFT is simply pumping stale air into the lungs of an
audience that would be better revived by going out
occasionally to see one of the works of a truly living
cinema, be it "Memories of the Underdevelopment," "Day
for Night," "The Long Goodbye," "Sleeper," "Mean Streets,"
or "Heavy Traffic."[47]

With notions like these, he takes on some of the anti-elitist qualities

of Kael.

These longer pieces represent Canby working at full capacity, under

the least pressure. They mark a departure from the style of the weekday

---

[46]Vincent Canby, "When Is a 'Rhinoceros' a Turkey?," pp. D-1 and D-30.

[47]Ibid., p. D-30.

reviews, which are more hurriedly prepared. What is more, relentless editing seems to be the order of the day, even at the _Times_. Renata Adler once described the editorial procedures of her critical "year in the dark" this way:

> Being a film critic for the _New York Times_ . . . was for me a particular kind of adventure--with time, with tones of voice, with movies, with editing, with the peculiar experience it always is to write in one's own name something that is never exactly what one would have wanted to say. . . .
>
> The idea at the _Times_ is that reviews are not edited at all, but the reality was a continual leaning on sentences, cracking rhythms, removing or explaining jokes, questioning or crazily amplifying metaphors and allusions, on pieces that were not that good in the first place.[48]

One wonders if Canby would echo these sentiments.

The Sunday think piece is less tampered with than the weekday column though. Aside from having to submit it five days early, there is little pressure on the Sunday arts-and-leisure essayist. The relaxation shows, as does, more obviously, the expanse. Canby, when granted twenty-odd paragraphs, is more fluid and seems more perceptive than in the dailies.

One of the excerpts above, dealing with the American Film Theatre, hints at a side of Vincent Canby not yet observed. In his stingingly candid fault-finding, he shares quarters with the five other critics in this study, all of whom, to varying degrees, have taken time out from the rigidity of movie reviewing to revile a performer, a filmmaker, or an institution. Canby's occasional outbursts are not reserved for the AFT alone. Individual stars have felt his wrath too. Although Canby has his moments of cruelty,

---

[48]Renata Adler, _A Year in the Dark_, Random House, New York, 1969, pp. 9 and 12.

for severity they place a weak second to John Simon. Also, whereas
Simon villifies actresses, Canby stays with the male performers. Two
in particular who have met with a dose of vituperation are John Wayne
and Kirk Douglas. "The air must be cleared," Canby once insisted.

> The truth can no longer be covered up--no matter
> who it hurts. Someone must state the facts: John
> Wayne has reached the awkward age, which, in his case,
> is an official 66. . . .
>
> What has become increasingly difficult to accept
> is Wayne's peculiar physical presence.
>
> Unlike most people as they age, Wayne is not
> shrinking and shriveling, nor is he becoming in any
> way decrepit. Instead, he is swelling up like a
> balloon.[49]

Canby served an equally hefty portion of nastiness to Kirk Douglas. The
critic observed that as the actor "grows older, the dimple in his chin
begins to look more and more like a surgical mistake."[50] Canby, like so
many of his contemporaries, has had harsh words for Elizabeth Taylor, who
in George Stevens' The Only Game in Town is "so top-heavy . . . that she
has the . . . silhouette of an apple balanced atop a pair of tooth-picks."[51]

Canby especially enjoys films that are ambiguous and skeletal. Significantly, he is drawn to productions which require the viewer to "fill in"
for himself. Again and again, he has written his most lavish praise for
such movies: Ingmar Bergman's The Passion of Anna and Cries and Whispers,
Luis Buñuel's Tristana and The Discreet Charm of the Bourgeoisie, Eric
Rohmer's My Night at Maud's, Claire's Knee, and Chloé in the Afternoon,

---

[49]Vincent Canby, "Film: 'Cahill, United States Marshal' Stars Wayne,"
The New York Times, July 12, 1973, p. 46.

[50]The New York Times Film Reviews (1959-1968), Arno Press, New York,
1970, p. 3771.

[51]The New York Times Film Reviews (1969-1970), Arno Press, New York,
1971, p. 139.

and Claude Chabrol's <u>La Femme Infidèle</u> and <u>Le Boucher</u>. These films
all wound up on the best lists of their respective release years.[52]   Each
has a detached quality about it, showing "cool" characters, austere
individuals who keep their passions cloaked.   Such choices suit the
restraint and detachment that Canby has chosen for his own life style.
The choices, furthermore, are in harmony with Canby's belief that films
with large passions are overly sentimental.   <u>I Never Sang for My Father</u>,
Gilbert Cates' film of the Robert Anderson play, is one emotionally
charged film panned by Canby.   The script traces a son's search for the
love of his aging father.   As the critic admitted,

> "I Never Sang for My Father," is, by definition,
> a wonderful motion picture if you're prepared to
> respond with feelings of mingled surprise and curiosity,
> excited by something extraordinary, to the adolescent
> misery of Gene Garrison, a 40-year-old widower.[53]

But Canby was not prepared to respond in such a manner.   The uncompromising script and the honest look at faltering family communication was
far from detached.   The movie left Canby "cheerless," so it became "by
definition, a wretched motion picture."[54]

---

[52]By contrast, here are some of the big, emotion-filled movies which
have appeared on Canby's "ten-worst" lists: Elia Kazan's <u>The Arrangement</u>,
James Goldstone's <u>Winning</u>, Stanley Kramer's <u>The Secret of Santa Vittoria</u>,
Peter Hunt's <u>On Her Majesty's Secret Service</u>, Peter Yates' <u>John and Mary</u>,
Gilbert Cates' <u>I Never Sang for My Father</u>, and Stuart Rosenberg's <u>WUSA</u>.

[53]<u>The New York Times Film Reviews</u> (1969-1970), Arno Press, New York,
1971, p. 229.

[54]<u>Ibid.</u>, p. 229.

Unaccountably, the critic wrote a highly favorable critique for Arthur Hiller's Love Story, a film with a good deal of emotional wallop and sentimentality. The boy played by Ryan O'Neal was essentially a "warm," loving character, but perhaps Canby was fond of the cold, detached, but rock-solid character of the girl. Nonetheless, it is strange he was drawn to such an openly sentimental drama.

On the other hand, Canby isn't the first writer (or the only one in this study) to deal in inconsistencies. He is no more or less innocent on that count than most of the world's men of letters, past or present. Ultimately, his liabilities balance with his assets.

If for no other reason, Canby merits praise for his one distinguishing trait: his watchdog concern for the public. Canby makes a practice of returning to a film when it opens commercially. Although, normally, his initial viewing is at a critics' screening session, he goes a second (and sometimes third) time to check the quality of the print offered to the general audience.[55] For this purpose, he has re-seen and re-reported on everything from The Passion of Anna (which he originally saw at Cannes, where he had to read French subtitles)[56] to David Lean's Ryan's Daughter[57] to The Exorcist.[58] One can imagine, though, that Canby's repeated viewings aren't wholly selfless. Consumer-minded as he is, he obviously likes movies

---

[55] Harvey Aronson, "Movies and Their Critics," p. 163.

[56] The New York Times Film Reviews (1969-1970), Arno Press, New York, 1971, p. 172.

[57] Ibid., pp. 244-245.

[58] Vincent Canby, "Why the Devil Do They Dig 'The Exorcist'?" The New York Times, January 13, 1974, pp. D-1 and D-2.

for themselves. His passion, though not as pronounced as in his fellow critics, seems as genuine. He confesses that his adoration of the medium is so strong that occasionally he concludes an evening by watching a "Late, Late Show." Befitting his non-elitist demeanor, he declares, "I find many bad films more interesting than some good plays."[59]

Toward the end of her fourteen-month tenure on the _Times_, Renata Adler confessed, "Two months ago I thought that very soon I was going to run out of anything to say. . . . Frequently it seemed as though the same movie was coming out again and again under a different title."[60]

It would seem that Vincent Canby doesn't harbor those same misgivings. He has been at his _Times_ desk, churning out daily reviews and a Sunday specialty for five years now, working around deadlines, competing with deadlines, living with deadlines. And there is no end in sight--for either him, the deadlines, or the movies.

---

[59]"Going Critical," _Newsweek_, March 10, 1969, p. 87.

[60]_Ibid._, p. 87.

VIII. SUMMARY AND CONCLUSION

Two centuries ago, while pondering the complexities of taste, Edmund Burke concluded that there are three separate stages in the appreciation of a work of art. The initial reaction is sensuous. Next comes imagination, or consideration of how the work of art compares with other, previously created, works of art. Then comes judgment. The first reaction is automatic; the second and third result from reflection upon the art object. While Burke didn't have motion pictures in mind when he imparted his thesis, the cinematic art applies just as well as novels, essays, musical compositions, statuary art, and legitimate theatre. Every man, in his turn, hones his individual taste by traveling Burke's tripartite path.

Critical consciousness traverses the route as well. Each of the six writers explored in this study presents a case for his own taste. To convey the effect of a film experience, the critics publish accounts of the sensuous response, the imagination-stimulated reaction, and the reasoned opinion provoked by a particular film. The process, for these critics, is unavoidable. Simon, Kael, Kauffmann, Sarris, Crist, and Canby have many shared qualities. They also differ radically. A review of their expressions of taste, as indicated by stylistic traits, biases, and emphases, opens up numerous areas of comparison and contrast. Now is the time to summarize their significant similarities and differences. It is necessary to recapitulate these key matters pertaining to each writer: stylistic characteristics;

purpose of criticism and role of the critic (who the critic writes for and why); tone; biases; and emphasis in published reviews.

The most distinctive feature of John Simon's writing style is his ardor for metaphor, ornate rhetoric, and the unfamiliar, and consequently conspicuous, polysyllable. Given the choice between calling a film a Gesamtkunstwerk and an encompassing work of art, Simon would opt for the former. In fact, he did.[1]

Simon's analogies are equally esoteric. Most all the critics discussed here draw in references to other art forms; but it is particularly common to Kauffmann and Simon, the "highbrows." Even so, there are important differences of approach. Kauffmann's style is marked by the ease with which he employs analogies. Recall his citation of Archibald MacLeish in relation to Alain Resnais ("A poem should not mean but be; a film . . . should not mean but see.")[2] Equally to-the-point is the comparison of Resnais' film style to painting:

> Resnais has combined the loneliness of the di Chirico surrealist vista with the exploded time of Picasso's cubism, but with this simple yet important difference: he has not distorted any of his elements. It is as if he were willing to accept orderly surfaces because it is the disorder beneath those surfaces that interests him. He seeks the disorderly true reality under the orderly false reality of the surface.[3]

So goes Kauffmann's penchant for backing up his generalizations with illuminating examples. (Often, his descriptions are a close second-best

---

[1] John Simon, Movies Into Film, Dial Press, New York, 1971, pp. 23-24.

[2] Stanley Kauffmann, A World on Film, Harper & Row, New York, 1966, p. 249.

[3] Ibid., p. 249.

to the image itself.) Kauffmann's listing of similarities is integrated quite successfully with his text. This display of expertise goes in contrast with the method John Simon employs.

Simon's references are more obtrusive, his analogies more arcane. One senses they are deliberately so. His samplings from Diderot, Henry Mackenzie, Respighi, and Casella don't communicate with as wide an audience as Kauffmann's MacLeish-Picasso examples.

Pauline Kael, too, uses literary, musical, and fine arts references to clarify issues about a film. Her standard, though, unlike Simon's is to utilize those analogies which will help her readers visualize the movie. Kael's examples are always as vivid and as meticulously synthesized as Kauffmann's. In the words of Lee Bobker,

> Although some critics tend to intimidate their readers by their erudition, Miss Kael never talks down to her audience and avoids the ivory-tower, look-how-much-I-know approach. Her carefully chosen references are clear in their intent and fall within the experience of most readers.[4]

A classic case of the well-thought-out analogy is Kael's consideration of Walker Evans' Let Us Now Praise Famous Men photographs in her Bonnie and Clyde review.[5] The reference to Evans' photo-studies of the Depression gives readers a hint of Burnett Guffey's cinematography, which captures the starkness of the Thirties midwest and the squalor of the dispossessed Okies.

Even though one finds occasional literary analogies, including dramatic literature, in her film reviews, the majority of Kael's comparisons are

---

[4]Lee R. Bobker, Elements of Film, Harcourt, Brace & World, New York, 1969, p. 293.

[5]Pauline Kael, Kiss Kiss Bang Bang, Little, Brown and Company, Boston, 1968, p. 52.

cinematic. She differs, in that respect, from the steep literary inclination of Simon and Kauffmann. In most other respects, these three critics can be positioned fairly closely. Common stylistic tendencies such as involved analogies and animated analyses of stylistic and technical elements link them, while highlighting their isolation from Andrew Sarris, Judith Crist, and Vincent Canby.

The writing styles of these three, while distinctive, are much more routine than the prose of Simon, Kael, and Kauffmann. There is a decided reportorial air about the former group, and an attendant stinting of evocative imagery. Sarris, Crist, and Canby rarely describe scenes from movies in empathic detail. Their analyses focus on movies as a whole; praise or condemnation is apportioned accordingly. Simon, Kael, and Kauffmann, on the other hand, regularly study individual scenes and ponder at length such particulars as costume choices, the actors' vocal inflections, camera placement and movement, musical arrangements and orchestrations, and inept subtitle translations. These concerns don't altogether escape the reporter-critics. They just don't merit very much space in their columns. Emphasis is elsewhere, and that dictates a different kind of style.

Andrew Sarris, the auteurist, has, as previously noted, an occasional skirmish with diction and syntax. His style is distinguished by self-manufactured qualifiers that propose to characterize a filmmaker's mode of work: "sub-Proustian visualization . . . facile Freudianizing,"[6] "steady stew of tromedy,"[7] etc. In this manner, the critic's prose sometimes turns

---

[6]Andrew Sarris, The American Cinema, E. P. Dutton, New York, 1968, p. 190.

[7]John Simon, Private Screenings, Macmillan, New York, 1967, p. 318.

congested and ambiguous. Once in a while the reader senses that Sarris

uses esoteric phrases as a smoke-screen for unintelligibility, perhaps

even as a desperate last gasp for concealing a dearth of thoroughly formu-

lated judgment. If John Simon tosses an eccentric phrase into a commentary,

he normally develops the analogy. The reader at least understands why

the comparison was made, even if, due to its obscurity, he doesn't appre-

ciate the kinship. Sarris, by contrast, lets his arcane analogies lie.

It is fairly apparent that Sarris is aware of his past grammatical

mistakes and stylistic breaches. Often in his reviews he gives his detractors

a nod. In his report on the woeful 1974 Academy Awards ceremony, the forty-

sixth, Sarris referred to John Simon and Ethel Strainchamps, frequent critics

of his diction:

> Oscar is just about as old as I am, but he looks
> positively ancient on television, and this year's presen-
> tation was clearly the most stupefying to date. Like
> the man said (incorrect usage, I know, Strainchamps and
> Simon), you've got to believe, and belief seems to have
> given way to bravado among the Malibu moaners.[8]

Judith Crist's most distinctive stylistic traits are her information-

embedding and her hip Variety-inspired jargon. These factors make her prose

instantly recognizable. Almost equally recognizable is her attitude of

investigative reporter (i.e., the impression one has of her tracking down

a movie's production background, even though much information is handed to

the critic gratis by way of the producing company's press book).

Ms. Crist's information-embedding is brought about by interrupting

sentence flow to present side-comments. Her notices abound in parenthetical

---

[8]Andrew Sarris, "Films in Focus: Streaking Toward Senility," The
Village Voice, April 11, 1974, p. 77.

inserts, double dashes, and ellipses. Just as prevalent, from a
stylistic standpoint, is the critic's fondness for slang; every relevant
coined word of the last decade--everything from "blaxploitation" to
"spaghetti western" to "chop-socky"--has landed in her New York column.

Vincent Canby, one might think, would be afflicted with rampant
Varietyese too. His six years with the trade journal would suggest it.
But now, working for the staid, respectable Times, Canby's trade lingo is
largely a thing of the past. He leaves the jazzy hyperbole to Judith Crist,
Pauline Kael, and Rex Reed. Canby practices a traditional writing style
with no distinguishing flourishes. His diction is that of the literate
man on the street, intelligent but not overly specialized.

As the style of these critics is diverse, so is their self-view.
Each one, either implicitly or according to published account, sees himself
in a particular way. In their self-analyses, they shed light on the purpose
of criticism in general--and who their criticism is directed toward. What
role, then, does each critic play: historian, dispenser of an individual
opinion, molder of public opinion? The safe answer is that they all wear
a variety of masks. Even so, there are distinct role preferences.

How does John Simon cast himself? Doubtless, he sees many purposes
in his chosen profession, but the part he plays most vehemently is that
of chronicler for the ages. Once and again he has proclaimed he writes
for posterity, not exclusively for today, which means that he refuses to
ally himself with schools and fads. Writing for the ages, his view is
long-sighted: his purpose is to upgrade the medium of motion pictures,
whether by campaigning for improved subtitles or by poking fun at buffs or

by discrediting critics he considers unworthy of assessing movies. He

bestows praise only to those few films that, in his estimation, have

staying power, those which in x number of years will survive.

This predilection explains Simon's frequent and "passionage jeremiads."[9]

So few films will survive, he insists. His historical perspective also

accounts for his negative view of mass audiences. He challenges his readers

to

> look up in the authority of your choice . . . the number
> of surviving plays from any season ten or more years ago
> . . . [and] decide whether the number conforms more to
> the seasonal number of raves dished out by me or by--
> you supply the name.[10]

In this excerpt Simon was speaking of stage plays, but it doesn't take

too large a leap of the imagination to know he would say the same about the

cinema. Popular taste (and critical taste that discovers a movie master-

piece every other week) is reprehensible to him. His sulfurous remarks

directed to actresses, colleagues, and audiences are indicative of the venom

that wells up in him. In disdaining the average moviegoer, Simon elevates

himself well above mass taste. His uncompromising criteria consequently

give his essays a dogmatic tone.

It is clear that Simon does not address himself to the multitudes.

It is just as clear that Pauline Kael has a broad readership among inveterate

movie fans because her tone is so unlike Simon's. Kael writes for people

like herself: the afficionados, men and women profoundly concerned with the

---

[9] John Simon, "Who Pens the Poison?," New York, August 21, 1972, p. 39.

[10] Ibid., p. 39.

heritage of the medium, its developments and innovations, and the social implications of individual works, but also deeply involved with the genuine fun of filmgoing. Kael's approach is to open herself up to the film experience, with no prescribed guidelines, and become a single, although abundantly informed, voice for her audience. That audience, many of them impassioned fans, sticks by the critic for several important reasons. First of all, her passion for films and her desire for their improvement are so moving. Her obvious commitment is evinced in her style (vernacular, imagery, references) and that style, in turn, generates a highly conversational tone. This attitude of a one-to-one conversation of equals separates Kael from the other critics in this study, especially Simon.

Also unlike Simon, Kael never snarls at her public. Her obscenities are reserved for film people alone. As a rule, her fury is warranted and rarely out of proportion to the object of attack. The same can be said for all the writers studied here except one. Anybody's rancor is insubstantial in comparison with a heavyweight like John Simon. Interestingly, Kael has become increasingly bitter and vicious in recent months to old-guard stars like Katharine Hepburn and Lucille Ball.

The critic wrote that Hepburn's performance in The Glass Menagerie was

> like a compendium of the remembered mannerisms of her earlier movies. She's beginning to destroy her early performances for us, since gestures that belonged to her earlier characters--gestures that by now belong to us--are turning up promiscuously. The desecration is painful.[11]

---

[11]Pauline Kael, "The Current Cinema: Survivor," The New Yorker, December 21, 1973, p. 51.

Not to appear partial, Kael saved a heaping helping of sarcasm for
Lucille Ball's enactment of Mame Dennis:

> Why did Lucille Ball do "Mame"? After more than
> forty years in movies and TV (and five years of chorus
> work before that)--after conquering the world--did she
> discover in herself an unfulfilled ambition to be a
> drag queen? She doesn't have what it takes--hardly
> a tragedy. . . . Decked out in Theodora van Runkle's
> abominations, she isn't a mirror of style; she's just
> a smirking, badly overdressed star. She throws up her
> arms, in their red giant-bat-wing sleeves, crying
> out "Listen, everybody!," and she really seems to
> think she's a fun person. But we in the audience are
> not thinking of fun; we're thinking of age and self-
> deception. When Mame's best friend, Vera Charles
> (Beatrice Arthur, television's Maude), asks her "How
> old do you think I am?" and Mame answers "Somewhere
> between forty and death," one may feel a shudder in
> the audience. How can a woman well over sixty say
> a line like that, with the cameraman using every
> lying device he knows and still unable to hide the
> blurred eyes?[12]

Kael's rage is infrequent, but when it surfaces it is not of minor intensity.

Straight across the board, Stanley Kauffmann can be and has been
compared to John Simon. Both are in the "highbrow" league; both have multiple
professional concerns beyond movie reviewing; and neither one hides his
liberal arts education. But on closer observation, some distinctions do
arise. Kauffmann is admittedly the gentler of the two; in thumbs-down
notices, his sting is rarely as lethal as Simon's. Kauffmann, even as a
highbrow, avoids the soap-box issues--namely the lamentable-state-of-popular-
taste war-cry--that gain enemies for Simon. Finally, Kauffmann's ability
to analyze surpasses Simon, who has had none of the practical experience
in acting, directing, and fiction-writing that his New Republic counterpart
has. Those special insights are Kauffmann's calling cards.

---

[12]Pauline Kael, "The Current Cinema: A Brash Young Man," The New Yorker,
March 11, 1974, pp. 122-124.

For whom, then, does he write? Certainly for an educated, well-read audience. Considering his forum (The New Republic), his readers are probably very politically conscious.

We can infer, too, that Kauffmann writes essentially for people who have seen the film under discussion. The critic fearlessly divulges information about character development and plot resolution, which Judith Crist, for one clear contrast, doesn't. Crist, for instance, wouldn't describe Dustin Hoffman's death scene in Midnight Cowboy. It is also unlikely that Canby, with his "consumer reports" columns, would reveal such an essential turn of the story. Crist and Canby provide bite-size samples to readers who may decide to taste the entire spread for themselves later. As advance men, they don't want to spoil the effect by disclosing too much. Normally, Kauffmann transcends the hors d'oeuvre stage and provides the main course on the spot. Because he furnishes a good deal of detail in his film criticism, Kauffmann is always better as a post-view (in line with the conversation-with-equals approach) rather than as a preview.

Andrew Sarris' audience is composed primarily of buffs and habitual moviegoers. His cinematic references are sometimes so esoteric they would only be appreciated by the cognoscenti. Sarris' tone makes it clear that he assumes his reader has enough background to keep up with the conversation. Names, particularly directors' names, are dropped at the drop of a hat, and without any of the parenthetical biographical aids of Judith Crist.

Sarris is a self-proclaimed "consumer cost consultant,"[13] but, if he is, he is market-testing for a relatively select group. (The Village Voice

---

[13]Harvey Aronson, "Movies and Their Critics--Whoops, We Mean Reviewers," Cosmopolitan, August 1972, p. 136.

doesn't have the readership of The Times.) John Simon may write "for history, not just for the moment";[14] but Sarris is little concerned with that view. The only historical perspective he deals in is the directorial one.

Judith Crist's sense of purpose is particularly well-defined. She sees herself as preacher and teacher, definitely speaking to the masses--as opposed to Simon, Kael, and Kauffmann. Her self-vision is given credence each week in the pages of New York.

Crist has proclaimed that the small-circulation magazine (of Kauffmann or Sarris, let's say) and the esoteric FM station (once utilized by Kael) are not part of her strategy. It is the mass audience for her. "I am a journalistic critic . . ." she has written. "I speak for the movie-lover rather than the cinéaste, for the audience rather than the industry."[15] But even as a preacher and teacher, she has no pretensions of elevating the taste of the common man. ("I have a sneaking suspicion that the public can elevate its own taste, given half a chance. . . .")[16] In her conversational, albeit flip and hip, manner, Crist is one critic who speaks for the public.

Vincent Canby shares certain traits with Crist. Both have an aura of the reporter still surrounding them. Crist stays on top of data about shooting, post-production work, editing problems, distribution, and box-office receipts. Canby's reportorial skills emerge whenever he alerts his

---

[14]Harvey Aronson, "Movies and Their Critics," p. 136.

[15]Judith Crist, The Private Eye, the Cowboy and the Very Naked Girl, Holt, Rinehart and Winston, Chicago, 1968, pp. xiv-xv.

[16]Judith Crist, "What Good Is a Movie Critic?: A Critic's Credo," TV Guide, August 29, 1970, p. 8.

readers to studio promotion gimmicks, box-office price changes, and the
discomforts of some New York theatres. With a few modest exceptions, the
Times reviewer takes a non-elitist, mass-oriented view. Canby describes
the critic's purpose as "to explore your own reactions in an honest way."[17]
Surely on this single point, all six writers would agree. Exploring one's
reactions, conceivably through each of Edmund Burke's levels of taste, is
what criticism is about.

The operative word in Canby's description of purpose is "honest."
Doubtless all six strive for that personal honesty; but in the long and
tedious process from initial viewing of a film to publication of the critique,
perplexities can occur. A habitual student of these writers can ultimately
detect biases and special areas where the critics show favoritism. These
biases, sometimes implicit, sometimes explicit, are worthy of a brief note.

John Simon, over and over again, divulges his prejudice. An aristocratic
attitude pervades his writing. He goes to films with rigidly preconceived
notions of art and condemns productions for not matching the mold. The
drawback here is obvious: he is in danger of being too limiting. In
advocating that only the most artistic works survive, Simon often allows too
few chosen survivors. It is characteristic of his personality and his writing
style that he establishes restrictive dichotomies (Bach vs. the Beatles,
Kafka vs. comic strips, a great dancer vs. a tennis champion), further
proving how unyielding is his definition of art, how closed he can be to
new forms. Said one film publicist about this critic, "The only person to
whom his opinion means anything is Simon."[18]

---

[17]Harvey Aronson, "Movies and Their Critics," p. 135.

[18]Ibid., p. 135.

Pauline Kael's prejudices are more difficult to pinpoint because they aren't on view so frequently (at least in recent criticism). Foremost among the critic's pet peeves is the "art house" film, or was since the line between art films and mass-consumption movies is no longer so clearly defined. However, when these pictures were all the rage (Hiroshima, Mon Amour, Last Year at Marienbad, and the original Antonioni features), Kael published countless tracts announcing her disgust at their pretentiousness. Far more to her liking is the plotted, fun-loving, free-wheeling kitsch of Gunga Din, the Fred Astaire-Ginger Rogers musicals, the classic Hitchcock thrillers, The African Queen, Charade, and, more recently, Wild in the Streets and Planet of the Apes. The entertainment value of certain kinds of "trash" (her word) so far exceeds the "high culture" product that Ms. Kael leans constantly toward the former and away from the latter. All this is not to suggest that her reviews are flighty fan-mag pulp, for the critic issues probing analyses of all films, including "trash."

Some of Kael's dearest foes also scold her for another bias emergent in her criticism: "a parochial defensiveness about her old home. . . ."[19] Among recent pictures shot in or near the Bay Area are The Graduate, Petulia, and The Way We Were. All were lambasted rather severely by Kael for their inaccuracies and misuse of locale. (Richard Lester, director of Petulia, was derided for placing carnival barkers in Golden Gate Park, for inventing Sunday excursions to Alcatraz, and "for making San Francisco look like Los Angeles.")[20]

---

[19]Richard Corliss, "Perils of Renata, Pearls of Pauline," National Review, April 7, 1970, p. 370.

[20]Pauline Kael, Going Steady, Little, Brown and Company, Boston, 1970, pp. 118-119.

Stanley Kauffmann's prejudices are against singers-turned-actors, filmmakers' tampering unnecessarily with acclaimed novels, and laboratory dubbing of foreign language films. His criticism is dotted with fiery denouncements of each of these things. Kauffmann's precise observations of acting technique allow him to make informed judgments on the Crosby-Sinatra-Burl Ives-Elvis Presley syndrome; the inventory continues far beyond these four actor-singers or singer-actors; but in each case, the critic stands by to spot inadequacies and rue the fact his favorite actor, Brando, has few decent opportunities in film while the musical interlopers reap success in a medium other than the one they were born to. That, at least, is Kauffmann's sentiment, although matters have changed somewhat in the mid-Seventies: the actor-singer phenomenon has waned and Brando, on the basis of The Godfather and Last Tango in Paris, has regained a following.

Movie adaptations of literary works still exist, though. So Kauffmann's denigration of inexpert screen treatments is as potent in the Seventies (Catch-22, The Great Gatsby) as it was in the Fifties (The Doctor's Dilemma, The Sound and the Fury) and Sixties (Lolita, Falstaff, Goodbye, Columbus). Kauffmann, a scholar to the teeth, always makes astute comparisons with the original.

Kauffmann's third professional bias is dubbed films. Like many critics, he proposes that voice dubbing is an inferior second choice to subtitles because it cheats the auditor of the screen actor's real voice and the texture a good actor can provide to suggest both character and milieu. Dubbing studio employees who give English voices to Italian peasants, Russian

soldiers, and French shop girls are rarely good actors. Whenever Kauffmann's
aesthetic sense is jarred by a dubbed print, the regrettable fact is noted
in his column.

The biases betrayed by Andrew Sarris have to do, not surprisingly,
with directors. In the best _auteur_ tradition, he is most pleased with
filmmakers who place an indelible imprint on their work. "Directors,
not writers," he has written, "are the ultimate auteurs of the cinema.
. . ."[21] His illustrations lend support to his case.

Further bias erupts in Sarris' disposition toward American-made films
and in his concern for a movie's "look" rather than its statement. The
critic's collected reviews reveal the overwhelming favoritism he displays
for American movies: his position as an _auteurist_ is that most Hollywood
pioneers (from Griffith to Ford and Hawks) established a visual style that
is just as commanding as the style of critics' darlings like Akira Kursoawa,
who is, if nothing, an imitator of Ford and his contemporaries. This declaration
is directed to the visual potential of film, not what it says, and Sarris
argues with examples of montage, process shots, camera movement, lighting,
and _mise en scène_. Rarely does the critic direct his attention to a
screenwriter's words. The director and the "look" he gives his picture are
the predominant considerations.

Judith Crist's pet topics include detective and mystery thrillers,
while her pet peeves include films with gratuitous violence, "sexploitation"
and "blaxploitation" programmers, weepy romantic stories, and the melodramas

---

[21]Andrew Sarris, The American Cinema, p. 215.

of Otto Preminger. She is never disproportionately nasty. The only real targets of her malice are the pet peeves enumerated above. In an interview with David Paletz, Crist stated:

> The movies I have liked least are all the Hollywood sex binges, and the ones that really insult your intelligence like Baby the Rain Must Fall, Guess Who's Coming to Dinner, Hurry Sundown; the Natalie Wood dramas of life like Inside Daisy Clover and Love With the Perfect [sic] Stranger--that kind of thing. Then the great epic trash or trash epics. I think one time I called these "Joe Levine's trilogy of trash," that started out with The Carpetbaggers.[22]

More recent productions to receive thumbs-down from Crist for depiction of sex and/or violence are The Beguiled, Straw Dogs, Portnoy's Complaint, and Andy Warhol's Frankenstein. With her pans of The Wild Bunch, Straw Dogs, and Pat Garrett and Billy the Kid, she counterbalances Vincent Canby's great adoration of Sam Peckinpah.

As for Canby's biases? The Times critic, like his contemporary at The Voice, maintains something of an auteur point of view. (Hitchcock, as an auteur, is faultless; but Ken Russell--well, no year-end worst recap would be complete without him.)

When it comes to favoritism, Crist has her thrillers and Canby, although not observably addicted to a specific genre, has his films of detachment and enigma. Ultimately, his bias toward these pictures aligns with his directorial bias: works of certain filmmakers--because they deal in mystery and ambiguity, with "cool" central characters--will almost certainly get a positive notice in The Times. Chief among artists in this category are Ingmar Bergman, Luis Buñuel, Eric Rohmer, and Claude Chabrol.

---

[22]David Paletz, "Judith Crist: An Interview With a Big-Time Critic," Film Quarterly, Fall 1968, p. 34.

Indeed, with one notable exception (Chabrol's Ten Days' Wonder), their works have consistently been given good marks by Canby.

The factors for possible inclusion in a movie review are so assorted-- from acting and directing to cinematography to social implications--it is only fitting that the six critics in this study represent a wide assortment of approaches. In examining each writer one discovers predominant emphases and manners of presentation.

John Simon rarely gives loose or generalized criticism. A scholar, he chooses precise words to represent his feelings. As we have seen, he dwells on many of the specifics of filmmaking: his observations on musical scoring (for I Vitelloni), camerawork (for Sundays and Cybèle), script (for Lawrence of Arabia), and editing (Rachel, Rachel) bear this out. His critique of an individual film traditionally lingers on the three or four most important elements of that production. Only time will tell if Simon's transfer from The New Leader to Esquire will change his emphases. Other things have changed already. By joining the Esquire staff, Simon moved from a biweekly forum to a monthly one. An attendant problem associated with that kind of shift is keeping on top of current releases. The critic admitted the vagaries of Esquire's deadlines at the outset of his February 1974 column: "As I write this, I should really be telling you about The Exorcist and The Day of the Dolphin, neither of which is as yet available for critical viewing. And what is, is nothing to write home, or columns, about."[23]

---

[23]John Simon, "Films," Esquire, February 1974, p. 54.

Pauline Kael's emphasis comes in her sociological overviews. She approaches movies in relation to the psychology of watching them and the sociology of response to them. The reaction of the audience, either an actual or a hypothetical-typical one, often becomes part of Kael's critique. Audience response concerns her almost as much as her personal outlook. Kael loves movies and wants them to remain a popular, non-elitist art. Her conversational notices, detailing viewer response along with her own sensations, are fully congruent with the woman for whom movies are "the most total and encompassing art form we have."[24]

In the manner of John Simon, Stanley Kauffmann rarely descends to generalities in his criticism. They both freely discuss most of the elements of a film; but Kauffmann, while performing his critical duties, goes Simon one better. Because of his training with the Washington Square Players (in addition to any academic experience he may have had), Kauffmann can provide especially eloquent commentary on screenwriting, directing, and acting--the theatrical elements of cinema with which Simon is conversant but not professionally trained.

Andrew Sarris is a most radical departure from Simon and Kauffmann. To repeat, the visual components (cinematography, editing, costumes, lighting) figure more heavily in Sarris' notices than do aural factors (words, music, sound effects). This choice is certainly in league with the critic's _auteur_ perspective. Perhaps if all critics had passed a year in the Cinémathèque Française basement they too would insist on a visual emphasis in criticism. Luckily, for the sake of variety, they didn't.

---

[24]Harvey Aronson, "Movies and Their Critics," p. 137.

Judith Crist, it would seem, betrays no primary emphasis. Her critiques are neither specialized in the Andrew Sarris sense nor intensive in the tradition of Simon, Kael, and Kauffmann. Crist's critiques tend to be elaborations of the particular topics she thinks relevant to each film. Consequently, emphasis shifts. In most reviews, though, she displays the critic-as-mass-reporter habits of the movie man for The Times.

Vincent Canby, well aware of his readership, pays a good bit of attention to New York City's moviegoers. His sympathies lie with the customer, not the motion picture industry, not the distributor, certainly not the exhibitor. He has registered so many complaints against Manhattan movie houses that he must be one of theatre owners' least favorite people. Topics such as admission prices, out-of-focus projection, and air-conditioning thermostats gone awry frequently invade his Times reports. Sometimes one gets the impression Canby is New York filmgoers' walking, breathing consumer protection plan. That is to his credit.

On the debit side is this: if Canby shares his colleagues' concern for and acquaintance with the different departments of filmmaking, then his critiques belie the fact. Only the barest details are mentioned. (In Canby's short reviews, six to eight paragraphs, at least half the space centers on story summary.)

In accordance with his journalistic origins, Canby is a reporter's reporter. A dedicated writer, he delivers the facts, ma'am, and lucidly, but he lacks expertise. The difference between Canby and Simon, Kael, and Kauffmann is the difference between a two-hundred level survey of nineteenth-century poets and an upper-division seminar narrowing in on

Byron. Canby charts the overview; the other three add much more intensive highlight and detail. As for Crist and Sarris, they fall somewhere in the vast middle ground, remote from either extreme.

It is important, in conclusion, to demonstrate that despite everything, all these critics do have commonalities. Andrew Sarris' wife, Molly Haskell, calls his prose "personal and autobiographical."[25] So is the writing of all critics. The personal, autobiographical angle is inescapable, even for Vincent Canby who seems to employ it less than anybody.

Pauline Kael recounts her lovers' quarrel before seeing Shoeshine and, in reviewing Petulia and The Way We Were, recalls her childhood and adolescence in the Bay Area. Kael, of the six in this study, is the most conspicuous autobiographer. Yet the others whether consciously or not, join her. John Simon's Harvard education, for example, envelops him like a mist. Every piece of criticism betrays, for good or bad, his militant erudition. Canby reveals his Protestant heritage in one review and tells us he can read French in another. And in more than one review, Crist talks about her childhood movie preferences, her leisure reading habits, and exhibits (by implication) her political persuasion. So it goes.

Writing about this autobiographical slant for Take One magazine, John Hofsess observed that

> what counts least in film criticism is the film itself: what matters most is the vantage point from which it is seen. Critics are not writing about an object outside them, but writing marginal jottings and whole chapters of their spiritual autobiography, of their relationship to movies at a given point in time.

> Critics may seem to be separating the good from
> the bad, and the excellent from the merely good, they
> may even aspire to make historic judgments of movies as
> if every film should be measured against the Western
> Intellectual Tradition from Homer onwards; but they
> are, nevertheless, writing the autobiography of their
> tastes, though rarely do they let us know what their
> standards are, or by what psychological process their
> tastes were formed. Critics may pose the question,
> "Is Summer of '42 a good film?" but the legitimate
> inquiry would be, "What combination of experiences,
> memories, film theory, etc., allow me to enjoy it?
> or, alternately, why don't I enjoy it?"[26]

Beyond their autobiographical tendencies and despite their widely divergent

critical inclinations and abilities, what do these six reviewers have in

common? To begin with, they are gifted writers. They offer lively, exciting,

sometimes thought-provoking commentary. Secondly, they truly adore movies.

In fact, with the exception of Simon and Kauffmann, they are somewhat mono-

maniacal. One gets the impression movies are their sustenance. Most of

them view films all day long, then go home for a prime-time telecast, then

stay for a late-show rerun.

Simon and Kauffmann are the only ones whose published work reflects

any interests other than cinema, although movies seem to be where their

passions lie. Kael, Sarris, Crist, and Canby, whatever their extracurricular

concerns, write exclusively about film. Time and again, all six have demon-

strated their devotion to the medium. Their words, if nothing else, are

affidavits of their love. Andrew Sarris has said, "If I wasn't making a

penny from writing about them, I'd be going to the movies as much--in fact,

I'd probably be seeing more." Specialty reviewer and mass reporter, intel-

lectual and middle-brow, auteurist and elitist--it seems clear they would

all agree with that sentiment.

---

[26] John Hofsess, "The Mind's Eye," Take One, June 3, 1971, p. 34.

More than perhaps any other living writers these six have refined the craft of motion picture criticism. In so doing, they have helped to elevate the medium itself. More and more, film is viewed as a serious art--and its seriousness is mirrored in the erudition which John Simon and Stanley Kauffmann apply to their analyses. It is mirrored in Kauffmann's precise and experience-based diction. And it is mirrored in Sarris' recognition of the auteur, in Canby's recognition of and sympathy with the movie patron, in Crist's preaching and teaching, and in Kael's questioning the motives of film producers and directors.

All of this is a delayed backlash to the vacuousness and puffery of earlier film criticism. Simon, Kael, Kauffmann, Sarris, Crist, and Canby, whatever their shortcomings, are not puff artists.

Taken collectively, this "second generation" of movie critics has made solid advancements over their predecessors, and for dedication, expertise, zeal, and plain talent, they excel all current competition. Their energies augur well for the profession. As these six writers move into old-guard strata, their productivity continues. We can doubtless look forward to their pronouncements for decades to come. As to their eventual demise--no cause for alarm. By now, the influence of these six is so widespread that a productive and energetic third generation is only a motion away.

BIBLIOGRAPHY

I. Books

Adler, Renata. A Year in the Dark. Random House, New York, 1969.

Armes, Roy. French Film. Studio Vista/Dutton Paperback, London, 1970.

The Author's and Writer's Who's Who. Hafner Publishing Company, Darien,
        Connecticut, 1971.

Bobker, Lee R. Elements of Film. Harcourt, Brace & World, New York,
        1969.

Crist, Judith. The Private Eye, the Cowboy, and the Very Naked Girl:
        Movies from Cleo to Clyde. Holt, Rinehart, and Winston,
        Chicago, 1968.

Diamonstein, Barbaralee. Open Secrets: Ninety-four Women in Touch With
        Our Time. The Viking Press, New York, 1972.

Gelmis, Joseph. The Film Director as Superstar. Doubleday & Company,
        Garden City, New York, 1970.

Graham, Peter, ed. The New Wave. Doubleday & Company, Garden City,
        New York, 1968.

Harte, Barbara and Carolyn Riley, ed. Contemporary Authors, Volumes 21-22.
        Gale Research Company (The Book Tower), Detroit, Michigan, 1969.

Kael, Pauline. Deeper Into Movies. Little, Brown and Company, Boston, 1972.

------. Going Steady. Little, Brown and Company, Boston, 1970.

------. I Lost It at the Movies. Little, Brown and Company, Boston, 1965.

------. Kiss Kiss Bang Bang. Little, Brown and Company, Boston, 1968.

------, Herman Mankiewicz, and Orson Welles. The Citizen Kane Book. Little,
        Brown and Company, Boston, 1971. This double-feature volume
        includes the shooting script for Citizen Kane and Kael's "Raising
        Kane," which originally appeared in The New Yorker.

Kauffmann, Stanley, ed. American Film Criticism (From the Beginnings to Citizen Kane). Liveright, New York, 1972.

------. Figures of Light. Harper & Row, New York, 1971.

------. A World on Film. Harper & Row, New York, 1966.

Macdonald, Dwight. On Movies. Prentice-Hall, Inc., Englewood Cliffs, New Jersey, 1969.

The New York Times Film Reviews (1959-1968). Arno Press, New York, 1970.

The New York Times Film Reviews (1969-1970). Arno Press, New York, 1971.

Rehrauer, George. Cinema Booklist. The Scarecrow Press, Metuchen, New Jersey, 1972.

Rilla, Wolf. A-Z of Moviemaking. The Viking Press, New York, 1970.

Sarris, Andrew. The American Cinema: Directors and Directions 1929-1968. E. P. Dutton, New York, 1968.

------. Confessions of a Cultist. Simon and Schuster, New York, 1970.

------, ed. The Film. The Bobbs-Merrill Company, Indianapolis, 1968.

------. Interviews With Film Directors. The Bobbs-Merrill Company, Indianapolis, 1967.

------. The Primal Screen. Simon and Schuster, New York, 1973.

Simon, John. Acid Test. Stein & Day, New York, 1963.

------. Ingmar Bergman Directs. Harcourt, Brace, Jovanich, Inc., New York, 1972.

------. Movies Into Film. Dial Press, New York, 1971.

------. Private Screenings. Macmillan, New York, 1967.

Terkel, Studs. Hard Times: An Oral History of the Great Depression. Pantheon Books, New York, 1970.

Truffaut, François. Hitchcock. Simon and Schuster, New York, 1967.

II. Periodicals.

Aronson, Harvey. "Movies and Their Critics--Whoops, We Mean Reviewers," Cosmopolitan, August 1972, pp. 134-163.

"As N. Y. Film Fest Fades," Variety, October 17, 1973, p. 6.

Avant, J. A. Library Journal, January 15, 1971, p. 96.

Barrett, Gerald R. "Andrew Sarris Interview: October 16, 1972," Literature/Film Quarterly, July 1973, pp. 195-205.

Beaver, Frank E. "Early Film Criticism: Some Prevailing Attitudes and Problems," The Central States Speech Journal, Summer 1972, pp. 126-131.

"Big Rental Films of 1971," Variety, January 5, 1972, p. 9.

Bogdanovich, Peter. Book World, November 5, 1967, p. 6.

Canby, Vincent. "'Ash Wednesday' Opens," The New York Times, November 22, 1973, p. 50.

------. "'Catonsville Nine' Begins Run as Film," The New York Times, May 16, 1972, p. 48.

------. "Crack in the Mirror," Variety, May 11, 1960, p. 6.

------. "End of Innocence," Variety, September 7, 1960, p. 16.

------. "Film: 'Cahill: United States Marshal' Stars Wayne," The New York Times, July 12, 1973, p. 46.

------. "For 'The Long Goodbye,' A Warm Hello," The New York Times, November 18, 1973, pp. D-1 and D-6.

------. "Giulietta de gli Spiriti," Variety, November 3, 1965, p. 6.

------. "Has Movie Violence Gone Too Far?," The New York Times, January 16, 1972, pp. D-1 and D-11.

------. "Let's Make Love," Variety, August 24, 1960, p. 6.

------. "The Men Who Tread on the Tiger's Tail," Variety, January 27, 1960, p. 6.

------. "Screen: Alfred Hitchcock At His Best," The New York Times, December 20, 1969, p. 36.

------. "Screen: 'Paper Chase,'" The New York Times, October 17, 1973, p. 55.

------. "The Screen: Robbers vs. Robbers," The New York Times, October 20, 1973, p. 27.

------. "The Screen: 'West World,'" The New York Times, November 22, 1973, p. 51.

------. "Segal and Jackson Star in 'A Touch of Class,'" The New York Times, June 21, 1973, p. 52.

------. "Tango--Erotic or Exotic?," The New York Times, January 28, 1973, pp. D-1 and D-3.

------. "The 10 Worst Movies of 1972," The New York Times, January 7, 1973, pp. D-1 and D-11.

------. "Threepenny Opera," Variety, July 13, 1960, p. 6.

------. "'Under Milk Wood' Arrives on Screen," The New York Times, January 22, 1973, p. 20.

------. "Whatever Became of Burton?," The New York Times, June 13, 1971, pp. D-1 and D-20.

------. "When Is a 'Rhinoceros' a Turkey?," The New York Times, January 27, 1974, pp. D-   and D-30.

------. "Why the Devil Do They Dig 'The Exorcist'?," The New York Times, January 13, 1974, pp. D-1 and D-2.

"Canby: 'Movie Going an Ordeal,'" Variety, January 24, 1973, p. 5.

"Cinema: The Film Maker as Ascendant Star," Time, July 4, 1969, pp. 46-51.

Coleman, John. Book World. April 11, 1971, p. 8.

Cooper, Arthur. "Critic as Superstar," Newsweek. December 24, 1973, pp. 96-98.

Corliss, Richard. "Perils of Renata, Pearls of Pauline," National Review. April 7, 1970, pp. 369-370.

Crist, Judith. "Movies: Archy Redivivus," New York, April 12, 1971, pp. 62-63.

------. "Movies: Bang! Bang! You're Dead," New York, November 27, 1972, p. 83.

------. "Movies: Below Zero," New York, February 4, 1974, p. 57.

------. "Movies: Best of Both Worlds," <u>New York</u>, February 21, 1972, pp. 60-61.

------. "Movies: Billy Pilgrim's Progress," <u>New York</u>, April 3, 1972, pp. 58-59.

------. "Movies: Crime Doesn't Pay--Or Does It?," <u>New York</u>, May 17, 1971, pp. 60-61.

------. "Movies: Current Shock," <u>New York</u>, October 29, 1973, pp. 80-83.

------. "Movies: Dial R for Rotten," <u>New York</u>, June 7, 1971, pp. 58-59.

------. "Movies: Dick and Jane Shoot Up," <u>New York</u>, July 19, 1971, pp. 58-59.

------. "Movies: Good 'Egg,'" <u>New York</u>, June 5, 1972, p. 62.

------. "Movies: Grounds for Complaint," <u>New York</u>, July 3, 1972, pp. 52-53.

------. "Movies: The Movies Didn't Get Bigger, the Festival Got Smaller," <u>New York</u>, October 4, 1971, pp. 62-63.

------. "Movies: Of Cops and Copouts," <u>New York</u>, May 31, 1971, pp. 60-61.

------. "Movies: Production Politic," <u>New York</u>, April 16, 1973, pp. 86-87.

------. "Movies: Pure Honey," <u>New York</u>, December 31, 1973, p. 77.

------. "Movies: Reupholstery," <u>New York</u>, December 13, 1971, pp. 76-78.

------. "Movies: Seasonal Slurp," <u>New York</u>, September 24, 1973, pp. 90-91.

------. "Movies: Shangri-La-De-Da," <u>New York</u>, March 19, 1973, pp. 70-71.

------. "Movies: Some For the Cachet, Others for the Cash," <u>New York</u>, October 9, 1972, pp. 72-73.

------. "Movies: The Tempora, or Maybe the Mores, Are Out of Joint," <u>New York</u>, May 10, 1971, pp. 70-71.

------. "Movies: This Crow Ain't Fit for Eatin'," <u>New York</u>, April 23, 1973, pp. 72-75.

------. "Movies: To Set the Tube Aglow," <u>New York</u>, January 28, 1974, pp. 58-59.

------. "Movies: Truth Unvarnished, Guilt Ungilded," <u>New York</u>, March 20, 1972, pp. 68-69.

------. "Movies: Uneasy Rider," <u>New York</u>, October 11, 1971, pp. 66-67.

------. "Movies: The Year of Something for Everyone," New York, January 1, 1973, pp. 50-53.

------. "Movies: You Can Go Home Again, If You Know the Way," New York, March 27, 1972, pp. 74-75.

------. "Movies: 'X' Should Be for Execrable," New York, January 24, 1972, pp. 64-65.

------. "This Week's Movies," TV Guide, March 16, 1974, p. A-7.

------. "What Good Is a Movie Critic?: A Critic's Credo," TV Guide, August 29, 1970, pp. 6-9.

Deedy, John. "News and Views: Canby and Berrigan," Commonweal, June 30, 1972, p. 346.

Denby, David. "Movies: Revival of the Fittest," New York, August 9, 1971. pp. 56-57.

Dienstfrey, Harold. Book Week, June 12, 1966, p. 10.

Downing, Robert. "'Defy Herd,' Judith Crist Says," The Denver Post, July 29, 1971, p. 31.

Ebert, Roger. "Movie Critics Role: What Does It Demand?," The Denver Post ("Roundup"), February 10, 1974, pp. 39-41.

"Going Critical," Newsweek, March 10, 1969, pp. 86-87.

Goldstein, Laurence. The New York Times Book Review, May 15, 1966, p. 6.

Grenier, Cynthia. "The New Wave at Cannes," The Reporter, July 23, 1959, pp. 39-41.

Haskell, Molly and Andrew Sarris, "Couple-Speak: Happy Marriage," Vogue, June 1971, pp. 106-161.

Higham, Charles. "Suddenly, Don Siegel's High Camp-us," The New York Times, July 25, 1971, p. D-11.

Hofsess, John. "The Mind's Eye," Take One, June 3, 1971, p. 34.

Kael, Pauline. "The Current Cinema: A Brash Young Man," The New Yorker, March 11, 1974, pp. 119-124.

------. "The Current Cinema: Movieland--The Bums' Paradise," The New Yorker, October 22, 1973, pp. 133-139.

------. "The Current Cinema: Pop Versus Jazz," The New Yorker, November 2, 1972, pp. 152-158.

------. "The Current Cinema: Survivor," The New Yorker, December 31, 1973, pp. 47-51.

------. "The Current Cinema: Tango," The New Yorker, October 28, 1972, pp. 130-138.

Kauffmann, Stanley. "Film Negatives," Saturday Review, March 1973, pp. 37-40.

------. "On Films," The New Republic, October 14, 1972, p. 22.

Landry, Robert J. "Variety's Four-Letter Signatures, the Dog-Tags of Its Critics," Variety, January 9, 1974, p. 26.

"Letters to the Editors," The Nation, November 18, 1944, p. 628.

MacGowan, Kenneth. "The Artistic Future of the Movies," North American Review, February 1921, pp. 260-265.

Macklin, F. Anthony. "Everyone Is An Auteurist Now, More or Less: An Interview With Andrew Sarris," Film Heritage, Summer 1973, pp. 26-36.

------. "Film To Me Is Another Art: An Interview With Critic Stanley Kauffmann," Film Heritage, Fall 1972, pp. 16-36.

Magid, Marion. "Observations: Auteur! Auteur!," Commentary, March 1964, pp. 70-74.

Morgenstern, Joseph. "The Moviegoer," Newsweek, February 23, 1970, p. 100.

Mount, Douglas N. "Authors and Editors: Pauline Kael," Publishers' Weekly, May 24, 1971, pp. 31-32.

"Movie Mailbag," The New York Times, July 29, 1973, p. D-8.

Paletz, David. "Judith Crist: An Interview With a Big-Time Critic," Film Quarterly, Fall 1968, pp. 27-36.

Peck, Seymour. "The Director Is the Star," The New York Times Magazine, February 18, 1962, pp. 24-25.

Rosenthal, Stuart. "The Terse, Sardonic, Pragmatic Loner in Donald Siegel's Unacclaimed Films," St. Louis Post-Dispatch, May 2, 1971, p. 5-C.

Ross, Ruth. "Perils of Pauline," Newsweek, May 30, 1966, pp. 80-82.

Samuels, C. T. The New York Times Book Review, February 22, 1970, p. 6.

Sarris, Andrew. "Films in Focus: Living the Private Eye Genre," The
     Village Voice, November 8, 1973, pp. 83-96.

------. "Films in Focus: Lost Tracks, Found Trends," The Village Voice,
     August 30, 1973, pp. 57-67.

------. "Films in Focus: Muffled Comings, Jagged Goings," The Village
     Voice, November 29, 1973, pp. 81-84.

------. "Films in Focus: The Perils of Papillon," The Village Voice,
     January 10, 1974, p. 57.

------. "Films in Focus: Streaking Toward Senility," The Village Voice,
     April 11, 1974, pp. 77-92.

------. "Notes on the Auteur Theory in 1962," Film Culture, Winter 1962-1963.

------. "Sixties Cinema," Rolling Stone, November 22, 1973, pp. 45-47.

------. "Whatever 'Lola' Has, Sarris Wants," The New York Times, April 20,
     1969, p. D-15.

Simon, John. "Abelard's Loss--and Ibsen's Too," New York, March 29, 1971,
     p. 57.

------. Book Week, April 14, 1965, p. 4.

------. "Films," Esquire, February 1974, pp. 54-60.

------. "In Praise of Professionalism," New York, September 18, 1972,
     p. 68.

------. "On Screen: Mailer's Mystic Marriage," The New Leader, September 17,
     1973, pp. 21-23.

------. "Strindberg on the Mat," New York, June 21, 1971, p. 60.

------. "Unstrung Quartet," New York, April 12, 1971, p. 58.

------. "Who Pens the Poison?," New York, August 21, 1972, p. 39.

Sinclair, Andrew. The New York Times Book Review, January 14, 1968, p. 12.

Susskind, Pamela. "Critic Around the Clock," Newsweek, March 27, 1967,
     p. 95.

Talbert, Bob. "People," Detroit Free Press, November 25, 1973, p. 19-A.

Truffaut, François. "Politique des Auteurs," Cahiers du Cinéma, January
     1954 (No. 31).

Warshow, Paul. "Moviemakers," Commentary, October 1969, pp. 89-94.

Williamson, Bruce. "Judith Crist's Magical Mystery Tour," Saturday Review, March 1973, pp. 7-10.

The Arno Press Cinema Program

THE LITERATURE OF CINEMA

Series I & II

Agate, James. **Around Cinemas.** 1946.

Agate, James. **Around Cinemas.** (Second Series). 1948.

American Academy of Political and Social Science. **The Motion Picture in Its Economic and Social Aspects,** edited by Clyde L. King. **The Motion Picture Industry,** edited by Gordon S. Watkins. *The Annals,* November, 1926/1927.

L'Art Cinematographique, Nos. 1-8. 1926-1931.

Balcon, Michael, Ernest Lindgren, Forsyth Hardy and Roger Manvell. **Twenty Years of British Film, 1925-1945.** 1947.

Bardèche, Maurice and Robert Brasillach. **The History of Motion Pictures,** edited by Iris Barry. 1938.

Benoit-Levy, Jean. **The Art of the Motion Picture.** 1946.

Blumer, Herbert. **Movies and Conduct.** 1933.

Blumer, Herbert and Philip M. Hauser. **Movies, Delinquency, and Crime.** 1933.

Buckle, Gerard Fort. **The Mind and the Film.** 1926.

Carter, Huntly. **The New Spirit in the Cinema.** 1930.

Carter, Huntly. **The New Spirit in the Russian Theatre, 1917-1928.** 1929.

Carter, Huntly. **The New Theatre and Cinema of Soviet Russia.** 1924.

Charters, W. W. **Motion Pictures and Youth.** 1933.

Cinema Commission of Inquiry. **The Cinema: Its Present Position and Future Possibilities.** 1917.

Dale, Edgar. **Children's Attendance at Motion Pictures.** Dysinger, Wendell S. and Christian A. Ruckmick. **The Emotional Responses of Children to the Motion Picture Situation.** 1935.

Dale, Edgar. **The Content of Motion Pictures.** 1935.

Dale, Edgar. **How to Appreciate Motion Pictures.** 1937.

Dale, Edgar, Fannie W. Dunn, Charles F. Hoban, Jr., and Etta Schneider. **Motion Pictures in Education: A Summary of the Literature.** 1938.

Davy, Charles. **Footnotes to the Film.** 1938.

Dickinson, Thorold and Catherine De la Roche. **Soviet Cinema.** 1948.

Dickson, W. K. L., and Antonia Dickson. **History of the Kinetograph, Kinetoscope and Kinetophonograph.** 1895.

Forman, Henry James. **Our Movie Made Children.** 1935.

Freeburg, Victor Oscar. **The Art of Photoplay Making.** 1918.

Freeburg, Victor Oscar. **Pictorial Beauty on the Screen.** 1923.

Hall, Hal, editor. **Cinematographic Annual,** 2 vols. 1930/1931.

Hampton, Benjamin B. **A History of the Movies.** 1931.

Hardy, Forsyth. **Scandinavian Film.** 1952.

Hepworth, Cecil M. **Animated Photography: The A B C of the Cinematograph.** 1900.

Hoban, Charles F., Jr., and Edward B. Van Ormer. **Instructional Film Research 1918-1950.** 1950.

Holaday, Perry W. and George D. Stoddard. **Getting Ideas from the Movies.** 1933.

Hopwood, Henry V. **Living Pictures.** 1899.

Hulfish, David S. **Motion-Picture Work.** 1915.

Hunter, William. **Scrutiny of Cinema.** 1932.

Huntley, John. **British Film Music.** 1948.

Irwin, Will. **The House That Shadows Built.** 1928.

Jarratt, Vernon. **The Italian Cinema.** 1951.

Jenkins, C. Francis. **Animated Pictures.** 1898.

Lang, Edith and George West. **Musical Accompaniment of Moving Pictures.** 1920.

London, Kurt. **Film Music.** 1936.

Lutz, E [dwin] G [eorge]. **The Motion-Picture Cameraman.** 1927.

Manvell, Roger. **Experiment in the Film.** 1949.

Marey, Etienne Jules. **Movement.** 1895.

Martin, Olga J. **Hollywood's Movie Commandments.** 1937.

Mayer, J. P. **Sociology of Film: Studies and Documents.** 1946. New Introduction by J. P. Mayer.

Münsterberg, Hugo. **The Photoplay: A Psychological Study.** 1916.
Nicoll, Allardyce. **Film and Theatre.** 1936.

Noble, Peter. **The Negro in Films.** 1949.

Peters, Charles C. **Motion Pictures and Standards of Morality.** 1933.

Peterson, Ruth C. and L. L. Thurstone. **Motion Pictures and the Social Attitudes of Children.** Shuttleworth, Frank K. and Mark A. May. **The Social Conduct and Attitudes of Movie Fans. 1933.**

Phillips, Henry Albert. **The Photodrama.** 1914.

Photoplay Research Society. **Opportunities in the Motion Picture Industry.** 1922.

Rapée, Erno. **Encyclopaedia of Music for Pictures.** 1925.

Rapée, Erno. **Motion Picture Moods for Pianists and Organists.** 1924.

Renshaw, Samuel, Vernon L. Miller and Dorothy P. Marquis. **Children's Sleep.** 1933.

Rosten, Leo C. **Hollywood: The Movie Colony, The Movie Makers.** 1941.

Sadoul, Georges. **French Film.** 1953.

Screen Monographs I, 1923-1937. 1970.

Screen Monographs II, 1915-1930. 1970.

Sinclair, Upton. **Upton Sinclair Presents William Fox.** 1933.

Talbot, Frederick A. **Moving Pictures.** 1912.

Thorp, Margaret Farrand. **America at the Movies.** 1939.

Wollenberg, H. H. **Fifty Years of German Film.** 1948.

RELATED BOOKS AND PERIODICALS

Allister, Ray. **Friese-Greene: Close-Up of an Inventor.** 1948.

Art in Cinema: A Symposium of the Avant-Garde Film, edited by Frank Stauffacher. 1947.

The Art of Cinema: Selected Essays. New Foreword by George Amberg. 1971.

Balázs, Béla. **Theory of the Film.** 1952.

Barry, Iris. **Let's Go to the Movies.** 1926.

de Beauvoir, Simone. **Brigitte Bardot and the Lolita Syndrome.** 1960.

Carrick, Edward. **Art and Design in the British Film.** 1948.

Close Up. Vols. 1-10, 1927-1933 (all published).

Cogley, John. **Report on Blacklisting. Part I: The Movies.** 1956.

Eisenstein, S. M. **Que Viva Mexico!** 1951.

Experimental Cinema. 1930-1934 (all published).

Feldman, Joseph and Harry. **Dynamics of the Film.** 1952.

Film Daily Yearbook of Motion Pictures. Microfilm, 18 reels, 35 mm. 1918-1969.

Film Daily Yearbook of Motion Pictures. 1970.

Film Daily Yearbook of Motion Pictures. (Wid's Year Book). 3 vols., 1918-1922.

The Film Index: A Bibliography. Vol. I: The Film as Art. 1941.

Film Society Programmes. 1925-1939 (all published).

Films: A Quarterly of Discussion and Analysis. Nos. 1-4, 1939-1940 (all published).

Flaherty, Frances Hubbard. **The Odyssey of a Film-Maker: Robert Flaherty's Story.** 1960.

General Bibliography of Motion Pictures, edited by Carl Vincent, Riccardo Redi, and Franco Venturini. 1953.

Hendricks, Gordon. **Origins of the American Film.** 1961-1966. New Introduction by Gordon Hendricks.

Hound and Horn: Essays on Cinema, 1928-1934. 1971.

Huff, Theodore. **Charlie Chaplin.** 1951.

Kahn, Gordon. **Hollywood on Trial.** 1948.

New York Times **Film Reviews,** 1913-1968. 1970.

Noble, Peter. **Hollywood Scapegoat: The Biography of Erich von Stroheim.** 1950.

Robson, E. W. and M. M. **The Film Answers Back.** 1939.

Seldes, Gilbert. **An Hour with the Movies and the Talkies.** 1929.

Weinberg, Herman G., editor. **Greed.** 1971.

Wollenberg, H. H. **Anatomy of the Film.** 1947.

Wright, Basil. **The Use of the Film.** 1948.

DISSERTATIONS ON FILM

Beaver, Frank Eugene. **Bosley Crowther:** Social Critic of the Film, **1940-1967.** First publication, 1974.

Benderson, Albert Edward. **Critical Approaches to Federico Fellini's "8½".** First publication, 1974

Berg, Charles Merrell. **An Investigation of the Motives For and Realization of Music to Accompany the American Silent Film, 1896-1927.** First publication, 1976

Blades, Joseph Dalton, Jr. **A Comparative Study of Selected American Film Critics, 1958-1974.** First publication, 1976

Cohen, Louis Harris. **The Cultural-Political Traditions and Developments of the Soviet Cinema: 1917-1972.** First publication, 1974

Dart, Peter. **Pudovkin's Films and Film Theory.** First publication, 1974

Davis, Robert Edward. **Response to Innovation:** A Study of Popular Argument About New Mass Media. First publication, 1976

Facey, Paul W. **The Legion of Decency:** A Sociological Analysis of the Emergence and Development of a Social Pressure Group. First publication, 1974

Karimi, A. M. **Toward a Definition of the American Film Noir (1941-1949).** First publication, 1976

Karpf, Stephen L. **The Gangster Film:** Emergence, Variation and Decay of a Genre, 1930-1940. First publication, 1973

Lounsbury, Myron O. **The Origins of American Film Criticism, 1909-1939.** First publication, 1974.

Lyons, Robert J[oseph]. **Michelangelo Antonioni's Neo-Realism:**
    A World View. First publication, 1976

Lyons, Timothy James. **The Silent Partner:** The History of the
    American Film Manufacturing Company, 1910-1921.
    First publication, 1974

McLaughlin, Robert. **Broadway and Hollywood:** A History of Economic
    Interaction. First publication, 1974

North, Joseph H. **The Early Development of the Motion Picture,**
    1887-1909. First publication, 1973

Pryluck, Calvin. **Sources of Meaning in Motion Pictures and Television.**
    First publication, 1976

Rimberg, John. **The Motion Picture in the Soviet Union, 1918-1952.**
    First publication, 1973

Sands, Pierre N. **A Historical Study of the Academy of the Motion**
    Picture Arts and Sciences (1927-1947). First publication, 1973

Shain, Russell Earl. **An Analysis of Motion Pictures About War**
    Released by the American Film Industry, 1939-1970.
    First publication, 1976

Stuart, Fredric. **The Effects of Television on the Motion Picture and**
    Radio Industries. First publication, 1976

Wead, George. **Buster Keaton and the Dynamics of Visual Wit.**
    First publication, 1976

Wolfe, Glenn J. **Vachel Lindsay:** The Poet as Film Theorist.
    First publication, 1973